ADVANCE PRAISE

"*Spirituality and Abolition* is an invaluable collective contribution to thinking abolitionist theology and spiritual praxis, an open invitation to an abolitionist struggle being waged in the earthly and also the immaterial and spiritual realm, demystifying the ways in which colonialism and anti-Blackness shape carceral religiosity and also calling forth and evoking liberationist models of spirituality. Activists, spiritual workers, clergy, and academics in religious and Black and Indigenous and feminist, queer and trans studies as well will greatly benefit from this indispensable anthology."
—**Che Gosset**, Racial Justice Postdoctoral Fellow, Columbia Law School and Visiting Fellow, Animal Law and Policy Center, Harvard Law School

"This brilliant and absorbing collection of rigorous research articles, thoughtful political interventions, and innovative artworks is immensely important to the work of committed scholars, activists, and organizers. There is much that teaches, fortifies, motivates, and mobilizes here."
—**Laleh Khalili**, author of *Sinews of War and Trade: Shipping and Capitalism in the Arabian Peninsula* and *Time in the Shadows: Confinement in Counterinsurgencies*

"The Abolition Collective embodies the kind of work anybody interested in justice should aspire to reproduce. Astute, rigorous, and uncompromising, the collective seeks to bring radical perspectives to a wide readership within and beyond academe. With the publication of its inaugural issue, we are treated to the very best of revolutionary analysis. Anybody interested in upending a carceral and colonial order will find plenty of inspiration here. Something we all need and do well to pass along."
—**Steven Salaita**, author of *Inter/Nationalism: Decolonizing Native America and Palestine*

"The Abolition Journal project offers a unique, revolutionary lens through which to view, analyze and fight against capitalism and patriarchy on the terrain of the prison-industrial complex. It aims to combine an abolitionist message with a democratic production process that prioritizes participation of those directly affected by incarceration. What a welcome and needed approach! I am confident the project will help intellectuals build ties of solidarity across race, class, gender, nationality, and other borders that block liberation and in its finest moments will help teach us, as Mumia says, to 'fight with light in our eyes.'"
—**James Kilgore**, author of *Understanding Mass Incarceration: A People's Guide to the Key Civil Rights Struggle of Our Time*

"*Making Abolitionist Worlds* is an urgent reminder that theorizing and practicing abolition must take place across prison walls and the boundaries imposed by the colonial state, heteropatriarchy, settler colonialism, white supremacy, and capitalism. Finally, here is a journal providing a platform capacious enough to embrace the insurgent knowledge of activists, the analytical rigor of scholars, and the visionary power of artists."
—**Jackie Wang**, author of *Carceral Capitalism* and *The Sunflower Cast a Spell to Save Us from the Void*

"As the world we know is shattering more rapidly than we might have ever imagined, comes *Making Abolitionist Worlds*, an urgent call to build the new. These pieces movingly remind us that liberation will not transpire solely through opposition; it demands radical inquiry, imagination, creation. This collection brilliantly illustrates a core truth: we don't need 'alternatives to incarceration,' we need a wildly recreated society in which incarceration is unthinkable. *Making Abolitionist Words* will nourish and fuel struggles for transformation."
—**Maya Schenwar**, author of *Locked Down, Locked Out: Why Prison Doesn't Work and How We Can Do Better* and coauthor with Victoria Law of *Prison by Any Other Name: The Harmful Consequences of Popular Reforms*

"*Making Abolitionist Worlds* is a rich and compelling mixed-genre collection of radical perspectives that makes an urgent contribution to abolitionist world-making. Inspiring and incisive, these political interventions advance collective and transformative revolutionary praxis—what we need, now more than ever. On fire, indeed!"
—**J. Kēhaulani Kauanui**, author of *Hawaiian Blood* and *Paradoxes of Hawaiian Sovereignty* and editor of *Speaking of Indigenous Politics*

"*Abolishing Carceral Society* is an immense contribution to contemporary struggles for freedom. The pieces in this collection provoke new questions that inform resistance strategies, and deepen our understandings of the systems we are seeking to abolish and the social relations we are working to transform. This collection will be a profoundly useful tool in classrooms and activist groups. The conversation happening in Abolition is essential reading for those participating in the thorny, complex debates about how we dismantle structures of state violence and domination. The writers and artists whose work makes up the inaugural issue of Abolition, rigorously explore the most pressing questions emerging in liberation struggles."
—**Dean Spade**, author of *Normal Life: Administrative Violence, Critical Trans Politics and the Limits of Law*

"*Abolishing Carceral Society* is a wonderful mix of provocative ideas married with art, to help us consider a world without prisons, policing, and surveillance. Many of the submissions, however, are less concerned with dismantling what exists than they are with taking seriously that abolition is a project interested in building and in practical organizing. This comes through particularly in David Turner's essay, among others. *Abolishing*

Carceral Society asks us some questions that we sometimes prefer to ignore, like 'What does it mean to transform human relations?' This inaugural issue from Abolition pushes us to ask a number of questions that are important to moving us toward an abolitionist horizon."
—**Mariame Kaba**, author of *We Do This 'Til We Free Us*, founder of Project NIA, and cofounder of Chicago Freedom School, Chicago Taskforce on Violence Against Girls & Young Women, and Love & Protect

"Abolition is a crucial contribution to radical social movements. While fighting against prisons and the death penalty as instruments of class rule, the journal amplifies the voices of the incarcerated, actively engages with organizers on the ground, and builds bridges across multiple movements. The first issue, *Abolishing Carceral Society*, presents incisive interventions in the current debates about prison abolition and abolitionism as a political principle. It is a bold beginning for what will become an essential forum for all insurgent thinkers."
—**Silvia Federici**, author of *Revolution at Point Zero: Housework, Reproduction, and the Feminist Struggle* and *Caliban and the Witch: Women, the Body, and Primitive Accumulation*

"From slavery to prisons, abolition has always been a project of courage and breadth. *Abolishing Carceral Society* brings to bear the reflective, transformative urgency needed to confront today's violent world order. Of the struggle, by the struggle, and for the struggle: this auspicious collection offers not answers but pathways down which contemporary abolitionists travel en route to a future freedom. Check out their words, scope their visions—heed their calls."
—**Dan Berger**, author of *Captive Nation: Black Prison Organizing in the Civil Rights Era*

"*Abolishing Carceral Society* continues the radical, democratic tradition started by abolitionists to speak truth to power. In these dismal political times, it is a matter of the greatest urgency to create and sustain a counter-public sphere and an alternative print culture to sustain and expand American democracy. This remarkable and inspiring advocacy journal is poised to do precisely that for democratic activists as well as the broader lay public."
—**Manisha Sinha**, author of *The Slave's Cause: A History of Abolition*

"*Abolishing Carceral Society* is a bold journal mapping new roads out of the inferno in which we live. As the editors' Manifesto tells us, 'abolition' is a key strategy out of our carceral, slave-like society—the prison being the pivotal place for the perpetuation of an unjust political system. But the journal also sheds light on the many ways in which we're imprisoned beyond the prison's walls. With scholarly articles, poems, and artwork, in a beautifully designed text, it asks us to open our eyes and support a liberation struggle against jails and jailers."
—**George Caffentzis**, author of *In Letters of Blood and Fire: Work, Machines, and the Crisis of Capitalism*

Spirituality and Abolition
Ashon Crawley, Roberto Sirvent, Abolition Collective

© 2023 Ashon Crawley, Roberto Sirvent, Abolition Collective
This edition © 2023 Common Notions

ISBN: 978-1-942173-72-4 | eBook ISBN: 978-1-942173-82-3
Library of Congress Number: 2022951240

10 9 8 7 6 5 4 3 2 1

Common Notions
c/o Interference Archive
314 7th St.
Brooklyn, NY 11215

Common Notions
c/o Making Worlds Bookstore
210 S. 45th St.
Philadelphia, PA 19104

www.commonnotions.org
info@commonnotions.org

Discounted bulk quantities of our books are available for organizing, educational, or fundraising purposes. Please contact Common Notions at the address above for more information.

Cover illustration:
Ashon Crawley, "i did not know i could be beautiful (number 1)"—mixed media on canvas, 20"x20" (2021)

Cover design by Josh MacPhee
Layout design and typesetting by Graciela "Chela" Vasquez | ChelitasDesign

Printed by union labor in Canada on acid-free paper

SPIRITUALITY AND ABOLITION

SPIRITUALITY AND ABOLITION

Ashon Crawley, Roberto Sirvent,

Abolition Collective

ABOLITION: A JOURNAL OF INSURGENT POLITICS

ISSUE 3

Brooklyn, NY
Philadelphia, PA
commonnotions.org

ABOUT ABOLITION COLLECTIVE

Abolition: A Journal of Insurgent Politics is a collectively-run project supporting radical scholarly and activist ideas, poetry and art, publishing and disseminating work that encourages us to make the impossible possible, to transform beyond policy changes towards revolutionary abolitionism.

We are developing our capacity to work across carceral walls, and we encourage currently incarcerated people to send us their writings, submissions, and thoughts about this publication. We will try to respond to mail as quickly as possible. Given that we are a small, multitasking collective, our replies might be slightly delayed. Please note, at this time we are not able to offer legal support.

We thank you for your patience in advance and we hope to continue to connect *Abolition* with spaces of abolitionist and insurgent thought and work.

Abolition: A Journal of Insurgent Politics
https://abolitionjournal.org
abolitionjournal@gmail.com

TITLES IN THE
ABOLITION COLLECTIVE SERIES

CONTENTS

INTRODUCTION

A dialogue between the editors, Ashon Crawley and Roberto Sirvent.

Ashon

I came to *abolition* because I was hurting. A riff on bell hooks' discussion of what theory let her think about and think through, abolition as a concept resonated with me initially because I was confused, I was left wanting, I was in various kinds of pain.

I was hurting.

And I was hurting because of the deeply self-serving and egotistical practice of Christian preaching I was asked to do.

When I was a seminary student at Emory University, my field placement—a working course for students to learn on the job, called Contextual Education—was the Metro State Prison for Women, just outside Atlanta. Weekly, as student chaplains, we were asked to lead the Sunday worship service, a Christian church service that featured rousing hymns and worship songs, sometimes testimonies, and a sermon. Each of us chaplains were to preach a Sunday sermon. And, it too was a weekly reflection on the campus, a space that was far enough away from the prison that we could comfortably make declarations about what the women needed, about how the preaching and worship was necessary, about *how prison saved them from themselves*. These weekly reflections, along with the weekly worship, sermonizing, and, too, praying and counseling sessions with one of the women, formed the basis of our yearlong grade.

I still remember the sensory experience; it was the first time I'd spent in the carceral space of a prison. It felt like *Eat, Pray, Love* through the lives of others, we the seminarians having made the right decisions so much so that without any background in counseling, psychology or even homiletics, we could *practice our trade* on the less fortunate.

I despised it.

Why were we being asked to provide spiritual counsel when we were also in need? Why were we framed as the ones that had the correct knowledge to give, the women repositories that we could simply enter our spiritual practice into? And why was what we'd learn from them only to be obtained by paying attention to the purported *mistakes* they'd made such that they found themselves in the carceral space?

I'd read *Pedagogy of the Oppressed* by Paulo Freire years previous, in undergraduate Education courses, and the banking model for education was one I was familiar with and wanted to break away from. Yeh, I began to notice how that model for education was also a model for religious practices of my familiar, how preachers and pastors are often the ones framed as having the knowledge that was desirous—they heard from god more intensely and urgently and maybe more intentionally too, they were holy and sanctified and set apart, they were given leadership positions purportedly because they postured their lives through prayerful supplication and ongoing meditation on scripture. And even when they made purported mistakes—being "caught" in sin, more often than not, of the sexual kind—their position and identity as preacher, pastor, prophet then allowed for the easy justification of their behavior. The lay folks needed clergy because, as lay people, they are the ones that are empty vessels awaiting being filled by messages and perhaps even exonerations from clergy.

I was learning experientially that identity was taking the place of the practice of—and journey towards—justice. Our identities as chaplains and students meant we were given latitude with the mistakes and missteps we could make. The women's identities as prisoners meant they were given almost none, everything they did was analyzed through the unalterable identity of an incarcerated person that made dangerous mistakes.

Our engagements with the incarcerated women were supposed to be grounded in the banking model, it was the contextual background of our engagements with them. We knew the right path, made the right decisions, so we were required to lead and guide and counsel. Or at least this is how we were treated. We were not prepared to give or practice a relational model for care or concern, and the pedagogy of carceral aesthetics certainly did not allow us to presume that the ones with which we met and to whom we preached had anything of real value beyond the contemplative reflection their flesh and inhabitation within concrete walls could for us provide. Like the one person that played the keyboard weekly, sang, and directed the choir. Like the one that met with me weekly and talked about her life, love, and desires.

> You're not like the other chaplains. You don't just come in the room and pray with me.

> Do you want me to? was my reply.

She said no. Indeed. I don't think I ever prayed with her at all. I was connected with one of the women to meet with weekly, but we always talked about her family, her girlfriend at home, the fact that I actively questioned what it was I believed, that maybe I was an atheist or at least agnostic.

May I ask, are you gay?

She wasn't trying, she let me know, to be disrespectful. She said she felt an affinity with me based on what I did but also did not say when we weekly met. Felt a sense of camaraderie, and perhaps too, something like friendship.

I was being confronted with a reality I was not prepared for. My weekly travels to Metro State were the first time I'd had regular contact with a prison. I was stunned by the sheer weight of the physical premises, the concrete and gates, the heaviness in the air as the food was prepared. It all felt like too much. It was the first time I sensed, because of inhabiting the space, the ways incarceration is a literal attempt to sever folks from family, friends, fresh air, fresh food, and a sense for the familial and familiar. A specific kind of evil, the transporting of people away from their homes and livelihoods and creating a built environment that both creates and then underscores being enclosed and captured.

I had no language, then, for abolition. I had not read the people that one committed to abolition is supposed to read. I hadn't heard of Critical Resistance, Angela Davis was at that time still only *that woman, maybe a Black Panther? that has the afro, right?* But I knew, because I sensed it weekly, how terrible it was to be asked to do this kind of work that seemed to justify the status quo. I sensed it weekly, how there needed to be a different way to think about harm and violence and community and care.

I more than once got into heated disagreements, and sometimes explicit arguments, with the full-time chaplain. I'd be reminded over and over again that the work she did was unthankful, that she wasn't paid enough for the services she provided, that it was complicated, that she was a feminist. I'm sure all these things were true. But I also came to sense and feel the ways these justifications were not in the direction of a more just prison, to say nothing of a more just, humane, and free world.

I was hurting because I felt the solutions we were offering were not at all about the incarcerated folks, that the things we offered were for our personal student chaplain benefit.

Abolition is the thing that gave me the language for structural harm, for a feminist praxis that took seriously the intersections of race, class, gender identity, sexuality, disability, without ever attempting to justify the caging of people. Abolition gave me a way to think about what harm is, how it happens, and what is necessary to repair the breach after harm happens. Abolition is what convinced me the search for innocence is futile and a distraction, the search for innocence disallows the occasion to think against the various ways we harm because we occupy time and space in ways that are structured by inequity, exclusion, violence.

Roberto

I was never assigned an abolitionist text in college. Or in graduate school.

I came to abolitionist theory during my early years of teaching. I had been doing some research on American exceptionalism and the ethics of patriotism. I noticed that although liberals claimed to be more "honest" than conservatives about the "dark history" of the US, they still insisted that the US had noble "founding ideals." And that a true patriot tries to live up to our country's "greatest aspirations." It was only by stumbling upon abolitionist discourse that I came to understand the dangers of liberal patriotism. Abolitionists don't fight to build a kinder, gentler prison, so we shouldn't fight to make a kinder, gentler nation-state. You can't reform a plantation. This is what abolitionists taught me. The prison is a plantation. And so is the US. What are the *founding ideals* of a plantation? What are the *aspirations* of a plantation? What are the ideals and aspirations of a settler colony? I think we all know what a settler colony tries to do, what it *aspires* to do.

Some might say, with all the good intentions in the world, that the nation isn't broken, it's just *unfinished*. But what violence is necessary to *finish* the nation, to *finish* the national project? What violence is necessary to create a *more perfect union*? Mariame Kaba and a whole host of others have taught us that prisons aren't broken; they're working exactly as they're supposed to.

The same can be said of the US. The US is not broken. This is how it's designed. All this violence, all this cruelty. This is what the US does. This is what a capitalist state does. This is what an empire does. This is what a settler colony does. This is what a genocidal regime does.

It's how a plantation operates.

This language, this vocabulary, this grammar—they were instrumental in helping me think through American exceptionalism and the vices of patriotism.

My university education never taught me about the genocidal logics of America's "aspirations" and "founding ideals", but Assata Shakur and George Jackson certainly did.

Yet while I luckily, and gratefully, came to *abolitionist theory,* I can't say that I've actually come to *abolition.*

I don't live an abolitionist life.

Sure, I might be an academic who assigns radical texts in class. But to what degree can we describe this as an abolitionist practice? Something Keguro Macharia tweeted a while back really stuck with me. "I've often wondered what would have happened if I read the people I read as an undergrad—Fanon, Butler, Lorde, Rich, Spillers,

Irigaray, Foucault, Freud, Cone, and others—in classes," he wrote.[1] "I think I'd have a very different relationship to them."

"I think because I didn't—I assembled bibliographies and read on my own—I never thought of them in disciplinary ways. They were never attached to a field or department," he adds. "They were simply people who thought about and toward stuff I was learning to think about and toward."

Yes, my students get to read George Jackson, Assata Shakur, Amilcar Cabral, Audre Lorde, and letters from political prisoners. But they're reading them within a very violent institution: the university. No matter how hard I try or tell my students to not worry about their grades, the disciplinary structure of the classroom remains. There's still a worry about not pleasing the instructor, an expectation that an "expert authority" will *explain* the right interpretation to them, and a danger that the instructor—with so many institutional pressures—will whitewash or dilute any revolutionary message from the readings.

It's really difficult for an academic to be an abolitionist.

When I try to explain to my students that I don't consider myself an abolitionist or anarchist, even though these theories make up so much of my syllabi, I share with them a couple stories:

When I was growing up, we'd sometimes stop at a McDonalds or Pizza Hut after a baseball game or when we received our school report cards. After putting our order in with the person at the register or exiting the drive through, my dad would almost always tell my brother and me one thing: "If you don't study, you'll end up like one of them."

Like one of them.

This "advice" took on many variations. Sometimes it was framed as a question.

"Do you know why they're working at McDonalds?" my dad would ask?

"No, papa, why?"

"Because they didn't study," he said.

I had this bullshit ingrained in me from the time I was ten years old. I mean, how do you unlearn that? Hearing the same thing over and over again every time I go to a fast-food restaurant? It's toxic shit.

This isn't to blame any one parent or guardian. Despite this insidious "papa speech" as he would call it, my father is a man of many virtues. Yes, I grew up with some toxic shit drilled in my head. But who knows what kind of toxic shit I'll drill into my son's head?

It's true, as Morgan Bassichis says, that "the very systems we are

---

1. Keguro Macharia, Twitter Post, August 25, 2020, 2:37 p.m., https://mobile.twitter.com/keguro_.

working to dismantle live inside of us."[2] So yes, I'm not alone in having to unlearn and dismantle so many violent systems that live inside of me. But for some reason, I still can't consider myself an abolitionist.

An abolitionist I know recently had two friends released from prison. This abolitionist moved in with their partner, who is also an abolitionist, so their two formerly incarcerated friends could live in the now vacant apartment.

Who *does* that? An abolitionist does. And I have plenty of abolitionist friends like them. Heck, I even have friends who *don't* identify as abolitionists who would do the exact same thing.

Yet I wouldn't.

I'd like to think I'm the type of person who *would* give up my apartment for a formerly incarcerated friend. But I'm not. And I don't know why. Perhaps I'm way too attached to comfort, security (Ashon—I think you once so brilliantly called this the "ruse of security"), and predictability. An abolitionist life seems to require that I renounce all that.

And to be clear, it's not that I can't see myself as an abolitionist because I myself am not a community organizer or activist. Abolitionist practice—and abolitionist spirituality—occur in many spaces and places. As fahima ife writes so eloquently about their book, *Maroon Choreography*:

> *Maroon Choreography* is a performance in black study, so inherent in the book is a desire and practice to reclaim the local, small scale, the necessarily mundane tenderness of being together in person—walking and moving and wheeling together outside, offering shared attention to the earth, talking with each other, listening to each other, tending to each other, crying together, feeling each other, vocalizing desire, holding desire, remembering where we have already been, wanting and collectively trying to figure out how to end up somewhere else, partying inside a rented house, dancing together at midnight, loving and not loving, fucking and friction and rubbing, pleasure for pleasure's sake, smoking, being real fugitive together, drinking, convening, coming and coming again, black sensuality, preparing a meal together and eating it, sharing a home, laughter, the hours inside the clearing, the hours spent together recursively weeping, the hours spent retracing where we have already been, reclaiming the night, reclaiming the secret—so that mundane life becomes so intentionally and fully integrated in shared activity it stops being mundane, becomes marvelous. Being together in person as to create the possibilities for living in common, for sharing.

2. Morgan Bassichis, in Ann Russo, *Feminist Accountability: Disrupting Violence and Transforming Power* (NYU Press: New York, 2019), 2.

And in all that active and communal marvel we move beyond the impulse to refer to ourselves as "activists" and "community organizers" or even "artists" and instead try to figure out what it is we want to do together.[3]

The many abolitionist friends I look up to have been trained in a particular way. Maybe we can call it a form of spiritual discipline (of course, I know Ashon and I want to trouble this idea of "discipline"—perhaps find other words for this practice—given its common ties to punishment). They've developed certain *habits*, cultivated certain abolitionist *virtues*. Whatever it is, it probably came from the daily practice of saying "no to the traps of empire and yes to the nourishing possibilities dreamed of and practiced by our ancestors and friends."[4]

In what ways can we see this daily practice as a *spiritual* practice?

Ashon

Spirituality is the space between. It is the seemingly immaterial impression felt. Like a comforter or quilt on skin on a cold morning, the warmth of a layer between fabric textile and the epidermis, that miniscule space between is where the heat is felt. Another way to say it is that we never touch anything, our material makeup with atoms demonstrates this, that electrons orbit atoms, but they repel one another. Electron repulsion is the truth of the material world at the quantum scale, but this does not preclude us from feeling, from sense perception. We feel things, we sense things *because of the space between*. This space between, whether great or teeny tiny, is what allows the flow of relation. In a word, it's the spiritual.

So when I think about abolition being a spiritual practice, it means for me it is a striving that does not have reaching a *there* or an end point, but is a constant unfolding of relation in difference, a continual unfolding of the practice of justice in whatever here, whatever now, of its enactment. Abolition is a posture, it is something you must *do*, not an identity to claim as unalterable. This I learned at Metro State, that the concern and lament over identity is precisely because there is so little desire to do the work of justice.

Abolition has to be practiced daily, it must become daily habit and reflexive, it has to be the default position and ideology. And this because one cannot wait for moments of spectacular violence and

---

3. fahima ife, "BAR Book Forum: fahima ife's 'Maroon Choreography'," *Black Agenda Report*, 26 Jan 2022: https://blackagendareport.com/bar-book-forum-fahima-ifes-maroon-choreography.

4. Morgan Bassichis, Alexander Lee, and Dean Spade, "Building an Abolitionist Trans & Queer Movement with Everything We've Got," in *Captive Genders: Transembodiment and the Prison Industrial Complex*, ed. Eric Stanley and Nat Smith (Oakland: AK Press: 2011), 36.

harm to happen to attempt to put it into operation, one has to live the posture of abolition as a way to connect with one's deepest urges and longings, to connect more fully with others, to connect with earth and sea and sky and the creaturely worlds both known and not yet discovered.

Roberto

For me, abolitionist spirituality has impacted the way I think about friendships.

Not to overgeneralize, but I rarely found meaningful (or memorable) friendships in church. I was usually the person at church who asked way too many questions, and since doubt was often seen as a chief symptom of losing one's faith, there were always talks of people praying for me behind my back. And not in the good kind of way.

Don't get me wrong—I know these people cared. It just seemed like what they cared most about was me "getting it"—and by "it" I mean whatever narrow creed I was supposed to believe in to be a model Christian. My questions were a sign that I wasn't "getting it." Which explains all the care, concern, and prayers for someone who was "backsliding."

Friendship looks very different for me in abolitionist circles.

Abolitionists taught me the dangers of a particular ideology—what many organizers describe as "blood supremacy." Why, they ask, do we spend so much effort and energy investing in toxic relationships with our blood relatives, even to the detriment of our physical, mental, and spiritual health? Why do these blood relationships reign supreme? How often is the "family" card played in an attempt to control, abuse, or manipulate people? For example: "Hey, Roberto, it would mean a lot to us if you did X. After all, *we are family*. We stick together."

Abolition liberated me from blood supremacy.

Abolition taught me that I could find caring, loving, life-giving relationships with friends. And that I didn't have to feel guilty if they meant more to me than my "family." Abolition taught me that a relationship need not be permanent or even long to be meaningful (Ashon, your work has been so instrumental in helping me see this).

In what seems like some of the most random moments, I sometimes find myself crying tears of joy just thinking about my friends—and the extraordinary love, support, and encouragement they've given me. I don't know why I cry. But I do. And it's hard not to call it a spiritual experience.

My students always ask about my plans for raising my son Jayden. I'm honestly terrified of how ill-equipped and unprepared I am for the questions he's going to ask me, the struggles he'll face, the advice he'll seek from me.

My friendships make parenthood a little less terrifying. When it came time to pick Jayden's godparents, we picked eight people—many of them self-identified abolitionists, many of them not, but all who mean the world to me. I know I'll fail Jayden. And for the thousands of times when I really won't be able to help him the way he needs, I'll at the very least be able to point him to eight friends who will help him refuse the ways of the world.

The ways of the world. The church was supposed to help me resist these. To refuse wealth, power, privilege, status, fame. But it didn't.

Jayden's godparents (only two of which are part of a church) help me refuse the ways of the world. They are my models.

So, in a sense, an abolitionist spirituality of friendship does for me what the church couldn't—or wouldn't—do.

My friends Amber-Rose Howard, Colby Lenz, Dean Spade, Troizel Carr, Liz Murphy, and Hilary Malson show me this. Although it's common to find ego-driven people in every organizing space—even abolitionist ones—these friends of mine have no desire to be seen, recognized, or applauded by the world. They know there's nothing sexy about mutual aid. They know to be skeptical of organizers who "want to make a name for themselves", who want to "leave a legacy", or who want to be *seen* as a radical or revolutionary. Abolitionist spirituality demands that we renounce these desires. So, my friends are my sages. My friends are my spiritual counsel.

Finally, Ashon, I know we're both big fans of the show *Craig of the Creek*. I can't help but watch the show through the lens of friendship, abolitionist spirituality, and what K'eguro Macharia describes as "practicing freedom."

I see Craig, J.P., and Kelsey and I think: "I wish I knew how to be a friend like that when *I* was younger." But if I'm really honest with myself, I really wish I knew how to be a friend like that *right now*. I also wish I had their imaginations.

I keep thinking of that episode where the gang is playing tag, and after thinking through what the game is actually about, they realize the only thing they must do is not *play* the game or *win* the game, but *end* the game. What a beautiful picture of creative destruction – a destruction that is done collectively, courageously, and even joyfully. Truly a glimpse of freedom.

***

We began with this reflection conversation between Roberto and Ashon because *Spirituality and Abolition* is not, in the final assessment, an attempt at what is reductively considered to be "academic rigor." We are not trying to produce a set of arguments that will find their denouement in academic conferences, panels, and unread scholarly journals. We are attempting to make clear our arrival to abolition as a practice and conviction by discussing the relationships, the successes, the failures, that made such imagination irresistible. Because the conditions of confinement and depravation do not *create* imaginative possibility, imaginative possibility rises to the occasion of strictures of incarceration and structures of disrepair, violence, and unrelenting harm.

Abolition is a spiritual journey. It does not belong to any one religious tradition or orientation, though it certainly can be sensed, felt, and known within any given tradition either as affirmation or restive and resistant force. Abolition is spirituality precisely because it is a seeking for connection against the horizon, its thrust, of borders and enclosures and arrests. Abolition teaches us to *continue*, it teaches us that cataclysm and crisis does not have to be the modality by which we can realize a more just and livable future. It allows us to imagine that care and concern, joy, and regard, are perhaps the only ways towards justice, though inevitably fumbling—to use the language of Mariame Kaba—towards it we might be.

We do not accept that catastrophe, harm, violence and inequality are pedagogical, they do not have the capacity to allow us a practice of learning that is not punitive and unjust because catastrophe, harm, violence and inequality necessarily self-replicate and must continue and widen and spread in order to operate. We cannot accept the conditions of confinement, of incarceration, as having the ability to *rehabilitate*, to teach those of us that harm how to stop harming, because these institutional practices justify harm as a means to learn. Would not beauty and delight and care and reckless joy be more capacious and breathable ways to think about relation, and to work against harm occurring, and to produce ways to repair breaches and boundaries when harm happens?

Incarceration is a failure of imagination. It pretends we can put off for some otherwise future the question of harm, that what is most urgent is the replication of harm in the service of its undoing. But that desired undoing will be the undoing of us all. Abolition, however, teaches us to rest in the restiveness of being, to accept uncertainty and difficulty and to, together with others, come up with ways to live with and in and through uncertainties and difficulties. Abolition requires of us all to join in, put our flesh in the way of becoming together more caring and thoughtful and intentional with regard.

Regard. How you treat yourself. How you treat others. It, regard, cannot be based on how white supremacy, capitalism, heteropatriarchy, and—as Kameelah Mu'min calls it—religious chauvinism has engulfed us and attempted to sever the possibility for relating in dense and full and transformative ways with one another. Regard has to be spiritual, it has to be grounded in the noticing of material relations of what we have been told we can be, and the movement toward imagining otherwise. This is nothing other than a freedom practice, a freedom dream.

Divided into three sections, *Spirituality and Abolition* begins with "Practice" as the first section. "The Manual for Liberating Survival: Lesson 1. How Self-care Matters as an Embodied Practice of Abolition," coauthored by Rae Leiner and Jasmine Syedullah, focuses on how we cultivate new habits for abolitionist practice. Because abolition must become reflex and mode of relation, it cannot be called up only in moments of crisis and harm but must be the way we engage one another and the earth daily. In the ordinary ways. On the boring days. Grounded in queer-of-color activism and critique, what Leiner and Syedullah help us to sense are the ways carceral logics have been imbibed and internalized, structuring many of our relations not just with others but to ourselves as well. We cannot only be concerned with the Prison Industrial Complex and its many iterations and lives out in the world; we must focus attention on the way the *idea* and *structure of thought* that produces its occasion lives within. And after attention, how to repair. They teach us to practice "alternative ways to actively disrupt our own habituated relationships to safety, sustainability, and survival."

AK Wright's "Resurrection at the Fractured Locus: Incarcerated Black Trans Embodiment and Decolonial Abolition Praxis" thinks with the Christian theological idea of Resurrection as ascension, reunification and ultimately, an otherwise way, what Wright calls the *other-life of abolition*. Black trans life not as a learning implement and instrument to be exploited, but Black trans life as a living way that has the capacity to teach us all what it means to recognize the strictures and boundaries of the logics of incarceration, how it infects our quotidian and mundane operations, and how we might live and breathe and have joy in a different set of relational practices, "a world without the forces of the carceral state." We must live and live otherwise, we must life the other-life of abolition, of which for Wright, Black trans life is exemplary.

And Jared Ware's "Reversing the Fragmentation: Searching for an Abolitionist Spirituality" stages the theoretical and practical intervention of thinking the relation btween abolition and spirituality through Cedric Robinson's *Black Marxism: The Making of the Black Radical Tradition*. Not enough has been written about the various ways Robinson's text provides various points of connection within and against various disciplinary boundaries, histories and methodologies. Ware thinks with Robinson to imagine the possibility for abolition as a spiritual practice, posture, and mode of inhabitation. In this way, Ware demonstrates for us the ways the Black Radical Tradition is a living tradition, can be and often is found in the most cramped spaces and crevices forgotten, intentionally, and harmed. Having interviewed folks on the inside that participated in various strikes against conditions of confinement, Ware "illustrates how abolition spirituality manifests itself into potent force for radical change and component of revolutionary organizing."

Section II, "Testimony," offers three reflections from folks doing the work of spirituality and abolition both inside carceral spaces and against the constitution of such concrete spatial displacements, dislocations, and dispossessions. In "Spiritual Abolition: Or Something Like That," Fatima Shabazz writes as a formerly incarcerated person that had to contend with the search for stillness, calm, quietude, and peace, against the violence that the carceral state imposes and attempts to require of each of us. Currently organizing in Los Angeles with currently and formerly incarcerated Black trans organizers, Shabazz writes, "Spiritual abolition does not require a holier than thou approach, it simply requires that you recognize the power of spirit to move, inspire and to motivate. . ."

Jason Lydon offers us "A Prayer for Abolition." Founder of Black and Pink, an abolitionist organization training its attention to support incarcerated LGBTQ and HIV-positive folks and a Unitarian Universalist minister, Lydon draws from the writing of catholic theologian Andrew Prevot, who defines spirituality, "as the living out of prayer," Lydon argues that, "we can understand that our shared work towards abolition is both a collective spiritual practice and a common prayer." Common insofar as the breath we use is shared because of air, shared because of the necessary inhalation and exhalation processes that make our living possible. Such breathing is reflexive, we mostly do not actively think about the processes, but without it we cease. To think prayer as spirituality and spirituality as the grounds for abolition as the shared breath of our lifeworlds is to urgently find in the material flesh the need for another more just way to be.

And in Michael Cox's "Reflections on Spiritual Life and Abolition," Cox discusses his path toward Buddhism and how that path is in deep relation to abolition. The Executive Director of the Black and Pink Massachusetts chapter, sensing and feeling and breathing and thinking with Buddhism rounds out the section. Demonstrated in the three reflections, then, is the fact that spirituality, and abolition, do not belong to the overrepresented as if it were spirituality itself evangelical Christian tradition that is consumed with anxieties about converting other folks, missionizing and preaching "truth" as a marker of serious regard for their idea of god.

The final section, "Black Spiritual Study," completes our study but not our work or action. "Is, Was, and is to Come: Freedom Dreamworld Dispatches," by Andrew Krinks, argues that there is at least a double move that abolition requires—a negation of the current conditions and the affirmation of what is to come by active creation ongoingly. Negation is not a final end, it does not cease, but is a practice in the same way that creation must constantly emerge and revise itself, refresh itself against staleness and sedimentation. "Through shared rituals of prayer, song, and sacred reading under conditions of death, through vigil, communion, protest, and public grieving in the wake of state violence, through incantations for the earth consuming carceral machinery, through recollection of prison labor and prison rebellion, through imperfect struggles to establish police oversight and redirect funds from cops and cages to public goods, through neighborhood potlucks and fragmented accountability processes, through cursing at cops and shouting at lifeless concrete walls, another world reveals itself, even if only 'dimly'," Krinks offers. We have to keep seeking after another world, other worlds, worlds otherwise that negate the possibility of normativity and the harm that attends it. Dreamworlds get us there.

Hannah Bowman's "The Abolition of Hell: Abolitionist Interpretations of Jesus' Descent into Hell" is a reinterpretation of the idea of Jesus's death in the Christian narratives about his life. Known in the stories to descend into hell in order to "steal" the keys from the violent and harmful one known as Satan, Bowman argues that the stories of Jesus descending into hell to free captives can be reformulated into a picture of an insistent demand for freeing all prisoners in this world. And not in some future to come, but to free them, free us all, *now*. Arguing that one way to think about the life of Jesus is through the lens of solidarity with oppressed and harmed people, Bowman compels us to think the texture and weight of liberation, not just for those that have been harmed, but those that have harmed as well. Because if abolition is to mean anything, it must mean the liberation of all.

"God is Blackness: Mysticism of the Unowned Earth" by Peter Kline tarries with Fred Moten's thought and practice, applying his category of the "nonperformance" to refuse subject formation, to stay with the object, to be the entity that causes a dispossessive force against being possessed and owned and private property of western thought and material practice. "What the practice of abolition calls for," Kline writes, "is a 'mysticism in the flesh,' an unowning of individuation and subjection and a consent to the flesh of the earth." What does it mean to unown, to refuse, that which the normative world attempts to capture us by? Carceral logics as religious doctrine and theology, we have to refuse, we have to relinquish, we have to seek alternatives.

***

This volume of collected essays makes the argument that prison abolition—which is to say abolishing the institutions, the practices of punitive responses to harm and violence, and the epistemologies grounded in carceral logics—is a spiritual disposition and posture.

Not about particular religious traditions, rituals or ceremonies, we argue that abolition connects us to what it means to live an abundant, radiant, and exuberant life in relation with others, with the whole of creaturely existence, with the earth and, fundamentally with oneself. The goal of the collected volume is to connect the arguments for abolishing the various practices of harm and violence, of which incarceration is a fundamental component, with ways people inhabit religious and areligious customs and habits.

REFERENCES

Bassichis, Morgan. Quoted in Ann Russo, *Feminist Accountability: Disrupting Violence and Transforming Power.* NYU Press: New York, 2019, 2.

Bassichis, Morgan, Alexander Lee, and Dean Spade, "Building an Abolitionist Trans & Queer Movement with Everything We've Got," in Eric Stanley and Nat Smith, eds.. *Captive Genders: Transembodiment and the Prison Industrial Complex.* Oakland: AK Press: 2011, 36.

ife, fahima. "BAR Book Forum: fahima ife's 'Maroon Choreography,'" *Black Agenda Report,* January, 26 2022: https://black-agendareport.com/bar-book-forum-fahima-ifes-maroon-choreography.

Macharia, Keguro. Twitter Post. August 25, 2020, 2:37 p.m. https://mobile.twitter.com/keguro_.

SECTION I: PRACTICE

THE MANUAL FOR LIBERATING SURVIVAL:

LESSON I, HOW SELF-CARE MATTERS AS AN EMBODIED PRACTICE OF ABOLITION

Rae Leiner and Jasmine Syedullah

PREFACE

Our attention may be the most valuable currency on the market at the moment. How we spend it, ration it, or pay it forward on the day-to-day matters, not only to those who earn the privilege of basking in the grace of its glow, but also for our own sense of self, our sense of what matters, who matters, and how we honor that witness with words, acts, and allegiances.

In this moment of mass distraction, fake news, snake charmers, mad men, and spin doctors, it can be challenging to know where to place our attention, how best to focus our efforts and realize our dreams. The authors of this piece met the summer before the 2016 US presidential election. What we saw reflected in each other is still unfolding. This project is one about time. We had both been examining history as Black people hungry for liberation and were seeing that it was time to take the tools that we had each independently spent our lives gathering, marry them, and put them out into the world to make an offering to the communities that we love, the communities that we live in, to shape a space for liberation within the landscape of fear and increasing senseless violence.

This manual draws inspiration from the popular education realm of zines, curricular pamphlets, and downloadable toolkits for deconstructing the ways our communities have been working for the liberated survival of queer and trans communities of color through the work of abolitionist activism. This manual is a co-created emergent project, a queer Black feminist meditation on our imaginations of abolition and what all we have inherited by way of strategies of survival, care, adaptation, adoption, shapeshifting, and transformation from those who have come before us. How have the lineages, practices, and protocols of abolitionists who precede us imprinted themselves on, what Kesho Y. Scott called in her 1991 book, our habits of surviving in ways that keep our "strategies for life" on point in some moments and can keep us from thriving in the next?[1]

As Black queer folks seeking fugitive community and maroon promised lands for ourselves, our Black, Indigenous, and trans-of-color siblings, niblings, and all those with whom we live, work, build, study, learn, dance, feast, touch, transgress, talk, get lost, get out, find ourselves, and grow, we started this project to more easily track our learning. We are documenting how we are learning to teach each other how liberating ourselves from a survival mode abolitionist consciousness can make it more possible to give to ourselves and each other what we are accustomed to gifting to our activism.

We are both coming from siloed sectors of abolitionist formation—activism and academia—spaces where the undertow of capitalism pulls our best intentions into riptides of goal-oriented myopia. Many of our so-called winning strategies are shot through with the same carceral logics of surveillance, policing, punishment, and disposal we set out to fight against. While these logics drive and organize what prison abolitionists have come to call the prison industrial complex (PIC), a vast and tightly networked landscape of corporate investment and criminal (in)justice, we too often fail to see how our own efforts are implicated in this expansive collusion of personal, private, and public interests. The PIC is infecting our thinking about ourselves, safety, and belonging, extending the effects of mass incarceration far beyond brick-and-mortar prison walls and into our everyday acts of so-called personal freedom, privacy, and safety, even within our own movements.

Combining our shared experiences of abolitionist theory and practice from nonprofit-driven activism, grassroots organizing, and academic scholarship, this manual is comprised of exercises, meditations, manifestos, testimony, and social theory designed to democratize the lessons we are learning on the fringes, in the streets, from the earth, on the path, with our people, from our mothers, mothers, mothers, from the university and its undercommons, from our comrades, teachers, and spirit guides, from silence, from the sound of our own voices, from the stars, from science fiction and critical theory.

We invite you who choose to join us—as readers, as family, as kindred accomplices or as agnostic curious critics—into conversation with us as we workshop a contemplative approach to dismantling heteronormative white supremacist capitalist patriarchy as it lives in our planet, politics, society, common sense, felt sense, sinews, blood, and bones.

We hope it can come in handy wherever folks find themselves needing queer-of-color forward ways to connect the dots between

---

1. Kesho ⁓. Scott, *The Habit of Surviving: Black Women's Strategies for Life* (New Brunswick, NJ: Rutgers University Press, 1991).

historical trauma and how come movement making towards a world without walls can be so taxing.

We seek to center healing while highlighting patterns of harm that lie within and between overlapping histories of movement making, patterns of harm that come with the work of taking on the forces of organized state violence but also those we face in collaboration with each other as we move closer to freedom.

We also seek to center the magic alchemic joy and pleasure of embodied awareness, collective imagination, and sensory conscious-ness that are necessary to defend against the carceral logics of state violence and self-inflicted harm that infect our felt sense of safety and belonging.

We seek practical strategies for learning to better care for our-selves and each other in ways that push back against the enclosures of scarcity, shame, fear, isolation, and alienation, to reach for each other in times of crisis rather than allowing competition, burn out, broken hearts, and self-reliance to keep us keeping on far apart from those we first found ourselves with on the frontlines of our struggles.

We seek to further deepen the wake work of our collective healing towards an emergent understanding of the current moment and to realize the inherent dignity we hold in our breath and in our bodies. May this intention strike a mighty and righteous blow at the face of this beast.

I. SURVIVING THE CARCERAL LOGICS OF AN ABOLITIONIST CONSCIOUSNESS

> "In our work and in our living, we must recognize that dif-ference is a reason for celebration and growth, rather than a reason for destruction."
> —Audre Lorde

Imagine we were working together to make prisons obsolete. Imagine we were queer of color-led and organizing for community safety, food justice, universal housing, and an end to police brutality. Imagine we were spending more time fighting each other than we were fighting the expansion of the prison industrial complex.

Imagine we were effective enough to attract funding, private and public support to acquire 501(c)(3) status, sustaining donors and a local following. Imagine our hearts and heads were in the right place but we were coming from completely different points in the process of waking up to our place in our own "geographies of containment," as New Slavery Studies historian Stephanie Camp calls it.[2] Imagine we were all working our edge but from various points in our own processes of bringing awareness and compassion to our own unique intersections of trauma and survival, strategies born from bearing the bodies, histories, and kin we carry with us.

Imagine our mission statements were in alignment with the core principles of abolitionist activism that inspired the 1971 Attica rebellion but our organizational practices of hiring, decision-making, and conflict resolution more closely mirrored the technologies of care and accountability born of the carceral corporatism of the nonprofit industrial complex. Imagine we had grown too burned out to notice.

We have been here before, not just once, not just now, but time and again. Our movements for abolition are at a crossroads. We are the 21st century great grandchildren of the movement to abolish slavery and we draw strength from the past by coming together to learn what "improvising on reality" might look like today.[3] More than fifty years after the state-sanctioned violence that forcibly brought the Attica uprising to a violent end, we find ourselves at yet another moment of reckoning. We have a choice to make. Demands to name.

We draw on Cedric Robinson's legacy as expressed by Gaye Theresa Johnson and Alex Lubin in their definition of abolition. In their "Introduction" to *Futures of Black Radicalism*, they boldly proclaim that abolition is nothing less than the wholesale "destruction of racial regimes and racial capitalism."[4] We draw abolitionist strategies from the many iterative histories of the abolitionist tradition centering the fugitive as foundational. Our fugitive lineage is in conversation with the writings of Ruth Wilson Gilmore, Angela Davis, Joy

---

2. Stephanie Camp, *Closer to Freedom: Enslaved Women and Everyday Resistance in the Plantation South* (Chapel Hill, NC: University of North Carolina Press. 2005). I (Jasmine) taught my Abolitionist Activism class about Stephanie Camp's book and loved how one of my students described this concept. As Maggie Kennedy described it in her mid-term, Minnesota Nice (Spring 2019, 6) "We can also think of these hidden spaces as potential places and times within the geographies of containment we already live within—as truant spaces, or simultaneous alternative geographies, as Stephanie Camp pulls on . . . Truancy is a radical reinventing of the spaces we occupy, a form of navigation and pattern of movement throughout the spaces we are in that doesn't require leaving them altogether. To move truantly is to practice a counter-orientation in the geographies of containment one lives in—to move towards freedom through physical hidden spaces like dance floors and shared housing and protests, to improvise in building relationality in spaces like testimonios and time-sharing, to embody practices of interdependency through deconstructing carceral logics in our patterns and trying to practice queer and trans ethics of accountability."

3. Liz Samuels, "Improvising on Reality: The Roots of Prison Abolition," in Dan Berger, ed., *The Hidden 1970s: Histories of Radicalism* (New Brunswick, NJ: Rutgers University Press, 2010).

4. Theresa Gaye Johnson and Alex Lubin, "Introduction," in Theresa Gaye Johnson and Alex Lubin, eds., *Futures of Black Radicalism* (New York, NY: Verso, 2017), 12.

James, Mariame Kaba, Alexis Pauline Gumbs, and INCITE! Women of Color Against Violence—divergent approaches to the work of abolition that ask us to focus our attention on all the everyday ways carceral logics colonize every acre of our political landscapes.

Carceral logics produce the carceral effects of the prison industrial complex in ways that exceed the scenes of traffic stops, court houses, jails, and detention centers to reach into our private lives, to live in the very places we call home. We see how quickly carceral logics and practices of policing, surveillance, and punishment persist beyond the bounds of the PIC to enter our intimate places of refuge, shaping the relationships we have with our families, organizations, communities, and movements. Canceling people or cutting people out, policing each other's identities or politics, caretaking in ways that feel more like management than the intimacy of shared oppression—these practices are so familiar many of us take them for granted. As Reverend angel Kyodo williams claims, "Our bodies take the shape of, and thus illuminate, the contours of the most insidious force of systematic dehumanization and destruction ever imagined, one which has led the global community into a downward spiral of self-annihilation."[5]

To abolish racial regimes and racial capital we have to divest from the seduction of carceral logics. In their essay entitled, "Transforming Carceral Logics: 10 Reasons to dismantle the Prison Industrial Complex using a queer/trans analysis," S. Lambel writes:

> a queer/trans politics not only helps identify the role of imprisonment in perpetuating gender, racial, and sexual violence, but also provides tools for developing alternative community responses that better address problems of harm. . . . The prison system is literally killing, damaging, and harming people from our communities. Whether we consider physical death caused by self-harm, medical neglect, and state violence; social death caused by subsequent unemployment, homelessness, and stigmatization; or civil death experienced through police disenfranchisement and exclusion from citizenship rights, the violence of imprisonment is undeniable. . . Prisons remove people from their communities, isolate them from social support, and disconnect them from frameworks of accountability. . . . More importantly, imprisonment does not assist with the collective healing process nor does it work to prevent harms from recurring in the future.[6]

---

5. angel Kyodo williams, Rod Owens, and Jasmine Syedullah, *Radical Dharma: Talking Race, Love, and Liberation* (Berkeley, CA: North Atlantic Books, 2016), xxi.

6. S. Lambel, "Transforming Carceral Logics: 10 Reasons to Dismantle the Prison Industrial Complex Using a Queer/Trans Analysis," in Eric A. Stanley and Nat Smith, eds., *Captive Genders: Trans Embodiment and the Prison Industrial Complex* (Oakland, CA: AK Press, 2016), 237–245.

Rather than continue to imagine that the PIC is out there, we are accountable to queer of color activist narratives, archives, and scholarship along with ancient traditions of embodied contemplative practice to see how the PIC lives in our relationships to ourselves, each other, and our protocols of resistance to it. We are practicing alternative ways to actively disrupt our own habituated relationships to safety, sustainability, and survival. We are watching our own patterns, taking note, and ritualizing ways to remember how we imagine a world without prisons. We need tools that hold us accountable to that vision and its realization in this moment. We are committed to keeping up a practice of unshackling ourselves and disarming each other from the false security of the carceral logics of capitalist bureaucracy as daily defense against the rip tide of their pull on our lives.

Even as we practice, we face the death throes of capitalism and see how racial capitalism, settler colonialism, and white supremacy have pushed our planet and our communities to the limit. We are constantly under attack, physically, politically, environmentally, psychologically, and spiritually. Our activist and organizing communities are responding across the planet, fighting against policing, paramilitary presence, prison expansion, war machines, and global capitalism. We fight because we feel the effects of oppression are reaching a critical point. Our planet burns and the sounds of its destruction resonate in our bodies, in our hearts, in our bellies, in our heads. Oppression ignites us to take action, to fight and grasp for survival strategies, for notions of liberation, whatever they may look like.

The challenges we face are not only external but structural. Our movements are gaining traction with mainstream politics and public opinion, not enough to tip the scale, but more than enough to greatly increase risks of cooptation. Not unlike the institutionalization of the civil rights movement, the current moment presses upon us to institutionalize our movements from grassroots community organizing into centralized celebrity-driven "activist" corporations and the branding of our public intellectuals.

We struggle to sustain ourselves while our friends fall. We struggle to sustain each other as we hold our own overwhelming feelings, burnout, depression, anger, frustration, and rage within our beloved communities. There is little to no time to take care of ourselves or grieve or fall apart because the mechanisms of oppression do not take time off. We have unwittingly adopted the cultural practices of our oppressors that teach us to mock the idea of self-care and wellness. We call it bougie or "wypipo shit." We dehumanize ourselves in our practice of becoming workaholics for the movement. We are competitive about how busy we are in advancing it. We brag about it on social media and in person with each other. We practice competition rather than practicing accountability and care in our beloved communities. We tear each other down bypassing our own grief rather than prioritizing healing our wounded egos to uplift ourselves to stand up for each other.

Self-care is not just about treating yourself to mani/pedis and holidays on the beach, not that we'd refuse such options if they were offered to us! Self-care is less about the what and more about the why. It's more about the journey than the destination. It's about learning the limits of your capacity to hold space for that which drains us of the strength to endure. What if we think of self-care as something more than an individual act we choose to do as a personal reward for hard work, or even as something more than an act of collective self-restoration? What if we begin to take self-care seriously as a practice in expanding our capacity to be present to ourselves and our world—retraining our attention to tell time in ways that help us become more accountable to our goals and ideals for social justice in real time, in practice, as we are, in the moment and in relationship to our communities, especially those intricately intersecting structures of harm and degradation? What if self-care and wellness were the road to liberation?

Our movements are not offsetting the effects of oppression that are weathering our Black womyn leadership, as though what we already deal with from systemic violence, poverty, overpolicing, underfunded schools, living in substandard housing, fighting against environmental health injustices isn't enough! Our leaders are battling health issues under wraps, our collectives are fighting each other over vision and resources while acting like they aren't already burnt out. We are perpetuating the habituated practices of oppression within our movements for liberation, and we aren't always aware of it. We are doing it because it has been our pattern, our survival strategy, our way of making a home out of a briar patch from the auction block to the neighborhood block. How we imagine self-care and wellness as indispensable or disposable for ourselves and our communities is *the* key component to how we are going to get our folks free this time.

The technologies of repression we face today do not only aim to silence and execute, they are designed to stress us past the point of breaking-down, past repair when possible. The technological stress, as Ntozake Shange calls it, that bears down on us as we work to advance the cause of abolition is disabling the strength of our movements physically, psychically, and collectively. Some of us are so busy fighting we do not even notice how stress is undermining our efforts. Some of us are missing the warning signs, the writing on the wall, the messages in bottles passed down by those who came before cautioning us not to lose sight of the long view. Our practice of imagination is, itself, in desperate need of our rapt attention.

Imagine the walls fall. Imagine we win. Imagine we win without what we need to rebuild ourselves and our communities? Octavia

Butler has walked us through a parable of this possible future and asked us how we are making ready for it. We cannot wait to win to learn to heal. The time for healing is right now. Wellness is a critical part of our collective pathways to liberation.

Now imagine we are owning our shit and paying rapt attention to our patterns of implication in carceral logics. Imagine we are no longer shaming ourselves or punishing each other for forgetting we can choose how we want to be in this world, no matter how bad the world gets. Imagine that we are fueling our imaginations to defend against the distractions of dream-stealers and body snatchers. Imagine that our activist leaders are also survivors of trauma who have become shamans, alchemists, and wisdom teachers, healers who teach us to yoke our movements to skillful practices of liberation that can abolish our reliance on both prisons *and* the technological stress of surviving its carceral logics.

Imagine that we practiced centering truth and trust in our movements towards liberation.

> "We not only have to learn to grow healthy plants, but healthy soil."
> —Angel Gonzales, organic farmer, community organizer, and retired NYC school teacher

We are only just beginning to understand the degree to which "liberation is a collective practice," as disability justice scholar Mia Mingus writes.[7] We are forming a sacred, congregational space of creative movement against the momentum of collective alienation, criminalization, and disposability. Mingus writes, "this is not about perfection, but practice. Falling down and getting back up. Spectacular failures and learning how we can be and do better. Resilience in the face of fear; humility in the face of ego; faith in the face of hopelessness. This is about understanding organizing as a spiritual practice that is just as much about our souls as it is about our goals . . . How do we cultivate the kind of commitment to each other that can withstand failures, heartbreak, disappointment, gossip, mistakes, and conflict?"

We turn to Mingus again and again because her approach to abolition is rooted in a radical ethics of accountability to creating the conditions for us to be able to receive the care we need to get free. More than inclusive of those power marginalizes, it recognizes that too often the ways we work for social justice are not working for us, for all of us, for our whole selves.

---

7. Mia Mingus, "Still Choosing to Leap: Building Alternatives," Remarks from the closing plenary, "Revolutionary Organizing Across Time and Space," at the INCITE! Color of Violence 4 Conference, March 26-29, 2015, Chicago, Illinois, https://leaving evidence.wordpress.com/2015/03/31/still-choosing-to-leap-building-alternatives/

Getting out is itself an ongoing abolitionist practice that can, with dedication, keep us moving towards another kind of freedom. An "all of us or none of us" kind of abolition is an embodied practice of survival that requires we notice when our strategies of resistance fall out of alignment with the imaginations of freedom we say we want. This practice of noticing is distinct from policing because it is not accountable to the power of rule, but to an impractical, nearly impossible process of building trust, building relationships out of all the fractured pieces of ourselves. It's a practice not a perfect as Rev. angel Kyodo williams, Sensei constantly reminds us. And we certainly ain't perfect.

II. BEING IN OUR FEELINGS

Part of the challenge of liberation has to do with our foundational relationship to feelings; not just to pain and suffering but also to pleasure and joy. Feelings work is much in the same vein as survival work; we can be in a habituated or liberated relationship to either. On one hand, we know feelings are socially constructed, for example, think of a woman clutching her purse as a Black man enters an elevator—being socially conditioned to respond to certain kinds of stimuli associated with undesirable social traits in certain ways that subject both herself and the person she fears to dehumanization. On the other hand, feelings are critical measures of one's condition or information about what might be coming, for example think of that moment you know you are too mad to talk, and you need to leave a situation or that sixth sense that you are in danger and need to seek safety.

As adrienne maree brown frames it, "we are in an imagination battle" and must "practice the future together" to move towards a more just, free campus and world.[8] brown's philosophy of emergence is central to our orientation to abolition and social justice more broadly. The idea is that we have to prepare ourselves to be agents of change, to hold space for grief, loss, rage, and shame, the inconvenient feelings that come with confronting racism where it lives in our lives. Without preparation we are left to whatever habituated devices of support and survival we have been conditioned into to cope with extremes of feeling. On our worst days, we represent two extremes of how lack of preparation can have the worst consequences. Whether you are hindered by social conditioning to stay in your feelings or not, we all still struggle to be in choice about them. For example, Jasmine can be so "in her head" that she cannot easily access her feelings and

8. adrienne maree brown, *Emergent Strategy: Shaping change, changing worlds* (Oakland, CA: AK Press, 2017), 18-19.

often functions as if everything is okay even when it is so clearly not. Rae on the other hand can be so in their feels that they move like the weather right along with them, whether it is called for in the moment or not. The kind of imagination that abolition requires emerges out of a practice of preparation, intention, and choice, not habit, compulsion, or reactive behavior. It requires the ability to create space within ourselves such that we can feel like ourselves enough to begin to really feel with each other. This is where self-care comes in. It is a way to make room when the noise of our thoughts or feelings can get so deafening, we can no longer connect to each other or what is happening as it arises. When we are so in our heads or so in our feelings that we cannot sense what time it is, time stops and we get stuck, in old patterns, in the past, in expectations, and it can be hard to find a way out.

In this section we are piloting a course for liberating survival that draws on years of cumulative learnings from activist and organizing spaces, from time we both spent with Critical Resistance in New York and in Oakland, with the movement for Black Lives in the Hudson Valley, with the School of Unity and Liberation, Community Voices Heard, People's Institute for Survival and Beyond, the Radical Dharma Team, the Warriors for Embodied Liberation (WEL), and years of learning from queer/trans organizing legacies like Marsha P. Johnson and Sylvia Rivera who founded STAR. Rae Leiner is working locally to cofound the first queer of color-led LBGTQ+ Center in the City of Newburgh with their cofounder Maria Ramirez. We are funneling these learnings into a popular education curriculum and calling it *The Manual for Liberating Survival*.

The Manual offers opportunities to deepen individual embodied responses to how oppression lives in our bodies, how we perpetuate it through habituated behavior, and how to deepen our sense of accountability to connect across lines of difference and move closer to freedom with every breath. The next sections draw from two of our teaching modules. The first, an orientation to embodied practice, and the other, a deep dive into embodied practices for building accountable communities.

> "I'm feelin' myself, I'm feelin' myself
> I'm feelin' my, feelin' myself . . . ."
> —Nicki Minaj, "Feeling Myself"

There are ways to be in our feelings that lead to authentic communication and mindful navigation of pressure-filled situations and there are ways they can lead to shutting ourselves and others down and burning out. There are ways to be accountable to yourself and your feelings without being attached to them and by learning to read the patterns like a forecaster might the weather. While habituated relationships to our feelings "feel good" while we are experiencing them, they repeat a lot, spinning us through the same cycle of drama over and over again without much chance for shift, change, or even slowing down (think about being hangry, or triggered, or stressed out). We are often aware of how these feelings are made up of physiological responses to our environment but are often not cognizant of the fact that all feelings are rooted in the body and what the body is trying to tell us she needs! People are afraid to feel, to be connected to their feelings and being in the moment and would rather fall back on practiced behavior even when they know those practices do not work.

People, especially in the West, have been taught to privilege mind over matter, science over experience, mechanistic behavior over animalistic behavior. When "people" are not able to connect to their own empathy and compassion for themselves, they cannot connect to other people—right when they need connection most. When we fear embracing our feelings or indulge in compulsive cycles of habituated practice in an emotion, we move away from being in choice with our actions at the very moment we need to be paying attention. When we are pushed to a place of severe disconnect—from the wholeness of ourselves, from the complex mix of joy/disgust/pain/lust/rage/loneliness/fear, when we cut ourselves off from pieces of ourselves that we don't like or are ashamed of—we revert to our reptilian brain in those instances and allow our default mode to take over for us. While these moments might feel like we are doing something like escape or fixing the problem, we often find we are leaving ourselves behind. Our survival instincts become the mechanism that move us away from the pieces of ourselves we most need to pay attention to. We move away from ourselves in order to maintain the pattern of suffering we have become most comfortable with, be it "getting it right," aversion to suffering, dependence on external affirmation, or whatever habituated practices of survival we have cultivated to make us feel safe.

As Black identified people, we both embody our awareness in ways that are linked to our survival and differ greatly from the experience of our white counterparts. Our connection to feelings is a complex mix linked to survival, hypervigilance, hyperempathy, and dissociation from violence, grief, and harm.

We are about the work of reclaiming our orientation to time as a practice of self-care that can support us to integrate our hearts/minds/bodies/spirits/speech/actions/intentions while reconditioning our whole selves to matter and to be in choice! It is a practice inspired by what Rev. angel Kyodo williams calls "Fearless Warrior Practice." It is a practice inspired by what Rusia Mohiuddin calls "Embodied Liberation". As their students, we are building off their work to say that to *be in choice* means we can discern the difference between what we are calling habituated and liberating protocols of survival—to know how that difference feels, how it resonates in the body, in the thoughts the mind entertains, in the relationships the heart returns to, and in the choices we make.

To build sustainable liberated communities, we need a new foundation, a way to practice feeling our feelings in sincere ways that aren't performative but authentic because they are our own and we have taken accountability for them, taking seriously the social conditions and histories that contribute to their formation.

First, this means learning to value ourselves and listen to ourselves as full human beings, not just talking heads, tokens, or problems. So much of what we are habituated to think are stories we hear over and over. Stories that live in our bodies far before they become conscious narrative, personal accounts of our story, or the truth. Our bodies are constantly communicating with us, but we are not always listening, or even fluent in the language of the body. Working with embodied practices and communities committed to those practices teaches us to mind our bodies, learn her language, and settle down enough to listen to her vast and valuable resources of information.

Second, once we are in practice and in communication with our whole selves then we can begin to discern between what is ours and what is not ours. Namely we practice noticing the difference between authentically feeling *our* feelings versus feeling someone else's feelings or a socially prescribed feeling that we are socialized to feel but are not truly connected to.

Third, we practice care and accountability for what we are feeling, for building the liberated kinds of relationships to feelings—pleasure, joy, pain, and suffering—that move us towards each other rather than further into isolation. By asking questions and noticing how we are habituated to orienting ourselves to feeling our feelings we begin to shift these foundational relationships to them. We begin to shift how we are taught to build responses to our trauma. We begin to honor our trauma, our joy, pleasure, and *use them* to build connection, and empathy with the feelings of others. We learn to use our feelings as barometers, a language for learning how we are processing the information our body is trying to tell us. We begin to learn to distinguish between feelings that are habituated and how to have a liberating relationship to them. We learn to dance with all that information to be both in sync and in choice all at once.

III. A TASTE: EMBODIED PRACTICES & AIMS

"How many times have we heard the same scenarios.
He had a gun. They feared for their lives.
We cannot trust white news media nor the pigs' version of the story.

We must rely on the community"
—Jasmine Abdullah Richards, May 18, 2019

We know the scenario. "I thought he had a gun." "He was like the hulk." Anti-Black rhetoric, stereotypes, and narratives are embedded in our culture, in our language, in our relationships and in our bodies. The aim of embodied practices is to connect how the cognitive dissonance of these scenarios impacts our ability to be present in a moment, to be in choice. Take for example the context of police encounters. Police narratives suggest the presence of Black bodies, masculine bodies, large bodies, gender non-conforming to standards of white gender norms for bodies are, in themselves, triggers, criminal threats that can and have resulted in an escalation of violence. Police accountability fails to draw connection between internal bias and the use of excessive or deadly force in action. Embodied bias travels through our bodies and actions and moves us in ways we usually only have an explanation for long after the moment passes. We rationalize. We justify. We reason. In so doing we naturalize conditioned responses, enactments of discriminatory narratives that erase Black people's humanity. Our reliance on policing to keep "us" "safe" results in the extension of policing behaviors in our everyday lives and culture. This increases our usage of the weapons of policing in our mediation of conflict: the use of surveillance, verbal or physical abuse, and isolation. If the very systems and institutions that are responsible for keeping structural inequity and vulnerability to violence in place are far reaching and slow to change then how do we "get free?"

We have a chance in this iteration of the movement for abolition to build from the unchecked blind spots of the past and heal how we have been hurt by our movements. In the past we have seen how liberation movements have reproduced the kinds of harm, domination, and violence they are seeking to leave behind. The antebellum antislavery abolitionist movements of the Northern US were not all antiracists mobilizing in solidarity with formerly enslaved communities. Many white antebellum abolitionists did not care about the conditions, futures, or welfare of Black lives, but were rather more concerned with saving the country from a culture of sin. In the late twentieth century we saw antiracism movements perpetuating sexism, queer liberation movements that excluded trans bodies and people of color, women's liberation movements perpetuating racism and classism, antiviolence movements that rely on policing and prisons, anti-poverty initiatives that promote suspicion and criminalization of disenfranchised communities. These lessons of the past are reminders to us in this present moment to leave behind the nostalgia of those moments and to look at them with a critical yet kind lens. There are important lessons in these blind spots for us to consider as we engage in the deeper work of challenging what liberation looks and feels like.

It's not solely the land that has been colonized, it is our minds and ways of being that are occupied by colonization as well. How do we know this? When we ignore the suffering of people in our community at large, when we hoard resources and don't share, when we take a missionary approach to serving others while looking down on them as though they need us when what they need is equal footing in our society. As human beings, we typically get engaged with something because we have an agenda that serves us/our needs. There isn't anything wrong with having an agenda—we have to be driven from someplace. The problem is that we live in a culture that rewards us for paying attention to our own needs and penalizes us for supporting the needs of others. We have enough housing to not have people living on the streets, we have enough food for people to not be hungry.

Our aim is to get clear on the places we come from and how we can shift from patterns of individualism, competition, supremacy, and territorialism to support the kinds of liberation each other needs and deserves. We are moved to action through being connected to an issue, something that triggers us to want to make a change. We see it now, with the global rise of white supremacist activity. Our triggers are tied to our emotions, our feelings, and our beliefs.

What if you were to reflect on how your feelings are not just individual or personal but also conditioned by history, by our community, by our traditions and culture to react towards certain kinds of stimuli in certain kinds of ways in the name of survival? What if "what's good" is subject to the rule of those in power—in service to their interests, desires, fears, etc. and not in service to our own? What if you were to reflect on how your feelings are conditioned by stories and situations that narrate established habituated responses. An example of this is the myth of the hypersexualized Black man who is always looking to rape a white woman. Where did this story come from? Who invented it? What purpose does it serve in moving people to act? Most importantly, how true is this story? Our attention is the greatest currency of this moment—how we pay attention matters and we have to begin by paying attention to our own habituated patterns of survival.

EMBODIMENT PRACTICE I. BREATHING

Warrior Breathing is the practice we use most often to teach meditation to folks who have never done it before. It is a practice we learned from Rev. angel Kyodo williams, Sensei, first at the dharma center she founded, the Center for Transformative Change. Her teaching style is unique and specifically oriented towards preparing practitioners to engage fully and directly with injustice in the world as they encounter it, in the moment, in our movements, without hesitation, bringing our whole selves to the table, being in choice, "to lead the life of a warrior," as she writes in the Warrior Spirit Prayer. Over the years of teaching, it and practicing it, we have found it generative in a number of practical ways. It helps us learn to follow the breath and rely on the breath as a constant friend who is always there to help bring us back to what really matters as Rev. angel teaches. As we have begun to teach it in courses and the community, we have come to see it as a prophetic practice for learning to tell the times, own our truth, and act from that place of knowing without apology.

In Warrior Spirit Breathing we follow the flow of the breath, noticing the in breath and out breath. We practice bringing the end of the out breath as close as we can to the in breath, so there's barely a break between them. In this practice the breath follows a continuous loop, smooth as a ribbon. At the sound of the bell no matter where we are in the course of the breath cycle, we breathe out fully and completely with a gently constricted throat, (lips closed) with a sound like the ocean.

We sit in continuous breathing practice, breathing out at the sound of the bell for five to ten minutes, until the practice leader rings the bell twice and brings the practice to a close. Afterwards we take note of what we noticed. Where did the mind go? Does the bell bring attention back into focus? Does the breath? Are we anticipating, managing, or controlling the experience? What is our pattern? So often when we hear the sound, the bells, ringing, and alarms we contract, from breath to bone. Rather than contract and get tight, with this practice we are training ourselves to have a different kind of response to having our attention pulled. It is a practice that bends our attention towards a kind of focus that is steady but not so rigid it remains closed to the world as it is. We are training ourselves in a practice of self-protection that remains receptive rather than incarcerating and shut down, open and ready to respond with our whole selves when the occasion requires. When the bell sounds, we can shift focus, putting down what we've been holding or what's holding us and respond to new information about what time it is now.

There are many ways we learn to tell time, many ways we learn to be present to what is needed in this moment. Internal discernment, being in choice, has to be honed. It is a practice of shifting the way we pay attention, the way our body responds to new information, even if we are not "ready," even if there are other things that are competing for our attention, even when the moment we are facing seems like one we have encountered time and time again—one that we can mail in, rush through, or do sleeping. Warrior Spirit Breathing is a practice that helps us "reprogram, deprogram and get down," to quote

Janelle Monae—to wake up to each moment like it is a new one, to shift gears clearly and completely, in an instant.

EMBODIMENT PRACTICE II. STEP-UP

Step-Up is a tool used and taught by Universal Partnership principal rusia mohiuddin through the Warriors for Embodied Leadership (WEL) program. The purpose of the Step-Up exercise is to create awareness of what it feels to be triggered into our basic default mode. We understand that survival mode shows up for individuals in four ways: 1. Fight, 2. Flight, 3. Freeze, 4. Appease.

Our survival instincts have helped to keep us alive through a number of psychological and physiological stimuli. When we are triggered into survival mode, we lose the ability to access the rational part of the brain, clouding our "better" judgment and our ability to be in choice. There are all kinds of stimuli that can trigger the amygdala, the oldest part of our brain that reacts to our surrounds and alerts us that we are in danger, putting us into survival mode. We learn how confrontation feels, slowed down, beat by beat. Where does the mind go when we feel the presence of the other, stripping back the story and paying attention to our own projections?

The purpose of this exercise is to make participants aware of when/how they can be triggered and to identify what feelings come up for them, where those feelings live in your body. We can be triggered into our survival instinct without being in real physical danger but through everyday interactions that we experience all the time. If we are being triggered into survival mode all the time and relying on these instincts at any given moment during moments when we are not truly in danger, then we are primed to attack at any given moment. These instincts are important, they have protected us and kept us alive for a long time but that doesn't mean they are always serving us. It doesn't mean we are in control or are even aware that we have been triggered. We generally think that this behavior is normal, and we accept it. But if we are always coming from a place of survival, it means that we can also be missing the larger picture and we are robbing ourselves of the ability to be in choice of our actions and responses when it most counts. When we are triggered into survival mode the brain is producing cortisol and adrenaline, both are toxic chemicals that the body produces in order to kick us into survival mode. Our appetite decreases, our blood flow increases, pupils dilate, and we start breathing heavily. When we are triggered into survival mode the brain is producing the toxic chemicals cortisol and adrenaline. We know that prolonged exposure to adrenaline or cortisol impacts the body in ways that create damage to our glands, our cognition, decision making, and overall weariness that settles into the body.

Now imagine you are a low-income person of color dealing with issues of housing stability, being paid minimum wage, and working two jobs, always on the edge of just making it by. Being triggered into survival mode is a normal existence for you, but actually isn't normal and wears you down quickly. Layers of oppression contribute to a social group's exposure to being triggered into survival mode and impacts that group's outcomes including life expectancy, overall physical and mental health. The deeper we cultivate a relationship to how and under what circumstances we are triggered into survival mode and how it robs us from being in choice.

WE KEEP FUELING OUR RADICAL IMAGINATION—
"I AM A BLACK UNICORN!"

Remember how to play pretend (or fake it 'til you make it!)? The practice of radical imagination comes from, first, a place of escapism. As children, we were both captivated by *The Last Unicorn*, which was a movie released in 1982 and we interpret as a story about the policing of Black women's magic and the carceral logics of the containment of Black magic. Separately, we came to this story because of its beautiful artistry and compelling story but stayed because of the opportunity it afforded both of us to escape the realities of systemic and interpersonal violence that we grew up in.

Radical imaginations fueled through flights of fancy are so generative—think about the myth passed down through enslavement of the people who could fly and take their liberation—they can play to the trope common in all story formulas about problems and solutions but are often accompanied by something of the supernatural or mystic. Things that have fueled our imagination for problem solving coach us to think outside of the box, to envision new possibilities. We read books, watch plays, movies, popular television shows that gave a much-needed refuge and break in our day-to-day moving. Books by Roald Dahl, Toni Morrison, and Octavia Butler, to name a few. Movies ranging from *Crooklyn* and *Daughters of the Dust*, to *Star Wars* to *X-Men*, *Labyrinth*, *The Dark Crystal*, and almost anything from the world of Jim Henson. Plays such as *For Colored Girls*, *The Vagina Monologues*, *Three Sisters*, and *Brewster Place*. Musicals like *Tommy*, *RENT* and *CATS*. Television shows such as *Mr. Roger's Neighborhood*, *Reading Rainbow*, *Sesame Street*, *Steven Universe*, *Misfits*, and *A Different World*. These are really just a few and a taste of what helps to inspire and support the possibility of dreaming, creating, envisioning, informing, and growing a mindset for pushing the boundaries of what is into the possibilities of what can be.

"Emergent strategies are ways for humans to practice complexity and grow the future through relatively simple interactions."
—adrienne marie brown, *Emergent Strategies*

Q: How do you show up as an abolitionist in your organizing?

Rae: I was six years old when the police came into my home in a section of the Bronx called Riverdale to arrest my seventeen-year-old brother for jumping the turnstile on a New York City subway to get home at 3AM. I can't remember the time of year or sequence of events that followed afterward but I do remember a deep sense of violation in my own home. That my home wasn't sacred. That our sanctuary away from all of the hustle and bustle of city life was violated. That it could be again. That police could enter my home at any time for any reason as long as it was deemed legal by a court of law. I remember thinking about how absurd it was that my brother was being arrested for something as trivial as jumping a turnstile when I knew that white children in our neighborhood were up to far worse deeds than running out of money and trying to figure out a way home late at night. That many of my brother's white friends were guilty of the same "crime" yet they were not violated in such profound ways, their families terrorized, and their sense of security shaken. I felt marked by this system.

Growing up I saw how other people in my community were marked and targeted for overpolicing, for outrageous tickets and fines because of racial profiling. I saw them get harassed, robbed, and roughed up by police in the street of El Barrio on the East Side or the PJs over in the South Bronx. What was most palpable were the feelings of dread and the reverberation of trauma that I felt in my community. I would come to know deeper about the impacts of trauma, stress, and being in a heightened state of survival mode, what that does to the body and the cognition of a person much later in life. These early childhood understandings of policing, the desire to dream another possibility outside of the carceral logics that we have institutionalized in our society have led to an understanding about the deep seeded trauma of systemic and interpersonal racism afflicting myself and my community. It raises questions about where trauma lives, because it is still living in my body. How has it manifested in my action? How has it impacted how I want to show up in the world? How has it robbed me of my ability to align my values and my actions in my life? I came to the work of embodiment because I am deeply hurt, fractured by the internal and external forces of how racism, sexism, heterosexism, queer and trans hate, classism and ableism have impacted me. I grapple with these questions as I am forging my own pathway to health and wellness, to resting when my body tells me it needs to and taking care of my needs. I am doing this because when people call on me to support them or fight alongside them, they expect me to be there. And I want to be there.

It took me a long time to understand how to connect to my story. What I mean is, it took me a long time to be in practice to reflect with myself on the stress I encountered in everyday life that kept me in a heightened state of awareness, how that impacted my decisions, actions, and attitude. How I embodied this type of oppression and how it showed up in my social justice work but most importantly my life. It took me a long time to observe how I was vomiting rage, as my teacher rusia mohuiddin would say and discuss in her article series appropriately entitled *Vomiting Rage*.[9] How deeply the stress and anxiety I experienced growing up in my predominately white mix of Irish, Jewish, and WASP neighbors and neighborhood filled with police officers, firemen, service men, white collar folx were the background of my otherness. How my Blackness despite being multiracial, light skinned and proximity to whiteness was made invisible yet hypervisible simultaneously. It didn't take me a long time to understand the basic tenets of abolition as a concept, how societies have lived with other means of conflict resolution and safety standards without these monolithic institutions, what took me a long time to realize where I was not even close to living abolition in my body.

I came to practice because of how deeply I did not understand the complexity of how policing had settled as a normal function of everyday, how frequently I am triggered into survival mode and stay on alert but most importantly how it has settled and taken up residence in my body. What I have come to understand and practice is how I handle these feelings, triggers, emotions and experiences in my body what I need to do to care for myself so that oppression doesn't take up residence. How I am seeking to heal the deep wounds of oppression I carry in my genes and navigate around inherited disease that can claim my life.

Q: What does it mean to bring abolition into the classroom?

Jasmine: In the university, in the classroom, the lion's share of information we have about systemic injustice—those intersecting structurally reinforced cultures of violence and oppression—focuses on victimhood, on injury, suffering bodies, death. We turn survivors into objects we would sooner study than learn from. Mine is not that kind of approach. My method of research and teaching centers the knowledge and insights of survivors; it centers the insights of their

9. rusia mohuiddin, "Vomiting Rage," *Universal Partnership*, October 12, 2015, https://universalpartnership.org/vomiting-rage/.

triumphs over these cultures of violence and oppression, however provisional, contingent, or temporary.

I am the first in my extended family to get a PhD. My grandmothers were both domestic workers. I grew up as a preacher's daughter in the Midwest, Tulsa and Cincinnati, before we moved to Brooklyn in the late 1980s. The Central Park Five protests and Crown Heights riots colored the backdrop to my Brooklyn Heights oriented acculturation to New York City race relations. In college, I volunteered in the local medium security prison and facilitated creative writing workshops with the women inside. Sharing stories together transformed my own sense of what freedom means and what the loss of it costs. I moved to California the year after 9/11 and started working with youth in the Bay Area, reporting on and supporting activism against gentrification as a student of the mother-daughter dream team of Poverty Scholars at POOR Magazine, Dee and Tiny. Around the same time, I caught up with a badass crew of spoken word poets-of-color and we started making theatrical street art, first at rallies and marches against the criminalization of youth, against the war, against street violence, and eventually in a black box theater in the Mission District, Brava! Theater for Women. We were Colored Ink, the group that makes ya think! We were in the streets when the US went to war against Iraq and Afghanistan. The helicopters buzzed like dragonflies around San Francisco while swarms of police in riot gear flooded the Tenderloin outside the window where I worked at the Y and downtown, armed with automatic rifles that shot endless rounds of rubber bullets. They came by bus loads. I studied Tupac and Dead Prez with the same tenacity with which I'd studied Kant and Nietzsche in college. Between undergrad and graduate school, I learned what school could not teach me—how to listen to myself and know my voice, who I was, who I was not, and what really matters most. I found that what I care about most are the stories we tell each other—how much we are free to share, how we know what we know in as many creative ways as we can so as to be transformed in the process, to echo the mandate as I would hear it from Mary Hook some years later. Co-Director of Southerners on New Ground, Hook's mandate promised to "to avenge the suffering of our ancestors, to earn the respect of future generations, and to be transformed in the service of the work."

Re-entry to the academy as a graduate student five years after undergrad was rocky. When a beautiful Latinx graduate student from LA asked how I was doing, I had to admit I felt out of place. Like I don't belong there. Susy Zepeda, now professor of Chicano Studies at University of California, Davis responded with words she'd learned to survive the academy. She reminded me that this place wasn't made for me. She and many other incredible marginalized artist activist queer-of-color academics taught me we can create the spaces we need to survive the spaces we were never meant to enter. I joined Critical Resistance in Oakland and helped lead the last couple years of an over forty-year struggle for Critical Race and Ethnic Studies at UC Santa Cruz. By graduation I felt myself emerging from school with a cohort of activist-oriented academics who were learning, teaching, and researching from within the interstitial spaces of our academic containment, the garret spaces, the joining places in-between disciplines, between the university and the community. What we were finding was that the most vulnerable, most easily disappeared, disavowed, and disposable populations not only live on the margins of our cities, communities, and institutions in theory, in practice, in reality we live our lives, work our resources, find our refuge, and move closer to freedom from within the very centers of public life. Our public truths of our lived experiences are not peripheral. We just are taught not to pay attention to them, not to hear ourselves speak. Without their words, wisdom, and witness how else would we work against the grind of politics as usual to fight the isolation of personal struggles and strive to work across lines of difference in the streets and in the academy to form these spaces of ethical allegiance, analysis, and study? This is why I teach my students at Vassar not to leave themselves out of their comprehension of social theory. This is why I invite them to approach themselves as objects of study alongside the sites of struggle we read closely. If we cannot keep our own account of what counts, if we are not writing ourselves into histories of struggle for liberation, then who will represent the truths we carry?

V. "ASK YOURSELF IF THIS HOW WE FALL APART?"

"Take a moment remind yourself to,
Take a moment and find yourself,
Take a moment to ask yourself if
this is how we fall apart?"
—Rebecca Sugar, "Here Comes a Thought," *Steven Universe*

We have been on this journey towards integrating embodied practices and abolitionist activism far before meeting each other. Now that we are on the journey together, the struggle to hold each other accountable is part of the work of integration. As we were preparing for this project of co-authoring what would become *The Manual for Liberating Survival*, we came across an incredible webinar with Mariame Kaba and two queer/trans leaders on "Building Accountable

Communities."[10] One section that resonated with us was a section where Shannon Perez-Darby was reflecting on the challenges of practicing accountability. She said, "My response to what accountability looks like related to state violence involves much of what we've talked about . . . . Thinking about accountability on such a huge scale is so overwhelming that I personally shut-down. I've seen movements and communities feeling defeated by it. It's such a huge scale with working out very basic skills. I use the example of dishes. I've never been in an environment where that isn't an issue. There's something about dishes. It's easy to think about. *If we can't plan for dishes, how do we hold the state accountable? . . .* Let's start where we are."

There is no place like home to begin the practice of liberating survival. This journey that we are on is not about discovering some new place, some far off destination, it's about the process, the practice of reorienting ourselves to where we are, where we live, and how we know what time it is. This prophetic journey that we are on is not a solo journey or one for just two people, or even just for chosen family, but it is for all of us. We are all on this journey together, whether or not we feel that way about it. Each activist, organizer, academic, or person who understands the yoke of oppression, the pressure of policing, the brutality of prisons, the carceral logics that keep us caught up in not knowing what time it is, are traveling along with us.

How do we make homemaking a radical abolitionist practice of all of us or none? How do we better take care of ourselves, to become more ourselves so that we can better take care of each other? We are each getting there in our own ways, and there is no one prescribed way of liberating survival. It is hard to know what liberation even means when so many of the movements that have struggled to get us free reproduce some of the very logics we seek liberation from. What does feel necessary is to take seriously how we read the legacies left to us by previous movements for building power, accountability, and liberation, from the abolition of slavery to the Civil Rights Movement to the power movements of the 1970s. There are lessons there, shining and messy and valuable moments that help us understand how we get free and impact how we practice liberation as defense against the cages, policing, punishment, and disposability that segregate the lives that must be defended from those that are just a problem. Liberation for the first indentured slaves in America was a practice of building Seneca village until it was burnt to the ground because the village acted as a unifier for oppressed people to stake their claim in building a new world. Liberation for emancipated Black folks after enslavement was a practice of creating collective resources for collective survival

10. Kiyomi Fujikawa, Mariame Kaba, and Shannon Perez-Darby, "Building Accountable Communities," webinar hosted by Barnard Center for Research on Women, October 26, 2018, http://bcrw.barnard.edu/wp-content/uploads/2018/06/Online-Event-Building-Accountable-Communities-transcript.pdf.

such as schools and collective housing, or as founder of the United Order of Tents, Annetta M. Lane, did. People provided alternatives to the personal responsibility for financing funerals and instead instituted a kind of life insurance commons where people pooled funds to honor their dead and support orphaned children. Rather than obsess about what liberation means, what if we sought out practices that got us in touch with how liberation feels? Liberation feels like this amorphic place, perhaps like utopia, but it is in fact a practice of paying attention to what we each need for our collective survival (remembering that medicine for some can be poison for others, that no one balm soothes all "genetic" or "environmental" allergies).

The enduring value of the abolitionist struggle for freedom born out of New World Slavery is a practice of moving towards liberation even within spaces of violence and oppression. As Barbara Lee said in a speech at Netroots Nation in 2019, "No one goes to the mouth of the shark unless there's more of a chance of survival there than at home." Even while living in the grips of slavery, even without personhood, even without a self to defend, enslaved communities found ways to resist the reach of the patriarchal institution in the South as much as they did in the North. For the enslaved truants and fugitives, there was no place like home precisely because "home" was not always a physical place but an embodied improvisational fugitive practice of reorientation to the idea of home, to the idea that freedom means having the right to hold another as property. It was a spiritual reorientation to the meaning of home as much as it is a political one.

Our movements for abolition are at a crossroads between the history we are waking up to and the futures we imagine. We have the chance to prophesize the present otherwise. All of us have an idea of freedom and how to get there. We have a choice to make about how we practice the kinds of freedom we say we want and how to do it collectively. How we integrate our imaginations of freedom with our practices of liberation matter.

What are your practices? Are you watching your own patterns? Some of the routes to freedom we have paved are rejuvenating or pay us back for the effort we take to practice them, others leave us depleted. How does the way you are embodying abolition feel? How do you prepare for it? Where do you sense it in your body? Who is with you? Are you alone? Do you have to be? What about this practice feeds you?

Even something as radical as abolition can become captive to habitual practices of surviving, just as some survival instincts become habituated practices that lead to prejudices, bias, the perception of threat when there isn't any. Habituated enclosures that sediment into the idea that we have no choice. We need some place to practice as if the walls are falling. No place, but another kind of relationship to placemaking, imagination, and realization that allows for something new to enter the frame. A loophole of retreat as Harriet Jacobs's slave narrative offers us. A place where we can be silent enough, be still enough, to hear the blood course, the skin breathe, and know we are alive. What do we hear here? How do we sit with what we hear? How can we stay with it long enough to unlearn the habituations of our desire to survive? How do we trust ourselves and each other enough to teach what we are learning from our breath, bodies, stillness, silence, pleasure, play, improvisation, repair, and patience and be changed in the process?

Mastery is not agency. Domination is not freedom. We need abolition to be a practice of liberation from the punitive isolation of habituated self-preservation. We need new habits of survival, ones that honor our differences as well as our common destinies. We need to center practices of flexibility, love, and trust as we move closer to freedom. We must learn to dance as one, or risk falling apart.

REFERENCES

brown, adrienne maree. *Emergent Strategy: Shaping change, changing worlds*. Oakland, CA: AK Press, 2017.

Camp, Stephanie. *Closer to Freedom: Enslaved Women and Everyday Resistance in the Plantation South*. Chapel Hill, NC: University of North Carolina Press. 2005.

Fujikawa, Kiyomi, Shannon Perez-Darby, and Mariame Kaba. "Building Accountable Communities," Barnard Center for Research on Women, Friday, October 26, 2018 http://bcrw.barnard.edu/wp-content/uploads/2018/06/Online-Event-Building-Accountable-Communities-transcript.pdf

Johnson, Gaye Theresa and Alex Lubin. *Futures of Black Radicalism*. Brooklyn, NY: Verso 2017.

Kennedy, Maggie. "MinnesotaNice" Midterm prepared for "No Selves To Defend: Gender, Sexuality, and Abolitionist Activis.n." Taught by Jasmine Syedullah, Visiting Assistant Professor of Sociology, Vassar College (Spring 2019).

Lambel, S. "Transforming Carceral Logics: 10 Reasons to Dismantle the Prison Industrial Complex Using a Queer/Trans Analysis" in *Captive Genders: Trans Embodiment and the Prison Industrial Complex* edited by Eric A. Stanley & Nat Smith. Oakland: AK Press, 2016.

Mingus, Mia. "Still Choosing to Leap: Building Alternatives," Remarks from the closing plenary, "Revolutionary Organizing Across Time and Space," at the INCITE! Color of Violence 4 Conference, March 26-29, 2015, Chicago, Illinois https://leavingevidence.wordpress.com/2015/03/31/still-choosing-to-leap-building-alternatives/.

mohuiddin, rusia. "Vomiting Rage," Universal Partnership, October 12, 2015, https://universalpartnership.org/vomiting-rage/.

Samuels, Liz "Improvising on Reality: The Roots of Prison Abolition" *The Hidden 1970s: Histories of Radicalism* edited by Dan Berger. New Brunswick, NJ: Rutgers University Press, 2010.

Scott, Kesho Y. *The Habit of Surviving: Black Women's Strategies for Life.* New Brunswick, NJ: Rutgers University Press, 1991.

williams, angel Kyodo, Rod Owens, and Jasmine Syedullah. *Radical Dharma: Talking Race, Love, and Liberation.* Berkeley, CA: North Atlantic Press, 2016.

RESURRECTION AT THE FRACTURED LOCUS:

INCARCERATED BLACK TRANS EMBODIMENT AND DECOLONIAL ABOLITION PRAXIS

AK Wright

"Whatever happens, whatever happened, we are deathless!"
—Ibeyi, "Deathless"

"Told you we aint dead yet, we been livin' through your internet
you don't have to believe everything you think
we've been programmed wake up, we miss you.
they call you indigo, we call you Africa.
go get baptized in the ocean of the people"
—Erykah Badu, "The Healer"

"As each new ancestor surges forward, my body screams.
My skin tears like it's being pulled apart. But I need it. I need them. Their voices begin to ring, a chorus of the living dead."
—Tomi Adeyemi, *Children of Blood and Bone*

In June of 2011, CeCe McDonald, a Black trans woman, defended herself from a violent transphobic and racist attack. Despite multiple accounts that she attacked in self-defense, attempted to leave the scene and only reacted when glass was smashed in her face, she was essentially forced to plead guilty for the manslaughter of her swastika-tattooed attacker to avoid a lengthy prison sentence. Like many trans individuals, she was placed in a facility that did not align with her gender.[1] McDonald, reflecting on her time in prison, writes, "In the beginning, I was scared—I was a trans woman surrounded by so many men, but they were really inviting and sincere. They want to know who I was as a person, as a trans woman, and they wanted to know my struggles as a trans woman. This surprised me

1. Matt Richardson and Omise'eke Natasha Tinsley, "From Black Transgender Studies to Colin Dayan: Notes on Methodology," *Small Axe* 18, no. 3 45 (January 2014): 152–53, http://smallaxe.dukejournals.org/content/18/3_45/152.abstract.

because the media portrays people in prisons as angry, evil, deceiving."[2] McDonald's transness and Blackness marked her as inherently criminal. These mythologies of criminality are conditions that led to her imprisonment and the imprisonment of so many Black trans individuals. Her imprisonment is a result of the construction of the United States as a state built and sustained through a raced and gendered form of carcerality.

A carceral state is one built upon imprisonment as a means of social control and regulation to address social conflicts that challenge the authority of the state to shape the lives of citizens.[3] The United States is a carceral state that often addresses ills that result from kyriarchal or hierarchical systems through punitive measures. The carceral state operates in a gender binary that renders those who do not conform to societal expectations of gender expression illegible, resulting in the endangerment of incarcerated trans folks, particularly those who are Black and Brown. Carceral logics can be carried out not only by the state and its agents such as police and border patrol but anyone who lives within the state.

Cece's assault occurred a four-minute drive away from my Minneapolis home. As a Black trans person, I know violence surrounds my existence. My very existence is a challenge to societal gender and racial norms as someone whose race and gender expression are doubly deviant, always out of place and out of order. As C. Riley Snorton notes, "To feel Black in diaspora, then, might be a trans experience."[4] One's existence is an act of transgression. Cece's narrative is one of many stories of quotidian antitrans violent encounters.

In this essay, I am interested in the implications and insights that can be drawn from decolonial theory in carceral studies regarding the experiences of Black trans folks. I am inspired by the graverobber methodology invoked in the work of Matt Richardson and Omise'eke Natasha Tinsley as they engage the work of Colin Dayan.[5] Richardson and Tinsley describe their graverobbing methodology as one in which they "delve into the purposely and accidentally immolated pasts of a variety of times and sites, in order to unearth the skeletons of racism, misogyny, and transphobia that dominant narratives keep invisible and disconnected in our understanding of times and places."[6]

2. CeCe McDonald, "Foreword," in Eric A. Stanley and Nat Smith, *Captive Genders: Trans Embodiment and the Prison Industrial Complex*, Expanded Second Edition (Oakland, CA, USA: AK Press, 2015), 1.

3. Marie Gottschalk, "Democracy and the Carceral State in America," *The ANNALS of the American Academy of Political and Social Science* 651, no. 1 (January 2014): 289.

4. C. Riley Snorton, *Black on Both Sides: A Racial History of Trans Identity* (Minneapolis: University of Minnesota Press, 2017), 8.

5. Richardson and Tinsley, "From Black Transgender Studies to Colin Dayan: Notes on Methodology," 153.

6. Richardson and Tinsley, 153.

Hence, I set forth on a critical intellectual curiosity of what can be unearthed from the past to elucidate our current carceral state and its significance for those marked as Black and trans.[7] What ideas can be "robbed" from the past to offer insight into the connection between coloniality and carceral logics? What theories and concepts provide the metaphoric shovel to complete this task?

Departing from Richardson and Tinsley, I wish to extend the act of theft, or the return of what is ours, using what was stolen in order to go beyond the grave. I consider abolition a process to save and recover lives, in a sense to engage with resurrection. Resurrection, as a spiritual understanding, as ascension, as reuniting, allows us to envision the other life of abolition creatively and passionately, a world without the forces of the carceral state. If as Ashon Crawley argues, Blackness is a decolonial abolitionist project that crafts possibilities and imaginaries that refuse quotidian violence and violation, then resurrection could be a project of abolition praxis. [8] Abolition creates what Crawley names as the "otherwise", the creation of a world without prisons, antiblackness and trans antagonism. [9] To meditate on resurrection allows us perhaps to also unearth abolitionist world making.

The resurrection of Christianity that culminates in Easter celebrations has been fascinating to me since I was a child in Caribbean Pentecostal churches. My childhood church, rebuking the idea of Easter as too pagan, encouraged members to call the day Resurrection Sunday. Therefore, I consider Easter and Resurrection Sunday two different celebrations. Resurrection Sunday was similar to a wake, what we Jamaicans call either the set-up/nine nights that occurs before the funeral except that this was a celebration of life that occurred after the body was buried and reborn. [10] A day filled with bright, colorful clothing, a lengthy church program that included song, dance, and prayers and that concluded with a feast. Resurrection Sunday was the celebration of a story of intense grief and mourning that gives way to redemption and joy. It was also an example of Black social life, the joy of spiritual hope that conveys that coloniality and white supremacist terror is not total. As Terrion Williamson notes, "To speak of black social life is to speak of this radical capacity to live—to live deeply righteous lives even in the midst of all that brings death close or, as Lucille Clifton puts it, to celebrate 'everyday/something has tried to

7. I define trans as any individual who does not identify as the gender that they were assigned at birth such as trans men and women and non-binary/gender nonconforming individuals.

8. Ashon T. Crawley, *Blackpentecostal Breath: The Aesthetics of Possibility* (New York: Fordham University Press, 2017), 4.

9. Crawley, *Blackpentecostal Breath*, 1.

10. According to spiritual oral tradition, the soul takes nine nights to arrive back at Africa to be with their ancestors.

kill me/and has failed.'"[11] Following Clifton, to engage resurrection is to understand that even if death succeeds, we can be reborn and hence death continuously fails. Communal joy that erupts in Black social life is deeply spiritual as it rebirths and nourishes the soul.

Despite the harm I experienced in my spiritual upbringing due to the castigation of my sexuality and gender expression, I still find it meaningful to my life. I am grateful for the work churches like the ones I grew up in provide to Black and Brown communities, especially those from poor and working-class neighborhoods. Though it is tempting to discard a space that harms queer and trans individuals like myself, this harm is not all that there is. To discard it would be to discard a part of myself. Noting the Black feminist practices of my family, I refuse to flatten the complex work done in their spiritual spaces to queer and trans antagonism.[12] It was in those spaces that communities crafted life and made space for Black Caribbean existence. It was the first place I saw how to heal spirit beyond the violences of colonialism and enslavement.

Building upon the spiritual practices of my childhood, I want to work with the concept of resurrection, thieving it away for a moment from the Christian narrative of Christ raising from the dead to link the concept with abolitionist praxis. How do we resurrect those who have passed, like the dozens of Black trans individuals who have been murdered in and by the carceral state or those who walk among us yet are marked for death due to their very existence?

Resurrection can also mean the coming back to life of the human dead before the final judgment.[13] What if we were to imagine this haunting image of rising beyond those packed in the earth to trouble the binary between life and death? What if "rising" meant everyone who the carceral state marks for death acted outrageously "to get the recognition they deserve"?[14] A recognition not asked of or given by the state. In this imagining, judgment falls upon the state to answer for its crimes and violent tendencies. In theology, resurrection can also be defined as material belief that yields to spiritual understanding. Perhaps we can think of spiritual understanding as the driving force of anti-carceral state resistance that becomes an act of resurrection

---

11. Terrion L. Williamson, *Scandalize My Name: Black Feminist Practice and the Making of Black Social Life* (New York: Fordham University Press, 2016), 9.

12. In her work, Terrion Williamson utilizes Black feminist practice which she defines as "radical commitment to the significance of black female life and the humanity of all black peoples, regardless of whether the practitioner identifies with feminism as a formalized ideological commitment or holds some views that might ultimately be deemed antithetical to feminism itself," *Scandalize My Name*, 8.

13. "Definition of Resurrection," *Merriam Webster*, Accessed April 17, 2018, https://www.merriam-webster.com.

14. Sharon Patricia Holland, *Raising the Dead: Readings of Death and (Black) Subjectivity* (Durham, North Carolina: Duke University Press, 2000), 120.

nested in abolition praxis. Abolition creates a resurgence and revival of Black trans souls demanding the right to live, flourish, and define their existence.[15]

How can we move beyond capitalist material realities that came from the brutal, bloody construction of racial colonial empire like the United States?[16] How do we move to spiritual healing that can create a harvest of understanding that helps us to tear down punitive sites and save souls? What would it mean for resurrected Black trans souls to hold as much significance and meaning as those risen from the dead in biblical text? How can understanding what Maria Lugones calls the "coloniality of gender" help us critically engage in this work?[17]

Lugones' work showcases that targeting the effects of coloniality allows for the dismantling of oppressive forces that are the foundation of the carceral state. One must deconstruct the carceral state as a colonial living-artifact that operates as a tool to reinforce racialized gender surveillance and regulation and that continues the dehumanization project of colonialism and slavery. I build upon Lugones' work by analyzing carcerality and Black trans embodiment because I believe the coloniality of gender is significant to understanding the U.S. as a carceral state and understanding what causes the policing and incarceration of Black trans individuals.

Building upon the Christian narrative of resurrection across three days, I divide this paper into three parts: the death, the tomb, and the revivification. First, I evaluate Lugones' theory of the "decoloniality of gender" through its understanding of racialized and ungendered bodies in colonized individuals and how understanding colonial legacies helps us understand why the carceral state marks Black trans folks for death. I then enter the grave through the entombment of incarcerated Black trans individuals in punitive sites. With my sight on the coming day of resurrection, I end with cogitations on the insights gained from decolonial feminist theory regarding carceral abolition praxis.

To do this project, I reflect on how we may communally rob the carceral grave of its bodies so that one day when nefarious agents of the state come looking, abolitionists may say in defiance: they are not here, they are not dead, they have risen.

15. Cedric J. Robinson, *Forgeries of Memory and Meaning: Blacks and the Regimes of Race in American Theater and Film before World War II* (Chapel Hill, North Carolina: University of North Carolina Press, 2007), xii.

16. Moon-Kie Jung, João Helion Costa Vargas, and Eduardo Bonilla-Silva, *State of White Supremacy: Racism, Governance, and the United States* (Stanford, California: Stanford University Press, 2011), 1.

17. María Lugones, "Heterosexualism and the Colonial/Modern Gender System," *Hypatia* 22, no. 1 (February 2007): 196.

Resurrection requires a discussion of death(s). A body must lose life, the ability to protect life forces, and/or be marked for premature death. To be marked for death does not require a physical death; death may occur in other forms where one cannot survive and flourish. Achille Mbembe argues that a state's sovereignty is defined by its ability to not only define control over morality but also to define life.[18] Coloniality, essential to the development of the US, becomes a means of attempting to control who lives and dies. In addition to the enslavement of Black people, Native genocide and erasure is central to carcerality of the state. Kelly Lytle Hernández argues, "Mass incarceration is mass elimination. . . . Incarceration operates as a means of purging, removing, caging, erasing, disappearing and eliminating targeted populations from land, life, and society in the United States."[19] Hernández notes the first individuals incarcerated in the state now known as California were unmarried Native women and girls who were locked in their dormitories in colonial missions in order to prevent them from becoming pregnant and hence creating future generations with claims to the land.[20] The carceral state is built upon logics cemented in coloniality which attempts to eventually eradicate Black and Brown communities.

Lugones defines coloniality as an ongoing process in which individuals are actively reduced and dehumanized to become shaped for a classification and subjectification that attempts to rob the colonized of their humanity.[21] This reduction of humanity, the reduction of colonial subjects to the status of unworthy life, creates an inferior group of people that validates the project of colonialism.[22] Lugones states that coloniality occurs when "all control over sex, subjectivity, authority, and labor are articulated around it."[23] Violences of coloniality become reminders of the continuation of dehumanization, theft and/or disrupting lives like a colonial poltergeist. In our current spatiotemporal existence, death is never far away for colonized subjects.

Colonial logic aggressively enforces narrow understandings of sex, gender, and sexuality through heterosexism and the gender binary,

---

18. Achille Mbembe, "Necropolitics," trans. Libby Meintjes, *Public Culture* 15, no. 1 (2003): 12.

19. Kelly Lytle Hernández, *City of Inmates: Conquest, Rebellion, and the Rise of Human Caging in Los Angeles, 1771-1965.* (Chapel Hill, North Carolina: University of North Carolina Press, 2017), 1.

20. Hernández, *City of Inmates,* 25.

21. María Lugones, "Toward a Decolonial Feminism," *Hypatia* 25, no. 4 (October 2010): 745.

22. Lugones, "Toward a Decolonial Feminism," 751.

23. Lugones, "Heterosexualism and the Colonial/Modern Gender System," 191.

resulting in the aforementioned types of death. Lugones argues that our understanding of gender is a result of a violent colonial introduction. She makes the case that colonized male and female subjects emerged with the introduction of a new gender system for the colonized.[24] As individuals were stolen, killed, robbed, and brutalized, "[t]his gender system congealed as Europe advanced the colonial project(s)."[25] Trans embodiment is antithetical to this colonial logic that states sex and gender as the same and biologically determined. Such understandings of gender and sex result in the gender surveillance and policing experienced by trans folks. CeCe McDonald notes that throughout her life she was policed by her family, schoolmates, and strangers for her gender expression.[26] The policing of her gender has continually placed her and other trans individuals in danger, marking them vulnerable to premature death. The defense of her life from this violent policing later became the reason that she was incarcerated. Her attacker and others who policed her adhered to the colonial logic of the carceral state.

Determining the gender and sexuality of colonial subjects becomes a means of control and regulation to benefit capitalist colonial projects invested in controlling the life and death of Black and Brown people. Like Lugones, Hortense Spillers also theorizes how colonialism and slavery affects the captive body. Spillers states that at the site of the captive body, "we lose at least gender difference in the outcome, and the female body and the male body become a territory of cultural and political maneuver, not at all gender-related, gender-specific."[27] Black cisgender women are not seen as women and hence do not gain the "benefits" of their "sex" such as labor reduction or protection from sexual violence. Even with the introduction of the colonial understandings of gender, such logics can be easily tossed to benefit the racialized, capitalist desires of the carceral state.

Coloniality acts paradoxically by simultaneously policing the gender of Black folks while ensuring that one cannot fulfill societal gender expectations due to their racial and ethnic identity. This paradox is necessary to act out colonial logic. Coloniality renders Black and Brown women genderless, according to Lugones, which also furthers their dehumanization.[28] Lugones firmly states, "No women are colo-

24. Lugones, "Heterosexualism and the Colonial/Modern Gender System,"186.

25. Lugones, "Heterosexualism and the Colonial/Modern Gender System," 206.

26. CeCe McDonald and Omise'eke Natasha Tinsley, "'Go Beyond Our Natural Selves' The Prison Letters of CeCe McDonald," *Transgender Studies Quarterly* 4, no. 2 (2017): 258.

27. Hortense Spillers, "Mama's Baby, Papa's Maybe: An American Grammar Book," *Diacritics* 17, no. 2 (1987): 67.

28. Lugones, "Toward a Decolonial Feminism," 745.

nized, no colonized females are women."[29] Only the civilized are men or women; only those who are white are human. Black and Brown folks are marked as un/human, non/gendered yet punished for gender deviancy. The carceral state criminalizes individuals for non-normative gender expression and acts: "Gender nonconformity in appearance or expression gives rise to police assumptions of disorder, violence, mental instability, among other qualities. Such presumptions of disorder are heightened when synergistically reinforced by equally powerful stereotypes based on race, class, or both."[30]

Gender conformity becomes a means of state control and regulation. The state has a vested interest in maintaining gender conformity. Vivian Mays argues, "Ostensible lack of gender, or aberrant or deviant gender, is then used to rationalize ungendered/degendered bodies being brutalized (as hypersexual or animal flesh), caged or incarcerated, exploited as surplus labor, or destroyed because they're expendable."[31] One's ability to pass and conform is contingent on norms, determined by white heterosexuality, which one's body is tested against.[32] I am reminded of a speech I attended a few years ago, by Black trans activist-actress Laverne Cox. She painfully reflected that when she identified as male, she was called a girl for being an effeminate boy and now that she identifies as a woman, due to her height she is masculinized and called a man. She can never truly be acknowledged as her gender identity or fulfill societal gender expectations. If Black cisgender women who are marked often as abnormally masculine and hypersexual fail to live up to the standards set forth by the state, it becomes extremely hard, if not impossible, for Black trans individuals to escape the clutches of the carceral state.

While Lugones argues that gender as we understand it is a colonial fiction, it is a fiction that holds tremendous power in shaping one's life and how one sees oneself.[33] It may be fiction, but it is powerful nevertheless. Significant in trans and gender nonconforming identity is self-identification and aligning one's gender expression in ways that are meaningful and comfortable to oneself. I am not interested in whether coloniality limits the validity of trans and gender nonconforming identity. Rather, I'm interested in how colonial conceptions of gender limit, shrink, or even eradicate a space for gender

---

29. Lugones, "Toward a Decolonial Feminism," 743.

30. Joey L. Mogul, Andrea Ritchie, and Kay Whitlock, *Queer (in)Justice: The Criminalization of LGBT People in the United States*, Queer Action/Queer Ideas (Boston: Beacon Press, 2011), 87.

31. Vivian M. May, *Pursuing Intersectionality, Unsettling Dominant Imaginaries* (New York: Routledge, Taylor & Francis Group, 2015), 204.

32. Toby Beauchamp, "Artful Concealment and Strategic Visibility: Transgender Bodies and U.S. State Surveillance after 9/11," *Surveillance & Society* 6, no. 4 (2009): 357.

33. Lugones, "Heterosexualism and the Colonial/Modern Gender System," 202.

variance and multiple understandings of gender. Why does gender nonconformity become a threat to the state and subject to regulation and surveillance through punitive sites?

The dichotomous hierarchy between the human (marked by whiteness and gender conformity) and the non-human (marked by race and gender nonconformity) which, as Lugones writes, becomes "the central dichotomy of colonial modernity," is reproduced through the strictly enforced dichotomy of Black and Brown people who live to prematurely die and white individuals who are entitled to life.[34] Saidiya Hartman argues that one must link slavery to the conditions of our current spatiotemporality of Blackness "because black lives are still imperiled and devalued by a racial calculus and a political arithmetic that were entrenched centuries ago. This is the afterlife of slavery-skewed life chances, limited access to health and education, premature death, incarceration, and impoverishment."[35] The racial calculus and political arithmetic that Hartman so eloquently invokes in her work is rooted in the emergence of the idea of race under modernity which cemented notions of Black immorality and criminality in the physiological landscape of the American empire. The aftermath of slavery vibrates in the racist underpinnings of the carceral state which both is built upon and reproduces anti-Blackness. Ruth Wilson Gilmore's definition of racism is most helpful in explicating anti-Blackness and its linkage to death. She defines it as "the state-sanctioned or extralegal production and exploitation of group-differentiated vulnerability to premature death."[36] In the lives of Black trans individuals, premature death becomes a given reality. The afterlife of slavery speaks to the epistemological power of racial ideas and their material repercussions for Black individuals. The erosion of the value of Black life is linked to a material and psychosociological investment in the perpetuation of colonial logic.

Systemic racism continues the colonial project of extracting economic benefits from Black bodies thus placing them in economic vulnerability. Julia Chinyere Oparah notes that just as slavery justified the dehumanization of African captives to maintain the economic system of plantation slavery, "the dehumanization of people of color through racialized and criminalizing ideologies legitimates the devastation wrought by capitalist globalization."[37] Black people

34. Lugones, "Toward a Decolonial Feminism," 743.

35. Saidiya Hartman, *Lose Your Mother: A Journey Along the Atlantic Slave Route*, 1st ed. (New York: Farrar, Straus and Giroux, 2007), 6.

36. Ruth Wilson Gilmore, "Fatal Couplings of Power and Difference: Notes on Racism and Geography," *The Professional Geographer* 54, no. 1 (February 2002): 28.

37. Julia Chinyere Oparah, "Maroon Abolitionists: Black Gender-Oppressed Activists in the Anti-Prison Movement in the US and Canada" in Stanley and Smith, *Captive Genders: Trans Embodiment and the Prison Industrial Complex*, 336–37.

are continually prevented from reaping the benefits of their labor in the building of the American empire and instead are kept in economically vulnerable positions. Black and Brown trans folks exist in the nexus of economic racialized violence and gendered vulnerability. The 2011 National Gay and Lesbian Task Force and National Center for Transgender Equality's "National Transgender Discrimination Survey" noted that 35 percent of Black trans respondents were living on less than $10,000 a year.[38] The same survey found that, far above the national average of 716 per 100,000 of the national population, one in two Black transgender people are incarcerated. A 2013 report from the National Coalition of Anti-Violence Programs found that 53.8 percent of anti-LGBT homicides were Black women, and 73 percent were LGBT people of color.[39] The colonial legacy of death continues to haunt Black and Brown queer and trans individuals. As Wilson Gilmore notes, in our current spatiotemporal geography, premature death becomes not an intolerable failure but an unfortunate given.[40] Angela Davis notes that racism as we know it today is so deeply embedded in institutional structures that they "now appear to be detached from the persons they harm with their violence."[41] In the current legal system and carceral state, gendered and racialized individuals cannot appear before the law without the system harming them.

No law or prison reform will work, only abolition—that eliminates the system altogether by cultivating a society that does not need such carceral systems will work. The criminalization of Blackness is so normalized that it is not considered an act of violence; coloniality has shaped the (in)justice system this way which is why an (extra)ordinary act of resurrection is required. Resurrection helps us to highlight, study, and enact resistance that cannot be fully prevented by carceral colonial logics. Resurrection is to be uncapturable by death, to believe that death is escapable.

Black trans embodiment lays at the center of what Lugones calls the fractured locus, a precarious location where one is marked as non-human, deemed not worthy of life and burdened by the weight of subjugation. Yet this location is where resistance begins. At this site, the seeds of resurrection sprout through the cracks and the subjectivity of the colonized subject comes through: "The fractured

---

38. Treva Elision, "The Strangeness of Progress and the Uncertainty of Blackness" in E. Patrick Johnson, *No Tea, No Shade: New Writings in Black Queer Studies* (Durham, North Carolina: Duke University Press, 2016), 325.

39. Elision, "The Strangeness of Progress and the Uncertainty of Blackness" in Johnson, 332.

40. Gilmore, "Fatal Couplings of Power and Difference: Notes on Racism and Geography," 17.

41. Angela Y. Davis, *Abolition Democracy: Beyond Empire, Prisons, and Torture* (New York: Seven Stories Press, 2005), 57.

locus includes the hierarchical dichotomy that constitutes the subjectification of the colonized. But the locus is fractured by the resistant
presence, the active subjectivity of the colonized against the colonial
invasion of self in community from the inhabitation of that self."[42]

Now that I have laid out the project of decolonial theory and the
coloniality of gender, I shall bring us closer to carceral sites of the
tomb and the project of abolition. Though prisons continue colonial
logics in their organization and structure, I believe the insights we
graverobbed through Lugones' theory of the colonality of gender and
decolonial theory helps us to not only examine the experiences of
Black trans incarcerated folks but also to build a decolonial abolitionist praxis.

DAY TWO: THE TOMB, CARCERAL LOGIC, AND GENDER DEVIANCY

Brick and mortar carceral tombs are punitive sites such as prisons,
jails, juvenile detention centers, and immigrant detention centers
that operate as forms of social control to fulfill the desires of the
neoliberal, heteronormative, white supremacist state. Coloniality
births carcerality and carceral tools that surveil, police, and target
Blackness. The state enforces societal norms through the usage of
carceral agents and carceral logics acted out by non-carceral agents.
Mark Neocleous argues that policing by the state originated due to
a loss of power by the bourgeoisie and nobility over poorer populations after the Middle Ages.[43] Those in power continuously seek to
remain in power. Neocleous states that policing became concerned
with "actively shaping the social body according to certain ends—
the ends of the state and the production of wealth."[44] The carceral
state uses policing as a form of control over the citizenry to shape
citizens to be what the state deems are good citizens and to extract
labor from incarcerated populations. For example, through the convict leasing system, freed slaves were leased out to private citizens
following the Civil War; a good Black individual was one in service to
their white counterparts. Hartman argues that post-slavery there was
the "resubordination of the emancipated, the control and domination
of the free Black population and persistent production of Blackness
as abject, threatening, servile, dangerous, dependent, irrational, and

---

42. Lugones, "Toward a Decolonial Feminism," 749.

43. Mark Neocleous, *The Fabrication of Social Order: A Critical Theory of Police Power*
(London; Sterling, Va.: Pluto Press, 2000), 2.

44. Neocleous, *The Fabrication of Social Order*, 6.

infectious."[45] Currently, in a time where the US rate of incarceration has risen, the crime rates have fallen.[46] What is happening? Michelle Alexander reminds us that punishment is a state tool of social control.[47] The normalization of carceral punishment aims to verify an alleged, inherent criminal nature of Black and Brown people, poor people, and/or queer and trans individuals.

Carceral punishment has also become a means to ignore and deflect from social, political, and economic ills that result from reverberating colonial legacies. States normalize carceral punishment because it exists as an ideal of functioning, modern nations: "The practice of putting people in cages for part or all of their lives is a central feature in the development of secular states, participatory democracy, individual rights, and contemporary notions of freedom."[48] In a nation such as the United States that prides itself on a mythology of liberty and honor, and yet has the world's largest prison and military, disappearing social problems is significant to the national image as the authority of justice and defender of freedom so that it may hold onto its place as the leader of the (un)free world. Wilson Gilmore argues that prisons are partial geographical solutions to a state perpetually in crisis.[49] Anyone deemed not a productive, normative individual is a threat to the state, becoming part of dispensable populations. Often societal removal through carceral logics at the hands of the state, its agents, and those who act out carceral logics, occurs violently. As Dean Spade argues, one cannot look to the state for protection through hate crime legislation and other measures because "state programs and law enforcement are not the arbiters of justice, protection, and safety but are instead sponsors and sites of violence."[50] You cannot convince the state to protect bodies that they have already marked for death.

The coloniality of gender becomes quite apparent upon examining carceral accounts by Black trans individuals where the gender binary is violently enforced. Trans individuals often account being placed in prisons by the sex they were assigned at birth and not by their gender expression. If they protest such treatment they are transferred into facilities for the mentally ill or into solitary confinement,

---

45. Hartman, *Scenes of Subjection: Terror, Slavery, and Self-Making in Nineteenth-Century America*, 116.

46. Michelle Alexander, *The New Jim Crow: Mass Incarceration in the Age of Colorblindness*, Rev. ed. (New York: New Press, 2012), 10.

47. Alexander, *The New Jim Crow*, 7.

48. Ruth Wilson Gilmore, *Golden Gulag: Prisons, Surplus, Crisis, and Opposition in Globalizing California* (Berkeley: University of California Press, 2007), 11.

49. Gilmore, *Golden Gulag*, 26.

50. Dean Spade, *Normal Life: Administrative Violence, Critical Trans Politics, and the Limits of Law* (Durham, North Carolina: Duke University Press, 2015), 21.

thus illustrating that carceral agents believe that they are pathologically inferior or dangerous and need to be separated from the general population. Elias Vitulli notes that when seeking medical treatment, "doctors often require trans people to conform to rigid and restrictive stereotypes, including white, heteronormative masculinity and femininity."[51] Hence, Black trans prisoners are continually measured against racial and gender norms that the state designs as unachievable due to their race and gender. The dehumanization that occurs in punitive sites speak to the continuance of the power of the state to objectify and dehumanize Black and Brown people.

Prison officials often argue that they utilize solitary confinement to protect trans folks from sexual assault. However, it instead becomes another form of carceral violence. Ashley Diamond, an incarcerated Black trans woman, described that, "if you report a rape, nothing happens, or you go to solitary confinement. I have spent a year and a half in solitary confinement just because I was raped. There was prior knowledge, and they knew."[52] Diamond's carceral enslavers decided to punish her for her own sexual assault. She spent a year and a half in isolation from other individuals because the guards had no interest in protecting her. Janette Johnson discusses a similar experience to Diamond. In order to negotiate for her own freedom, she had to choose between sexual violence and notifying others of the abuse. If Johnson had "chosen to stay 'protected' in solitary confinement by complaining to prison authorities about being sexually abused, the opportunities leading to early release would not have been available to her."[53] Sexual violence and exploitation that occurs in prisons are not a reason to keep prisons open and populations of people caged; instead, such violent acts convey that prisons harm individuals within their walls, survivors, perpetrators, and those who are both. Furthermore, prison officials are incapable of protecting these women who are labeled as disposable due to the colonial logic of the carceral state which exemplifies further the need for prison abolition.

Solitary confinement is the clearest example of entombment. Lisa Guenther notes that many incarcerated individuals describe solitary confinement as a form of living death.[54] Guenther argues such isolation is a form of social death where people are physically alive but lives no longer matter.[55] The narrative of Jazzie Ferrari, a Black trans

51. Elias Vitulli, "Racialized Criminality and the Imprisoned Trans Body: Adjudicating Access to Gender-Related Medical Treatment in Prisons," *Social Justice* 37, no. 1 (119) (2010): 55.

52. Kristin Schreier Lyseggen, *The Women of San Quentin: Soul Murder of Transgender Women in Male Prisons* (Berkeley, California: SFINX Publishing, 2015), 68.

53. Schreier Lyseggen, *The Women of San Quentin*, 3.

54. Lisa Guenther, *Solitary Confinement: Social Death and Its Afterlives* (University of Minnesota Press Minneapolis, 2013), xii.

55. Guenther, *Solitary Confinement*, xx.

woman, incarcerated for eighteen years for a crime she did not commit reflects this. In her words she has been left for dead by her family. When describing the horror of solitary confinement, she describes that "being in the SHU is like being underground."[56] To hold individuals in prison, especially in solitary confinement, is to rob them of life-giving forces that nurture and cherish their humanity. Prisons are a tool of the death-making carceral state that punishes Black and Brown trans individuals for their presumed deviancy and attempts to capture and bury them away from their communities.

The gender binary of prison housing is even more precarious for those who exist outside the binary and are gender nonconforming. There is no place for them in punitive sites that require one to be male or female. In many places, the local criminal (in)justice system refuses to recognize chosen names, gender identities, or even provide clothing that aligns with one's gender expression.[57] Oparah argues that the reduction of gender to what is believed to be biological sex violates one's right to self-determination.[58] Oparah interviewed Bakari who is Black and identifies as gender nonconforming.[59] S/he states. "You have male and female prisons. I ain't male or female, so which do I get to go to? And you're housed according to your genitalia, which to me does not connote gender."[60] Where does s/he go? S/he is illegible to the carceral state. Her/his gender identity exists outside carceral logics that attempt to reign in nonbinary gender identities. Bakari speaks to this misrecognition: "How they control you and mandate you to this gender binary is if you're in a women's facility, you must wear whatever society says is for women."[61] Her/His boxers were taken away from her/him and labeled contraband.[62] Yet the same piece of fabric would be acceptable in a facility designated for males. How do we make sense of this strange logic? Lugones discusses coloniality as a process of classification and subjectification.[63] Their boxers are a sign of an unruly colonial subject. The boxers convey self-determination, which the carceral states do not want to allow. Just as coloniality attempted to remove the ability to recognize

56. Schreier Lyseggen, *The Women of San Quentin: Soul Murder of Transgender Women in Male Prisons*, 215.

57. Mogul, Ritchie, and Whitlock, *Queer (in)Justice: The Criminalization of LGBT People in the United States*, 110.

58. Oparah, "Marron Abolitionists," in Stanley and Smith, *Captive Genders: Trans Embodiment and the Prison Industrial Complex*, 340.

59. Bakari chooses the pronouns, S/he or Her/Him.

60. Oparah, "Marron Abolitionists," in Stanley and Smith, *Captive Genders: Trans Embodiment and the Prison Industrial Complex*, 340.

61. Oparah, "Marron Abolitionists," in Stanley and Smith, 341–42.

62. Oparah, "Marron Abolitionists," in Stanley and Smith, 342.

63. Lugones, "Toward a Decolonial Feminism," 745.

genders outside of the binary, so do carceral sites erase gender-non-conformity and trans identity, violently assigning incarcerated folks to labels in "the attempt to turn the colonized into less than human beings."[64] How do we reclaim the humanity lost in coloniality? How do we rob the tombs?

Amid burial, all is not quiet. There is still life—the soil is animated, strengthening itself with nutrients, seeds are planting roots and allowing for new life to push through the dirt. Within colonial regimes, there is something fracturing its attempts to hold and control life. Cedric Robinson argues, "regime entropy ensues from the fact that because the regimes are cultural artifices, which catalog only fragments of the real, they inevitably generate fugitive, unaccounted-for elements of reality."[65] Robinson encourages us to find those unaccounted-for realities. Realities, like ivy that takes over a building and slips in and out of faults in the stone, that illustrate the violences of the carceral state is not the only narrative to tell. In August of 2014, an extraordinary collection of videos surfaced on YouTube, erupting through the cracks of the carceral state. Ashley Diamond, who was mentioned earlier as a survivor of sexual assault in prison, arrived in the digital ecology of the internet to tell her own story. Diamond, somehow despite the intense surveillance and regulation of prisons, was able to create a YouTube channel entitled, "Memoirs of a Chain Gang Sissy."[66] Diamond's videos tell her audience what she wants from them. She states, "It is my hope that we shake you and we stir you and we get you to do something. . . . Many of our stories go unheard or even never reach the right ears, it's time to stop this now."[67] After being held in prison with no access to hormonal treatments or other factors to help with her gender dysphoria, Diamond attracted national attention when she filed a lawsuit against the Georgia Department of Corrections (GDOC) in 2015. Once this occurred, Diamond faced intense backlash from the GDOC. Her accounts were frozen and the little mental healthcare she received were canceled. Diamond stated she was punished because she exposed the GDOC's treatment of trans prisoners: "They thought that I was just going to be just like any other person that they have destroyed, because I am not the first, nor will I be the last."[68] Amidst intense backlash, Diamond's YouTube channel and her lawsuit can be imagined as actions against carceral entombment; she would not be left in the tombs. She demands life, a life resurrected.

---

64. Lugones, "Toward a Decolonial Feminism," 745.

65. Robinson, *Forgeries of Memory and Meaning: Blacks and the Regimes of Race in American Theater and Film before World War II*, xiii.

66. Ashley Diamond, "Memoirs of a Chain Gang Sissy. A Monologue Describing Unjust and Inhuman Treatment of a Transgender," *YouTube*, July 31, 2014, https://www.youtube.com/watch?v=87jJ4T_Z1aY.

67. Diamond, "Memoirs of a Chain Gang Sissy."

68. Schreier Lyseggen, *The Women of San Quentin: Soul Murder of Transgender Women in Male Prisons*, 69.

The tools robbed from the graves of coloniality provide us a ruttier to guide us along the path to abolition. Now we may look towards resurrection.[69] Lugones' theory of the coloniality of gender helps us to understand that ending the effects of colonialism allows us to dismantle systems of oppression that are foundational to the carceral state. She argues that decolonizing gender is a necessarily praxical task.[70] She names that praxis as decolonial feminism which determines our actions upon understanding that the root of racialized gender-based oppression lies in colonialism. We must read the fractured locus "to learn about each other as resisters to the coloniality of gender at the colonial difference."[71]

What shall we read from the fractured locus? I reflect on the resurrection celebrations held by my Caribbean Pentecostal church. Celebrations began with my family cooking special dishes, buying new clothes for their children and themselves, and cleaning their homes. There was a mood of joy and celebration amid economic vulnerability. Everyone who came to Resurrection service and dinner became part of my family, an extension of the community. The joy and hope of resurrection required acts of care.

In Christina Sharpe's engagement with the politics of care, care becomes the challenge to envision new ways to prevent and deal with harm in the wake of anti-Blackness to acknowledge the humanity of Black individuals.[72] Her conceptualization of care alerts me to honor the life-making and lifesaving spiritual practices of my upbringing and to return to the concept of resurrection. I believe we find ways to build communities that challenge the existence of prisons by rejecting colonial logics that require certain people to be disposable and for us to police each other along gendered and racialized differences.

In this climate of anti-Blackness that attempts to harm our bodies and steal our breath, how do we have lungs to draw oxygen from the soil and breathe, allowing us to push through the dirt or move the stone? How do we nurture what Ashon Crawley calls black pneuma[73] and Sharpe names as aspiration[74]? Resurrection allows for breath. Crawley argues, "The fugitive enacts by enunciative force, by desire,

---

69. A ruttier is a map, often used at sea. I first encountered this term in Christina Sharpe's *In the Wake*.

70. Lugones, "Toward a Decolonial Feminism," 746.

71. Lugones, "Toward a Decolonial Feminism," 746.

72. Christina Elizabeth Sharpe, *In the Wake: On Blackness and Being* (Durham, North Carolina: Duke University Press, 2016), 121.

73. Crawley, *Blackpentecostal Breath: The Aesthetics of Possibility*, 38.

74. Sharpe, *In the Wake: On Blackness and Being*, 109.

by air, by breath, by breathing. Breath and breathing of air, in other words, not only make possible but sustain such movement."[75] The task of protecting Black life, guiding breath into Black lungs is a task of resurrection. Reflecting on care against premature carceral death, I divide the concept of resurrection into three parts: reclaiming the body and hence the soul, learning modes of communal care, and practicing those modes of care.

Care begins at the body. Resurrection begins at the body. The first step of this form of spiritual warfare is to simply reclaim. Alexis Pauline Gumbs writes in her speculative fiction work, "so they stole themselves, which was a break with everything, which was the most illegal act since the law that made them property, and they had to re-rhythm everything, re-tune bass in their chest, and immediately and perpetually they gave themselves away, the selves they had to give, the reclaimed flesh and bones and skin."[76] We must reclaim the body from the grasp of the carceral state. Reclaiming ushers in new ways of being for Black futurity. It requires new noncarceral, noncolonial ontoepistemologics and pedagogies. It requires a new hustle in order to complete this act of theft of life, to reclaim the Black trans body from carceral graves. As bell hooks argues, to call for the body is to reject "the legacy of repression and denial that has been handed down to us."[77] To claim the Black body is to reclaim a tool utilized for racialized capitalism. It is to declare oneself ungovernable. H.L.T Quan argues that there is much to learn from this declaration: "The ungovernable and ungovernability are theoretical spaces that can helps us think about life and the politics of living wherein ordinary people and communities assert their renderings of life and living rather than those of the state, capital and other dominion's terms of order."[78] Against the backdrop of the carceral state and its terms of orders, folks keep moving along, nourishing life that is protected and valued by themselves. Black ungovernability posits that we find new networks and maps for living, for breathing, for eating, for creating other narratives while living amid attempted social death. And this form of life has always existed, has always been happening.

As we have seen, the carceral state does not allow trans and gender nonconforming Black and Brown individuals the right to determine their gender identity and expression, just as their diasporic enslaved and colonized kin were robbed of the ability to define themselves.

---

75. Crawley, *Blackpentecostal Breath: The Aesthetics of Possibility*, 36.

76. Alexis Pauline Gumbs, *M Archive: After the End of the World* (Durham, North Carolina: Duke University Press, 2018), 100.

77. bell hooks, *Teaching to Transgress: Education as the Practice of Freedom* (New York: Routledge, 1994), 191.

78. "It's Hard to Stop Rebels that Time Travel: Democratic Living in the World and the Radical Reimagining of Old Worlds," in Gaye Theresa Johnson and Alex Lubin, *Futures of Black Radicalism* (Verso Books, 2017), 178.

Despite this, trans folks demand the right to be recognized by their own terms. Erica Meiners argues that "decolonization is gender and sexual self-determination."[79] For example, CeCe McDonald after the work of activists in a petition to the Minnesota Department of Corrections was given hormonal treatment—a means through which she could define and reclaim herself within entombment. Though a seemingly small victory for one individual, this achievement conveys why the carceral locus is perpetually fractured. Her supporters helped her to survive her incarceration, communal reclamation thus negated colonial logics of abandonment of populations marked as disposable. She writes: "Before I go, I just want to say that I love you all more than ever now. I couldn't be more conscious of the love and support you all give me—my family, and that's kin and chosen, and of course I have chosen all of you. You're all my family and I will love and cherish and appreciate you all until there's no more of me. We are the future, we are the revolution!"[80]

While we reclaim, we also learn. What must be done? And how will we do what must be done? The answer is in ourselves and each other. M. Jacqui Alexander asks, "How does spiritual work produce the conditions that bring about the realignment of self with self, which is simultaneously a realignment of oneself with the Divine through a collectivity?"[81] Alexander illustrates that collective and radical self-embodiment offers pathways to knowing how spiritual practices offer new conditions for Black life. We must learn what practices our souls and the souls of those around us require. By acknowledging our souls and the souls of those around us, we allow for resurrection because that soul escapes the clutches of carceral death forces. The task of listening and being in service to the soul places one in opposition to a carceral state that wishes to abuse and use our bodies in an attempt to limit our connection with the soul via forms of carceral dissociation. This learning requires "intention, a revolutionary patience, courage, and above all humility."[82] Abolition must be a collective force. We will find lessons in each other; we will be each other's students and teachers. If we attempt to run from this collectivity, we will always simply return to each other.[83] In collective learning, we find the tools of resurrection, a return to each other beyond the tombs.

The tasks of reclaiming and learning must be continuously practiced. Gumbs writes, "freedom is not a secret. it's a practice. it's

---

79. Erica R. Meiners, *For the Children? Protecting Innocence in a Carceral State* (Minneapolis: University of Minnesota Press, 2016), 20.

80. McDonald and Tinsley, "'Go Beyond Our Natural Selves' The Prison Letters of CeCe McDonald," 264.

81. M. Jacqui Alexander, *Pedagogies of Crossing: Meditations on Feminism, Sexual Politics, Memory, and the Sacred* (Durham, North Carolina: Duke University Press, 2005), 298.

82. Alexander, *The New Jim Crow*, 284.

83. Gumbs, *M Archive: After the End of the World*, 22.

contagious."[84] If we are to take seriously the project of abolition it must become a quotidian practice of actively embodying the world we want to create. We must practice again and again how we wish to be well.[85] My mother, when I spoke to her about her community organizing in her church, told me that her most important task was to build a relationship with those around her as those relationships were a way to embody the spirit. As Alexander states, "We have been neighbors, living in the raucous seams of deprivation. We have healed each other's sick; buried each other's dead."[86] McDonald used her time in prison to gain understanding of anti-prison activism through works by Black ex-prisoners like Assata Shakur, Huey P. Newton, and Angela Davis and now she is a prison abolitionist. Her time in a punitive site built her anti-state resistance, an example of decolonial practice. She grave-robbed tools to not only survive imprisonment but now works and practices abolitionist teachings towards making sure no one is also imprisoned.

Abolition requires a critical reimagining of the world—a form of visionary imagining. Abolition demands that the end goal cannot be simply to fix the carceral state. Instead, it demands envisioning ways to not rely on and strengthen a system that builds and perpetuates systemic violence.[87] Abolition requires addressing multiple forms of systemic injustices. Abolition requires a cultivation of not only alternatives to prisons but other ways of living, being in community, in relationship with each other and with the larger world. The high stakes of abolition are due to the shadows of the prison on our lives and the sinister ways in which carcerality invades all parts of life. Jackie Wang explicates the radical process abolition requires, "Imagining and working toward a world without prisons—which is the project of prison abolition—would not only require us to fundamentally rethink the role of the state in society, but it would require us to work toward the total transformation of all social relations."[88] Abolition demands a new ecology of existence in our partnership with each other, the seen and unseen universe, and ourselves. In a sense, to invest in abolition is to become communal healers—placing poultices on the wounds created by racialized capitalism and oiling the scars left by ancestral suffering in the name of coloniality. But it also means resurrecting the spirit as well.

To usher in a decolonial future, we must make a future for Black trans individuals. Freedom is the ability to not only walk out of the tomb but also to destroy it so that no one else may be buried there.

---

84. Gumbs, M Archive, 93.

85. Alexander, Pedagogies of Crossing: Meditations on Feminism, Sexual Politics, Memory, and the Sacred, 297.

86. Alexander, Pedagogies of Crossing, 298.

87. Mogul, Ritchie, and Whitlock, Queer (in)Justice: The Criminalization of LGBT People in the United States, 144–45.

88. Jackie Wang, Carceral Capitalism (South Pasadena, CA: Semiotext(e), 2018), 297.

Resurrection allows us to envision creatively and passionately the other side of abolition, a world without the forces of the carceral state. To believe in resurrection is to believe there can be an/other side. The roots of the carceral state lies in systems of oppression including queer, gender, class, and disability oppression. Building a decolonial abolition praxis requires ensuring the centering of the voices of Black trans folks. The violent erasure and disregarding of the lives and will of Black trans individuals cannot be replicated in abolition praxis. To do so plays into colonial logic and continues the coloniality of gender. Taking our cue from those who have engaged in care for Black people and hence Black life, breath, soul, and spirit, let us engage in spiritual practices that usher in an abolitionist world.

I start and end with McDonald because she exemplifies the necessary praxis for carceral abolition; how at the fractured locus the carceral state marks individuals like her for death and yet still becomes a site of resistance where communal resistance creates change. Following her, let us learn from the work done before us, grave robbing our way to resurrection, rising out of the tombs of coloniality.

REFERENCES

Alexander, M. Jacqui. *Pedagogies of Crossing: Meditations on Feminism, Sexual Politics, Memory, and the Sacred*. Durham, North Carolina: Duke University Press, 2005.

Alexander, Michelle. *The New Jim Crow: Mass Incarceration in the Age of Colorblindness*. Rev. ed. New York: New Press, 2012.

Crawley, Ashon T. *Blackpentecostal Breath: The Aesthetics of Possibility*. New York: Fordham University Press, 2017.

Davis, Angela Y. *Abolition Democracy: Beyond Empire, Prisons, and Torture*. New York: Seven Stories Press, 2005.

Diamond, Ashley. "Memoirs of a Chain Gang Sissy. A Monologue Describing Unjust and Inhuman Treatment of a Transgender. YouTube, July 31, 2014. https://www.youtube.com/watch?v=87jJ4T_Z1aY.

Gilmore, Ruth Wilson. "Fatal Couplings of Power and Difference: Notes on Racism and Geography." *The Professional Geographer* 54, no. 1 (February 2002): 15–24.

———. *Golden Gulag: Prisons, Surplus, Crisis, and Opposition in Globalizing California*. Berkeley: University of California Press, 2007.

Gottschalk, Marie. "Democracy and the Carceral State in America." *The ANNALS of the American Academy of Political and Social Science* 651, no. 1 (January 2014): 288–95.

Guenther, Lisa. *Solitary Confinement: Social Death and Its Afterlives*.

University of Minnesota Press Minneapolis, 2013.

Gumbs, Alexis Pauline. *M Archive: After the End of the World*. Durham, North Carolina: Duke University Press, 2018.

Hartman, Saidiya. *Lose Your Mother: A Journey Along the Atlantic Slave Route*. 1st ed. New York: Farrar, Straus and Giroux, 2007.

Hernández, Kelly Lytle. *City of Inmates: Conquest, Rebellion, and the Rise of Human Caging in Los Angeles, 1771-1965*. Chapel Hill, North Carolina: University of North Carolina Press, 2017.

Holland, Sharon Patricia. *Raising the Dead: Readings of Death and (Black) Subjectivity*. New Americanists. Durham, North Carolina: Duke University Press, 2000.

hooks, bell. *Teaching to Transgress: Education as the Practice of Freedom*. New York: Routledge, 1994.

Johnson, E. Patrick. *No Tea, No Shade: New Writings in Black Queer Studies*. Durham, North Carolina: Duke University Press, 2016.

Johnson, Gaye Theresa, and Alex Lubin. *Futures of Black Radicalism*. Verso Books, 2017.

Jung, Moon-Kie, João Helion Costa Vargas, and Eduardo Bonilla-Silva. *State of White Supremacy: Racism, Governance, and the United States*. Stanford, California: Stanford University Press, 2011.

Lugones, María. "Heterosexualism and the Colonial/Modern Gender System." *Hypatia* 22, no. 1 (February 2007): 186–219.

———. "Toward a Decolonial Feminism." *Hypatia* 25, no. 4 (October 2010): 742–59.

May, Vivian M. *Pursuing Intersectionality, Unsettling Dominant Imaginaries*. New York: Routledge, Taylor & Francis Group, 2015.

Mbembe, Achille. "Necropolitics." Translated by Libby Meintjes. *Public Culture* 15, no. 1 (2003): 11–40.

McDonald, CeCe, and Omise'eke Natasha Tinsley. "'Go Beyond Our Natural Selves' The Prison Letters of CeCe McDonald." *Transgender Studies Quarterly* 4, no. 2 (2017): 243–65.

Meiners, Erica R. *For the Children?: Protecting Innocence in a Carceral State*. Minneapolis: University of Minnesota Press, 2016.

Mogul, Joey L., Andrea Ritchie, and Kay Whitlock. *Queer (in)Justice: The Criminalization of LGBT People in the United States*. Queer Action/ Queer Ideas. Boston: Beacon Press, 2011.

Neocleous, Mark. *The Fabrication of Social Order: A Critical Theory of Police Power*. London; Sterling, Va.: Pluto Press, 2000.

Richardson, Matt, and Omise'eke Natasha Tinsley. "From Black Transgender Studies to Colin Dayan: Notes on Methodology." *Small Axe* 18, no. 3 45 (January 2014). http://smallaxe.dukejournals.org/content/18/3_45/152.abstract.

Robinson, Cedric J. *Forgeries of Memory and Meaning: Blacks and the Regimes of Race in American Theater and Film before World War II*. Chapel Hill, North Carolina: University of North Carolina Press, 2007.

Schreier Lyseggen, Kristin. *The Women of San Quentin: Soul Murder of Transgender Women in Male Prisons*. Berkeley, California: SFINX Publishing, 2015.

Sharpe, Christina Elizabeth. *In the Wake: On Blackness and Being*. Durham, North Carolina: Duke University Press, 2016.

Snorton, C. Riley. *Black on Both Sides: A Racial History of Trans Identity*. Minneapolis: University of Minnesota Press, 2017.

Spade, Dean. *Normal Life: Administrative Violence, Critical Trans Politics, and the Limits of Law*. Durham, North Carolina: Duke University Press, 2015.

Spillers, Hortense. "Mama's Baby, Papa's Maybe: An American Grammar Book." *Diacritics* 17, no. 2 (1987).

Stanley, Eric A., and Nat Smith. *Captive Genders: Trans Embodiment and the Prison Industrial Complex*. Expanded Second Edition. Oakland, CA, USA: AK Press, 2015.

Vitulli, Elias. "Racialized Criminality and the Imprisoned Trans Body: Adjudicating Access to Gender-Related Medical Treatment in Prisons." *Social Justice* 37, no. 1 (119) (2010): 53–68.

Wang, Jackie. *Carceral Capitalism*. 21. South Pasadena, CA: Semiotext(e), 2018.

Williamson, Terrion L. *Scandalize My Name: Black Feminist Practice and the Making of Black Social Life*. New York: Fordham University Press, 2016.

SEARCHING FOR AN ABOLITIONIST SPIRITUALITY

Jared Ware

In the first instance, abolitionism was the mode through which enslaved people resisted the slaveocracy's ability to relegate people to a form of property. Resistance took many forms, including but not limited to mutual aid, marronage, the development of communication networks and intercommunal organization, and rebellion. Through protracted struggle, this refusal would over time fracture the weak ideological foundation which upheld the institution of chattel slavery.

In *Black Marxism*, Cedric Robinson demonstrates that resistance to chattel slavery was not merely tied to the material conditions of slavery but was also based in the ontological totality of enslaved Africans and their descendants. Systems of belief, including African religions and spirituality, are key components of this ontological totality. Seeking to understand the character of this spirituality and the historical role of these belief systems might provide lessons in how enslaved African people organized themselves against chattel slavery and built a coalitional abolitionist movement strong enough to undermine an entrenched system of chattel slavery. The legacies of the racial regimes that produced slavery and the resistance against it continue beyond the 13th Amendment and the Civil Rights Movement, in what Saidiya Hartman calls "the afterlife of slavery," namely, "skewed life chances, limited access to health and education, premature death, incarceration, and impoverishment."[1]

Through a critical analysis of key abolitionist figures and ethnographies and histories of the culture and rebellion of enslaved peoples, I will examine links between spirituality and abolitionism. I conclude with an interview with an imprisoned organizer of the 2018 prison strike to examine the role abolition spirituality plays in the manifestation of potent forces for radical change and revolutionary organizing.

While certain white figures in the Northeastern US or Europe supported the idea of abolition and even vigorously promoted it, I do not share the view of history that considers abolitionism to have been a white movement at its source or in its most politically impactful. In my view these figures were, at best, responding to and rearticulating

---

1. Saidiya Hartman, *Lose Your Mother: A Journey Along the Atlantic Slave Route*, (New York: Farrar, Straus and Giroux, 2008), 6.

the abolitionism of the enslaved and former slaves for different audiences. As George Rawick states:

> Abolitionism was not primarily a product of the white New England Brahmin conscience many historians have claimed it to be. It was more accurately the product of the slave quarters of the plantation South, the border slaves, and the communities of Northern freedman who helped bring into being a movement which drew into it some of the most eloquent and outstanding whites of the period. Abolitionism came from the black community and its task was to liberate that community by whatever means were found to be necessary, violence included, as the slave revolts and the Civil War would demonstrate. In liberating that black community, abolition transformed American society and took the lead in creating a new America.[2]

Working from the understanding of abolitionism as a transformational movement by enslaved Africans and "freedmen," this essay examines the role of spirituality in this movement concretely altering the course of history in North America.

The spirituality of abolitionism, or abolition spirituality, does not align with dominant expressions of Western organized religion, yet at times it operates within forms or practices or spaces of Christianity out of necessity or utility. Abolition spiritualtiy emerged in opposition and resistance to the slaveocracy's articulation of Christianity, which could be described using Karl Marx's formulation: religion is the "moral sanction" of an "inverted world."[3]

Enslaved or "free" Africana abolitionists often believed divine sanction came from direct communion with spirits or God. Scholars of US history treat Harriet Tubman, Denmark Vesey, and Nat Turner as historically unusual. Historians often question their sanity or neurological health on grounds that their religiosity was extreme. Yet a review of historical work which examines the role of African religious beliefs in the New World suggests that while figures like Tubman, Vesey, and Turner were absolutely exemplary in their commitment to the struggle for the liberation of their people from the slave society, they functioned within a much broader set of spiritual traditions across the diaspora. These traditions were rooted in Africa, but were reforged and syncretized on slave ships, in slave quarters, in ring shouts and in maroon communities.

---

2. George P. Rawick, *From Sundown to Sunup: The Making of the Black Community* (Westport, Conn: Greenwood, 1971), 112.

3. Karl Marx, "A Contribution to the Critique of Hegel's Philosophy of Right," Marxist Internet Archive, 1843, https://www.marxists.org/archive/marx/works/1843/critique-hpr/intro.htm.

By examining these movements and figures, their particularities notwithstanding, I show that there were common practices, beliefs, and rituals within religions that Africans brought with them through the holds of the slave ships and onto plantations or into maroon communities.[4] From there, I argue these various groups syncretized new forms of a distinctly abolitionist spirituality.

Forms of organization fostered in the context of these syncretic processes enabled astonishing acts of resistance. The Haitian Revolution, Turner's revolt, and the Underground Railroad all emerged in proximity to these processes. So too did the organizing that enabled enslaved people to abandon plantations, travel through slave networks to the camps of the Union Army by the thousands, to eventually take up arms and strike down the Confederate Army, thus turning the tides of the Civil War to secure a legal emancipation from chattel slavery.[5] While this emancipation and any formal rights associated with it would be viciously and duplicitously contested and challenged through various means in "the afterlife of slavery," the organizational forms necessary to fight these new regimes of racial repression would continue to evolve and resurface in subsequent struggles.

I. ABOLITION SPIRITUALITY AND ITS RELATIONSHIP TO AFRICANA RELIGIONS IN THE NEW WORLD

There are many misconceptions that can attend an examination of religions from across Africa since their adherents did not see themselves as sharing one set of beliefs or a common culture. It is important to remember that African people at the onset of slavery were not a monolithic whole. Cedric Robinson reminds us that European racialization and chattel slavery first treated them as such. There are also inherent issues with researching the history of these religions as historical scholarship can be riddled with misconceptions, biases, and caricatures forged in slaveholder society, which historically has been partially based on denying the legitimacy of African and Native American beliefs and cultures. The slaveocracy did not generally concern itself with the beliefs of enslaved people, at least until they were

---

4. A full elaboration upon the different belief systems of West and Central African societies and the ways that distinct peoples related to the process of enslavement and worked towards alliance is beyond the scope of this paper. Fortunately, for those interested, there is amazing scholarship to engage. See, for example, the works of Maya Deren, Katherine Dunham, Bunseki Fu-Kiau, Kola Abimbola, Robert Farris Thompson, and Wole Soyinka.

5. W.E.B. Du Bois, *Black Reconstruction in America* (New York: Touchstone, 1995), 55–83.

used to foment insurrection. And since for many years the dominant historical trope was that most enslaved people were content in slavery, these episodes were rarely examined by scholars as historically substantial until dominant orthodoxy was challenged by historians in the 20th Century, often by African American or white radical scholars who began investigations to recover lost traditions or challenge dominant white perspectives of American history.

Despite the caveats above, there are common liberatory themes, practices, and expressions of abolition spirituality in Western and Central African religions and cultures as well as the development of diasporic communities forged by and against the transatlantic slave trade and enslavement. The role of African spirituality in the development of inter-ethnic solidarity among enslaved people should not be understated. Historian George Rawick noted:

> We shall here look at slave religion as a way of focusing upon a specific aspect of American slave thought and behavior. Close to the center of the slaves' lives from sundown to sun-up was religion. The African slaves in the New World had come from societies in which there was no distinction between sacred and secular activities. The holy and the sacred were experienced as a part of all activities. Divisions between this world and the next, between flesh and spirit, between the living body and the spirits of the dead were not conceived of as absolute. Men were thought to be able to slip across these boundaries with comparative ease.[6]

Various African societies had different forms of government, secret societies, and modes of self-organization which were not completely distinct from their religious systems. In other words, the spiritual was bound up with all aspects of their lives and key to West African values as well as how they related to each other and to gods, spirits, and ancestors. It is through this lens that we must understand that for enslaved people, syncretizing spiritual forms was a key mode of religious organizing. It was also inherently a mode of socio-political organizing.

In what follows, I briefly examine the manifestations of abolition spirituality that were at play in the Haitian Revolution due to its central relationship to abolitionism globally and abolitionist movements in North America specifically. Even by limiting my scope in such a way, I acknowledge that this piece may leave readers with more questions than answers, and my hope is that others will in turn seek answers to those questions and share their findings.

---

6. Rawick, *From Sundown to Sunup*, 32.

II. INSURRECTION AND SPIRITUAL RAGE

"That African religion served as a major reservoir of support for insurrection throughout the New World has been abundantly demonstrated in the literature, from South Carolina to Jamaica, from Louisiana to Haiti to Brazil."[7]
—Michael A. Gomez

Because Haiti was so central to the abolition of slavery, it is of central importance to any discussion of abolition spirituality. As the site of the only successful revolution of a slave nation, the religions of the enslaved, adapted to Haitian plantations and maroon settlements, were preserved with less dilution and repression than in many other contexts. The success of the revolution in Haiti served as a source of inspiration for enslaved Africans and their descendants across the diaspora. Its historical fact forever challenged any notion that slave systems were the will of an omnipotent Christian God. Just as the Haitian Revolution would have been a source of inspiration for the struggle of Africana abolitionists, it haunted the dreams of slave owners.

C.L.R. James' oft quoted claim that "[v]oodoo was the medium of conspiracy" at the dawn of the Haitian Revolution has been supported by other historians and ethnographers.[8] Because "vodou" is a term for spirits or gods among Fon and Ewe speakers, there are many spelling variations in the English language, and many related but variant forms of vodou that were and in many cases are practiced from West Africa to various parts of the New World. I will most closely examine Haitian Vodou or Voudoun as Maya Deren calls it.

Laurent Dubois reminds us that enslaved Africans were "[b]rought from different parts of Africa." Differences in language, culture, and belief were barriers to communication and a sharing of faith and ideas. But, as Dubois explains, "African slaves and their descendents on plantations and in towns, as well as in maroon communities, carved out spaces for worship, adapting their religions to the New World. They did so for the most part hidden from the eyes of planters and administrators who might have documented the process."[9] Dubois continues: "In their struggle to unite across differences, the slaves of St. Domingue developed new forms of religious coherence,

7. Michael A. Gomez, *Exchanging Our Country Marks: The Transformation of African Identities in the Colonial and Antebellum South* (Chapel Hill: University of North Carolina Press, c1998.), 249.

8. C.L.R. James, *The Black Jacobins; Toussaint L'Ouverture and the San Domingo Revolution.*, 2d ed., rev. (New York: Vintage Books, 1963), 86.

9. Laurent Dubois, "Vodou and History," *Comparative Studies in Society and History* 43, no. 1 (January 2001), 94.

bringing together rituals and imbuing them with revolutionary significance."[10]

Maya Deren concurs. "Voudoun," she explains, "was responsible for the unity that made the revolution possible." Per Deren, "Historians of Haiti agree on fixing the beginning of the revolution on a cult ceremony held on August 14, 1791."[11] The pig sacrifice that sparked the Haitian Revolution, as described in historical accounts of the ceremony, indicates that the ritual was a Petro ceremony. Petro is a strain or sect of Voudoun. The white fear of Petro is responsible for common misconceptions about its character and its perceived association with the demonic.

Deren speculates that Petro emerged as a response to the violence of enslavement: "It is not evil; it is the rage against the evil fate which the African suffered, the brutality of his displacement and his enslavement. It is the violence that rose out of that rage to protest against it." She continues:

> It is the crack of the slave-whip sounding constantly, a never-to-be-forgotten ghost, in the Petro rites. It is the raging revolt of the slaves against the Napoleanic forces. And it is the delirium of their triumph. For it was the Petro cult, born in the hills, nurtured in secret, which gave both the moral force and the actual organization to the escaped slaves who plotted and trained, swooped down upon the plantations and led the rest of the slaves in the revolt.[12]

Petro is significant because it is a distinctly "New World" manifestation, despite its mostly African roots. It was fostered in maroon camps on the outskirts of slave society. It was in league with runaway slaves from Indigenous Nations in the Caribbean who were brought to Haiti by European slave traders.[13] Maroon settlements served as one of the strongholds of African spirituality and were key sites for the syncretization of its different forms within the New World. Wherever colonists trafficked enslaved Africans, settlements of runaways, maroons, or *cimarrones* were formed by slaves who escaped plantation life and formed their own settlements, *quilombos* or *palenques*.[14] Robinson documented that history in sites of enslavement across the Western Hemisphere. "Marronage, of course, was a concomitant of slavery,"

---

10. Dubois, "Vodou and History," 95.

11. Maya Deren, *Divine Horsemen: The Living Gods of Haiti* (New Paltz, NY: McPherson & Company, 2004), 62-63.

12. Deren, *Divine Horsemen*, 62.

13. Deren, *Divine Horsemen*, 64–71.

14. Cedric J. Robinson, *Black Marxism: The Making of the Black Radical Tradition* (Chapel Hill: The University of North Carolina Press, 2020), 130–164.

he explained. "Brutality was as much a raison d'être of the former as it was a condition of the latter."[15]

As I will explain later, spiritual rage was crucial to abolition spirituality in the US. It is noteworthy that for the enslaved, religion was part and parcel of what the Black Panther Party saw as survival pending revolution. This is not to suggest that the spiritual make-up here is one of passivity while seeking to hide from a disastrous situation. Even within slavery, developing places of sanctuary and processes for care, release, and healing were necessary strategies for survival. Enslaved people organized themselves in particular ways to survive the daily onslaught of the slave system and to liberate themselves and their family members when possible.

III. ABOLITION AS GOD'S WILL IN VOUDOUN

A second essential component of abolition spirituality pertains to the moral order. Specifically, God represents a different system of morality than that conveyed by the religion of the masters. That system demands the destruction of the slave system in no uncertain terms.

Consider C.L.R. James' account of Boukman's sermon at Le Cap at the dawn of the Haitian Revolution. Boukman distinguished the white man's god from the god of the Africana people in Haiti:

> The god who created the sun which gives us light, who rouses the waves and rules the storm, though hidden in the clouds, he watches us. He sees all the white man does. The god of the white man inspires him with crime, but our god calls upon us to do good works. Our god who is good to us orders us to revenge our wrongs. He will direct our arms and aid us. Throw away the symbol of the god of whites who has caused us to weep, and listen to the voice of liberty, which speaks in the hearts of us all.[16]

Boukman invokes a God that intervenes in human affairs. Yet, per Deren, that is incongruent with West African religious traditions. However, Deren is instructive here:

> Voudoun would not have come into existence, nor would it still be flourishing so vigorously, if it had been governed by men rigidly dedicated to superficial sectarian distinctions. It is, in fact, a monumental testament to the extremely sophisticated

---

15. Robinson, *Black Marxism*, 139.

16. James, *The Black Jacobins*, 87.

ability of the West African to recognize a conceptual principle common to ostensibly disparate practices and to fuse African, American Indian, European and Christian elements dynamically into an integrated working structure.[17]

The ability to find common denominators helped stave off forced assimilation. That syncretic process was taken up by enslaved peoples among various New World slave regimes.

Let us return to Boukman's speech. The white man's god "inspires him with crime;" "our god calls upon us to do good works" and "orders us to revenge our wrongs." Further, the god of the African slaves "will direct our arms and aid us."[18] This vision of a God who intervenes in human affairs is likely borrowed from the Christian understanding of God. Per Deren:

> If religious belief can be understood to range from an almost abstract divinity at one pole to the manipulations of magic at the other, then the Christian deity—who was subject to persuasion by prayer, and who might intervene as a supernatural force—was much easier and more comfortable than the usual High God of Africa, whose absolute objectivity placed him beyond the pale of human reference.[19]

Africana people made a critical theological intervention by adapting the Christian God to abolition spirituality. They were able to articulate actionable and empowered abolitionist rhetoric. In that way too, spiritual rage was sanctioned by a God who refused to accept chattel slavery. That would prove to be a powerful weapon in inspiring resistance to the slave system.

IV. THE RING SHOUT AS SANCTUARY AND A SITE OF SYNCRETIZATION

Many historians discount Christianity's impact, regardless of efforts at adapting it. Gomez goes so far as to suggest that "when people of African descent converted, they knew what they were doing." There was also "an ecstatic legacy and component, whether it is owned up to or not." Dreams, visions, prophecies, spirits, and miracles are all Biblical traditions.[20] But nonetheless, the overwhelming majority of enslaved peoples practiced African religions or Islam.

---

17. Deren, *The Divine Horsemen*, 56.

18. James, *The Black Jacobins* 87.

19. Deren, *The Divine Horsemen*, 55.

20. Gomez, *Exchanging Our Country Marks*, 278–279.

Religion was a medium of spiritual rage and the moral sanction of abolition spirituality. It also provided refuge and was a site of syncretization. The ring shout or ring ceremony is exemplary in that regard. In the ring ceremony, worshippers move in a circular motion. The ritual is ecstatic and transcendent. The ring shout was a "sanctuary in every sense of the word."[21]

The ring shout was also a way for the enslaved to bring gods, beliefs, and traditions together. Sterling Stuckey claims that "ring shouts" were "the main context in which Africans recognized values common to them. Those values were remarkable because, while of ancient African provenance, they were fertile terrain for new forms."[22] Per Gomez:

> Although the focus of shout participants shifted over the years from the African gods to Jesus, and from Africa to heaven, the ring shout was performed throughout. Given the fact that it antedates the African's conversion to Christianity in North America, it is the Christian faith that was necessarily grafted onto the tree of African tradition. It is the Christian faith that had to undergo its own conversion prior to its acceptance by the African-based community. For some, that conversion began on African soil in Kongo; for the vast majority, however, the transition took place in America and to a significant extent by way of the ring shout.[23]

As I have explained, the tendency towards syncretization meant enslaved peoples could incorporate Christianity into their faith without surrendering completely to it.

Secretive prayer meetings where slaves would notably "[turn] down the pot" to muffle the sound of prayer and singing also served as a place of sanctuary and syncretization.[24]

V. GOD'S WILL IN THE CHRISTIANITY OF AFRICANA ABOLITIONISTS IN THE US

Abolitionist spirituality in the US shared the components outlined above: it was a medium of spiritual rage, a moral sanction for that

---

21. Gomez, *Exchanging Our Country Marks*, 269.

22. Sterling Stuckey, *Slave Culture: Nationalist Theory and the Foundations of Black America* (New York: Oxford University Press, 1987), 15.

23. Gomez, *Exchanging Our Country Marks*, 269.

24. Rawick, *From Sundown to Sunup*, 39–45.

rage, and a source of refuge. In addition, Nat Turner, Harriet Tubman, Sojourner Truth, and Denmark Vesey all claimed that God spoke to them directly. They cited prophetic revelations. Western scholarship on abolition spirituality in the US tends to be Eurocentric. But the Christianity of abolitionists was opposed to the Christianity of the ruling class and was likely a product of a process of translation between spiritual traditions.

Denmark Vesey's famous plot represents a powerful expression of abolition spirituality and white fear of it. Vesey, former personal slave of a slave-trader captain, bought his freedom after winning the lottery. Heavily influenced by the Haitian revolution, Vesey was known to make "[a]ppeals to the rights of man, couched in both theological and secular terms," including reference to "how the children of Israel were delivered out of Egypt from bondage."[25]

One unnamed slave quoted in Herbert Aptheker's account recalled Vesey telling him Black people "were living such an abominable life, they ought to rise."[26] William Freehling adds:

> At the church and in his home, Vesey preached on the Bible, likening the Negroes to the children of Israel, and quoting passages which authorized slaves to massacre their masters. Joshua 4, verse 21, was a favorite citation: "And they utterly destroyed all that was in the city, both man and woman, young and old, and ox, and sheep, and ass, with the edge of the sword."[27]

While plotting one of the most elaborate insurrectionary plots in US history, Vesey wrote at least twice to Haiti, "telling of his plans and asking for aid."[28] His plot included lieutenants who were leaders of various ethnic groups of Africa, including Gullah Jack who was believed by many potential rebels to be invulnerable and to have charms that could protect them from harm as well. Vesey and Jack would famously be betrayed before the plot was carried out, but due to the elaborate nature of the plans, and the state's hanging of dozens of alleged conspirators, news of it spread across the US. The plot struck fear in the hearts of South Carolina slave owners in a state where "blacks were the majority and constituted an African population."[29] It also demonstrated the danger presented by the African institution, in

25. Herbert Aptheker, *American Negro Slave Revolts* (New York: Columbia University Press, 1946), 269.

26. Aptheker, *American Negro Slave Revolts*, 270.

27. William W. Freehling, *Prelude to Civil War: The Nullification Controversy in South Carolina, 1816–1836.* (New York: Harper & Row, 1966), 55.

28. Aptheker, *American Negro Slave Revolts*, 272.

29. Stuckey, *Slave Culture*, 46.

this case the African Church, where much of the planning and religious justification for the plot was laid out. Stuckey explains, "When slaves erected their own house of worship, the African Church, in the suburbs of Charleston in December of 1821, it was labor that made them more conscious of their dignity as human beings and represented an effort to institutionalize their spiritual autonomy."[30]

Vesey showed a "lack of concern for material possessions, and the willingness to risk all in attempting to better the lot of one's people, through revolution or reform." He was an ostensibly "free man" of limited means. He had purchased his own freedom after winning the lottery and running a carpentry business, but he was not able to buy the freedom of his first wife and their children. He became a prime candidate for what Amilcar Cabral would theorize as "class suicide" over a century later.[31] Stuckey observed "a powerful strain in nationalist thought, in Vesey's time and later, and contained the seeds of socialism that flowered in the programs of Afro-American theorists in the twentieth century." In Vesey's era, the legacy of slavery "encouraged in blacks a powerful opposition to wealth acquired at the expense of others."[32]

To signal his "freedom" as a child in North Carolina, David Walker wore a badge of cloth with the word "FREE" on it. Stuckey writes, "His father's death in slavery and his mother's oppression as a free Negro must have been painful sources of strength for Walker when he reflected on the tragedy of their lives."[33] The revolution in Haiti led to "a law in 1795—Walker was then ten years old—calling for the suppression by force of any gathering of free Negroes and slaves aimed at challenging the servile positions assigned to each."[34] David Walker published his incendiary *Appeal* as an ostensibly "free" African descendant living in Boston. *Appeal* was written against the history of state repression after the Haitian Revolution and undoubtedly countless other struggles against the slaveocracy.

Appeal certainly seems authentic in its embrace of Christianity but takes up that mantle for decisively subversive purposes.[35] Walker's articulation of the Christian God in his *Appeal* was not making a moral case to his audience for white abolitionist propaganda. As Stuckey notes, "concepts of African autonomy and Pan-African

30. Stuckey, *Slave Culture*, 53.

31. Amilcar Cabral, "The Weapon of Theory," Marxist Internet Archive, 1966, .https://www.marxists.org/subject/africa/cabral/1966/weapon-theory.htm.

32. Stuckey, *Slave Culture*, 49.

33. Stuckey, *Slave Culture*, 110–111.

34. Stuckey, *Slave Culture*, 111.

35. Steven H Shiffrin, "The Rhetoric of Black Violence in the Antebellum Period: Henry Highland Garnet," *Journal of Black Studies* 2, no. 1 (1971): 55, fn 1.

revolt, so much a part of Walker's thought, did not have roots or currency among Europeans."[36] Walker's goal therefore was to convince Africana peoples, enslaved and otherwise, that God demanded abolition and that there will be a violent reckoning for those who do not heed this demand.

While it is impossible to know the full extent of *Appeal's* reach, the slaveholder class was greatly concerned that it might incite rebellion or had already done so, including Nat Turner's. However, there is a lack of reliable evidence about *Appeal's* reach because of the conditions of enslavement and the secrecy of enslaved organizing. For that reason, it is impossible to know how many insurrections Walker inspired or if his message ever reached Turner. Aptheker's research suggests great concern over its distribution in the South. Walker seems to have somewhat achieved his goal of distribution among slaves in the South.[37]

Nat Turner communicated revelations from God, notably in his 1831 *Confessions*. Fellow slaves believed he was a medium of divine prophecy. He stated in his confession that his power of influence came from his "communion of the Spirit whose revelations I often communicated to them, and they believed and said my wisdom came from God."[38] He convinced family and fellow slaves of his prophetic abilities when he had visions of past and future events.

After his rebellion, Turner confessed that his actions were derived from divine prophecy, stating "the Spirit instantly appeared to me and said the Serpent was loosened, and Christ had laid down the yoke he had borne for the sins of men, and that I should take it on and fight against the Serpent, for the time was fast approaching when the first should be last and the last should be first."[39] Turner's recounting of "spirit(s)," the "Holy Ghost," and the "Serpent" in his confessions are significant. They appear twice as frequently as "God," "Lord," and "Christ." Though ostensibly Biblical, they have analogues in African religions, and prominently within the spiritual syncretizations found in the New World, which incorporated elements of Christianity. There are spirits within the Bible to be sure, but this idea of lesser deities communicating with humans is common among African systems of belief. As for the Holy Ghost/Spirit, theirs is a Christian representation that has greater significance among African people in the New World than it did for European practitioners. Per Gomez, "Europeans

---

36. Stuckey, *Slave Culture*, 153.

37. Aptheker, *American Negro Slave Revolts*, 61, 82, 107, 288.

38. Thomas Gray and Nat Turner, "The Confessions of Nat Turner," *Zea E-Books in American Studies*, January 1, 1831, https://digitalcommons.unl.edu/zeaamericanstudies/11, 9.

39. Gray and Turner, "The Confessions of Nat Turner," 11.

may have provided the skeletal frameworks of Christianity, but it was the African who introduced the ways of the Holy Ghost."[40]

Confessions offered a Christian justification for revolutionary, abolitionist violence. Vesey's plot and Walker's appeal worried the slavocracy, but Turner's violent praxis and its documentation as the fulfillment of a Christian prophecy made their worst nightmares come true. Slave states enacted laws that banned slaves from holding public meetings and regulated the religious indoctrination of Black people in hopes of using religion to instill docility and contentment. Gomez explains: "Both Vesey and the prophet Nat were Christians, claiming to have been inspired by God to unleash a baptism of blood-letting and violence. That the Christian faith and the Bible could be used as tools of revolt was totally unacceptable to the slaveocracy, swift and decisive measures had to be taken to decouple Christianity from just war."[41]

Vesey's plot, the Haitian Revolution that unfolded during Walker's childhood, and Turner's revolt provoked a similar response: capital punishment for plotters; the repression of literacy and education; and bans on the congregation of people of African descent. The slave-ocracy also attempted to inculcate a Christianity that insisted upon the docility of enslaved people. That pattern of repression would continue well beyond the 13th Amendment as I will discuss later. It would infuse itself into the logic of the US prison system.

Henry Highland Garnet, a fugitive slave, minister, and orator, made a speech at the 1843 National Convention of Colored Citizens, where he argued that rebellion by enslaved people was not just morally permissible, but that it was a requirement of their Christian faith:

> The forlorn condition in which you are placed, does not destroy your moral obligation to God. You are not certain of heaven, because you suffer yourselves to remain in a state of slavery, where you cannot obey the commandments of the Sovereign of the universe. If the ignorance of slavery is a passport to heaven, then it is a blessing, and no curse, and you should rather desire its perpetuity than its abolition. God will not receive slavery, nor ignorance, nor any other state of mind, for love and obedience to him. Your condition does not absolve you from your moral obligation. The diabolical injustice by which your liberties are cloven down, neither God; nor angels, or just men, command you to suffer for a single moment. Therefore, it is your solemn and imperative duty to use every means, both moral; intellectual and physical that

---

40. Gomez, *Exchanging Our Country Marks,* 253.

41. Gomez, *Exchanging Our Country Marks,* 257.

promises success. If a band of heathen men should attempt to enslave a race of Christians, and to place their children under the influence of some false religion, surely, Heaven would frown upon the men who would not resist such aggression, even to death. If, on the other hand, a band of Christians should attempt to enslave a race of heathen men, and to entail slavery upon them, and to keep them in heathenism in the midst of Christianity, the God of heaven would smile upon every effort which the injured might make to disenthrall themselves.

Brethren, it is as wrong for your lordly oppressors to keep you in slavery, as it was for the man thief to steal our ancestors from the coast of Africa. You should therefore now use the same manner of resistance, as would have been just in our ancestors, when the bloody footprints of the first remorseless soul-thief was placed upon the shores of our fatherland. The humblest peasant is as free in the sight of God as the proudest monarch that ever swayed a sceptre. Liberty is a spirit sent out from God, and like its great Author, is no respecter of persons.

Brethren, the time has come when you must act for yourselves. It is an old and true saying that, "if hereditary bondmen would be free, they must themselves strike the blow." You can plead your own cause and do the work of emancipation better than any others.[42]

Garnet nodded to a tradition of resistance, citing Vesey's plot, Turner's rebellion, and the successful shipboard insurrections by John Cinque and Madison Washington, before invoking another thread within many forms of African spirituality: the voices of ancestors, still speaking. "Your dead fathers speak to you from their graves. Heaven, as with a voice of thunder, calls on you to arise from the dust," Garnet commanded.[43] Stuckey is unsure whether Garnet learned about ancestral communication from his father, who was the son of an African, from runaway slaves or from other Africans in the North. But he notes that Garnet's "formulation of reciprocity between the living and the dead, of the return of the dead from the afterworld to resume life among the living, is so remarkably akin to the African religious vision that he might have been aware of it."[44]

---

42. Henry Garnet, "An Address to the Slaves of the United States of America," *Electronic Texts in American Studies*, August 16, 1848, https://digitalcommons.unl.edu/etas/8, 5–6.

43. Garnet, "An Address to the Slaves of the United States of America," 9.

44. Stuckey, *Slave Culture*, 76.

Beyond ancestral communication, Garnet argued that death did not offer spiritual emancipation due to the intergenerational nature of the struggle for abolition: "Nor did the evil of their bondage end at their emancipation by death. Succeeding generations inherited their chains, and millions have come from eternity into time, and have returned again to the world of spirits, cursed and ruined by American slavery."[45] Garnet gestured towards a spiritual reward in his address, like the one offered by priests or houngans at the dawn of the Haitian revolution who promised slaves "that the souls of the dead would return to Africa."[46]

Furthermore, Garnet implicated the enslaved and the fates of future generations of slaves in the sins of the slave system itself. He argued that those who accepted their lot as slaves would not be welcomed into Heaven. Only those who rose up against slavery would be. This was a powerful theological intervention, particularly in opposition to the gospel of the slaveocracy, which, in the wake of the Turner rebellion, was committed to one catechism: "'Slaves, obey your masters as in the Lord! Cease, dark masses, from striving; look to God for heavenly reward!'"[47] It is against this pacifying interpretation of the Bible that Garnet calls for enslaved people to liberate themselves through every means at their disposal, even against their own probable demise: "Brethren, arise, arise! Strike for your lives and liberties. Now is the day and the hour. Let every slave throughout the land do this and the days of slavery are numbered. You cannot be more oppressed than you have been—you cannot suffer greater cruelties than you have already. Rather die freemen than live to be slaves. Remember that you are FOUR MILLIONS!"[48]

Walker, Vesey, and Garnet selected passages from the Bible that slave society did not want the enslaved to hear. These verses were not the spiritual bedrock of settler society or the slaveocracy of that era. They did not justify Manifest Destiny or the enslavement of "Hammites." Walker, Vesey, and Garnet fashioned the material at their disposal to call upon enslaved people not merely to wait for the Kingdom of Heaven, but to overthrow slavery by force as a necessary condition of their own humanity and spirituality under the ordinance of the Christian God.

VI. HARRIET TUBMAN AND ABOLITION SPIRITUALITY

Historical renderings of the spirituality of abolitionists often run the risk of pathologizing religious experience. Nat Turner, Gullah

45. Garnet, "An Address to the Slaves of the United States of America," 3.

46. Deren, *The Divine Horsemen*, 63.

47. Gomez, *Exchanging Our Country Marks*, 257.

48. Garnet, "An Address to the Slaves of the United States of America," 5–6.

Jack, John Brown, and the practitioners of Vodoun, to name a few, have been likened to madmen at one point or another. Kate Clifford Larson's biography of Harriet Tubman *Bound For The Promised Land* is a representative case in point. Larson attempts to connect the way Harriet Tubman communicated with God and the spiritual world into a symptom of a neurological disorder known as Temporal Lobe Epilepsy (TLE), a condition which would not be discovered until several decades after her death.[49]

It is common for accounts of Tubman's life to note that she suffered a head injury when an overseer hit her in the head with a two pound weight during an escape attempt by another slave.[50] Larson cites multiple accounts that suggest this incident coincided with Tubman's inability to maintain consciousness, to an increase in her religiosity thereafter, as well as what the modern medical community might deem auditory and visual "hallucinations." While TLE, a disorder of the nervous system, could serve as a plausible explanation for Tubman's visions and trances, it doesn't explain her gift for prophecy, nor does it explain the wider context in which enslaved people and "free" Africana people in abolitionist circles would have interpreted her spiritual gifts.

To her credit, Larson does acknowledge a connection between Tubman's spirituality and African religions passed down to her from her grandmother Modesty. Larson writes:

> Tubman and her family found ways to negotiate the cruelties of slavery and lack of control in their lives. Evangelical Protestant Methodism was one source of strength, blending smoothly with cultural and religious traditions that survived the Middle Passage. First-generation Africans, such as her grandmother Modesty, embodied a living African connection and memory for Tubman and her family. Tubman's religious fervor and trust in God to protect and guide her evolved from a fusion of these traditions.[51]

Tubman was exposed to Christianity as an African descendent who participated in revivalist camp meetings during slavery. Gomez writes, "people of African descent were allowed to enter the revivalist experience on their own terms. That is, they were allowed to respond to the preaching of the Gospel in a fashion that was entirely consistent with their roots in indigenous African religion."[52] Tubman would

---

49. Kate Clifford Larson, *Bound for the Promised Land: Harriet Tubman, Portrait of an American Hero* (New York: Ballantine, 2004.), 43.

50. Larson, *Bound for the Promised Land,* 42.

51. Larson, *Bound for the Promised Land,* 47.

52. Gomez, *Exchanging Our Country Marks,* 252.

have been familiar with African spiritual beliefs and with Africana religions syncretized with Christianity. More importantly, her visions and messages from spirits would have been welcomed within this tradition. Tubman's actions, visions, and prophecy did not exist as a total aberration, but connected her with an expansive tradition of abolitionists and enslaved rebels across the diaspora who were known to experience similarly vivid expressions of their spirituality, who believed they could pass through to other spiritual dimensions, and commune directly with holy spirits and gods.

Her tactical skill and spiritual gifts had an impact on John Brown. George Rawick explains, "Brown thought he could weaken the South by running off slaves, setting into motion a slave revolt, and then waiting for the entire system to crumble. This strategy he learned from the activities of the freedmen and such organizers of liberation as his friend, the runaway slave Harriet Tubman."[53] Tubman did not accompany Brown to Harper's Ferry as planned. Moreover, she did not use her abilities to attempt to foment mass slave insurrection. However, she put her prophetic abilities to use while liberating the 300 slaves she brought on her nineteen trips on the Underground Railroad.[54] During the Civil War, "Tubman employed her mastery of the terrain to guide and lead the Union companies," organized slave intelligence networks, scouted, raided and led Black and white union soldiers in battle.[55] With regards to the Underground Railroad, which the slaveocracy feared was an elaborate "national conspiracy," Robinson writes, "Tubman and her colleagues were the actual railroad." Although she likely would have aided John Brown if she had not fallen ill, Tubman's spiritual commitment was to abolition, not through an impossible uprising, but through daily praxis and protracted struggle. She continued that struggle after the war by setting up a home for freed people "too old or sick to support themselves."[56]

During the Civil War, multiple fruits of abolition spirituality came to bear. What Du Bois described as the "General Strike" was a manifestation of the organized network of enslaved people coordinating action on a scale that had never been seen north of Haiti. Rawick states, "Out of the independent black religion arose not only the slave revolts, but also the black secret fraternal organizations which, among other functions, became centers of resistance during the Civil War." Rawick details the way the slave community guided federal soldiers from prisoner of war camps in the South day in and day out, from slave quarters to the swamp to outposts in the woods and back

---

53. Rawick, *From Sundown to Sunup*, 111.

54. Cedric J. Robinson, *Black Movements in America* (New York: Routledge, 1997), 30.

55. Robinson, *Black Movements in America*, 31.

56. Robinson, *Black Marxism*, 31.

to Northern lines. They coordinated with Tubman and others a vast network of spies from enemy territory. Like Du Bois, Rawick also details the actions of hundreds of thousands of enslaved people who escaped plantations, traveled with the aid of the coordinated network of enslaved people, making their way to Union lines, simultaneously denying the South its labor force, and joining the Union army to fight for their own liberation.[57]

VII. REMNANTS OF ABOLITION SPIRITUALITY IN THE AFTERLIFE OF SLAVERY

When I set out to write this essay, I discussed it with a representative of Jailhouse Lawyers Speak. As someone with over a decade of abolitionist organizing experience in the prison system, I wanted to try and learn how abolitionist visions of spirituality might relate to prison abolition movements led by prisoners today. For his safety, and as a condition of his organization's oath of secrecy, his identity will remain anonymous, but for the purposes of this essay we'll call him Mike. We spoke in mid-April of 2019, a year after the violence at Lee Correctional Institution that immediately took the lives of seven prisoners, and left dozens more seriously injured. That incident led Jailhouse Lawyers Speak to issue a national call of ten demands in response to the conditions in US prisons.

For context on his perspective, it is important to understand that Jailhouse Lawyers Speak does not see slavery as having ever ended. They view the 13th Amendment as a reform, which produced new forms of enslavement within and related to what they call the Prison Industrial Slavery Complex (PISC). As a result, they consider themselves both slavery and prison abolitionists. These views are articulated more fully in other pieces that I have published in the past.[58] While it is not a replacement for their own historical analysis and theorization, there is scholarly work, notably by Angela Davis and Dennis Childs, around the "loophole" within the 13th Amendment, convict leasing, and the continuation of "prison slavery" more

---

57. Rawick, *From Sundown to Sunup*, 113–117.

58. Jared Ware, "'I'm for Disruption': Interview with Prison Strike Organizer from Jailhouse Lawyers Speak," *Abolition* (blog), August 20, 2018, https://abolitionjournal. org/im-for-disruption-interview-with-prison-strike-organizer-from-jailhouse-lawyers-speak/; Jared Ware, "Interview: South Carolina Prisoners Challenge Narrative Around Violence," Shadowproof, May 3, 2018, https://shadowproof.com/2018/05/03/ interview-south-carolina-prisoners-challenge-narrative-around-violence-lee-correctional-institution/; "Beyond Prisons — Episode 11: Jailhouse Lawyers Speak," Shadowproof, August 10, 2017, https://shadowproof.com/2017/08/10/ beyond-prisons-episode-11-jailhouse-lawyers-speak/.

generally which provides academic context for their analysis.[59]

Over the years, Mike has been reluctant to discuss his spirituality with me in-depth. He has always shared his analysis in secular terms. I was aware that he was a Muslim, which while not a religion that originated in Africa, is one of the religions that many slaves brought over to the New World on slave ships, and which has survived among Black people, in various forms, in America from colonial times to the present. In all of its iterations, Islam has long been surveilled and demonized by the state, a tradition which has continued within prisons.

I asked Mike what he sees as the role of spirituality within revolutionary movements in and out of prisons, and he described his views on the ubiquity of spirituality among revolutionary prisoners while citing some of his objections to organizing along religious terms:

> I haven't personally run across too many people these days, that does not have some sense of spiritual grounding among really hardcore type people. But I can remember doing some of my first political education, we were discussing comrade George Jackson, his viewpoints dealing with dialectical materialism and the godlessness aspect of it. We were just dealing with a lot of it, historical materialism and all that. And I can remember we just got in a discussion about some of the comrades out in the California area, Huey P. Newton as to some of his challenges with some of the East Coast, and people may not know but a lot of those revolutionaries were very cultured, Assata Shakur and all them. These wasn't no godless type people that didn't believe in something higher and spiritual. You know, they was Yoruba, they practiced a lot of Yoruba back then.
>
> That was within the Panther movement only and I'm bringing that up, but there was conflict in a lot of other revolutionary movement cadres as well, as it relates to spirituality, non-spirituality and the revolution. But I think in today's time period what we're finding in the prisons, one of the things we've done and we try to get other people to see is that it's going to always be a conflict when we start talking two religions. It's gonna become a conflict. So you can't talk religions.

Despite his hesitancy to bring religious views into national prison organizing work, Mike did have some additional insights on how spirituality relates to the struggle for abolition:

---

59. Angela Y. Davis, "From the Prison of Slavery to the Slavery of Prison: Frederick Douglass and the Convict Lease System," in *The Angela Y. Davis Reader* ed. Joy James (Malden, Mass.: Blackwell, 1998) and Dennis Childs, *Slaves of the State: Black Incarceration from the Chain Gang to the Penitentiary* (Minneapolis: University of Minnesota Press, 2015).

You just have to use it as your fire, that's the fire in the belly. My spiritual walk, which I don't really call it a religion, it's really spirituality, but my spiritual walk is in my belly, that's my fire. It helps you reason with what comes after. But not only does it help you reason with what comes after this, it helps me look at you different, it helps me look at even our enemies different. It makes me look at them different on another level. I want something better for all of us. And it is my spiritual walk which helps me see that there's something bigger than this and there's hope even in this particular realm that we currently exist in this material form.

The image of "fire in the belly" might call forth images of Haitian Petro to the uninitiated, but Mike's reflection here is actually much more in tune with the tradition of the Black Nationalist visions of Vesey, with the "seeds of socialism" that Stuckey outlined.[60] But just as Boukman, Walker, Vesey, Turner, Garnet, and Tubman were committed to using their faith to impact material conditions, rather than praying for a better afterlife, Mike is committed to that same spiritual tradition.

Mike went on to elaborate that although he has grown to view religion as an impediment to prison organizing, he does share lessons from the syncretization processes of enslaved Africans as a basis for organizing solidarity among what his comrades refer to as the prison class:

It's so much difference that we have to figure out a way to work together. It kind of reminds me of during the slave plantation time. A lot of times when we speak about New Afrikans, we have to remind ourselves in some of our study groups that a lot of our ancestors didn't come over here with the same beliefs, they came from many different nations, but nonetheless they went through that tragedy together and they found a way to work together and even to rebel together, regardless of their differences on those particular plantations.

I try to use that as an example, because in a lot of ways they were very successful. They were successful at surviving, they were successful at even some of the insurrections they had when they was rising up against the so-called plantation master and his forces. And they were ready to die, and a lot of them did die. A lot of them lost their lives in that particular phase of our battle.

One thing too that we always teach, is that all of these people from a spiritual perspective, and we don't talk about it

---

60. Stuckey, *Slave Culture*, 49.

much, but there was really no slaves, or those that were enslaved that really did not have no type of spiritual background, because all those that came from the African continent had some type of spiritual background, some form of spiritual grounding. And so we use that as an example, it's that fire in the belly and we're figuring out we have to work together we have to make it happen together.

When I asked about his favorite scriptures, Mike cited two passages from the Qu'ran about battling oppression. Asked why he selected them, he said it was because they showed the support of his faith for fighting oppression and let him know he's "on the right track" in his own struggle. In terms of what his faith provides him, he added:

> For me personally, it let's me know that I'm not alone, that there's something bigger than this, and that even if my life is lost now in this particular phase of the struggle, I also feel like it wasn't lost for nothing, but not only was it not lost for nothing, but I feel like my good deeds will be rewarded later. Whether that's karma, or however that may be, it will be rewarded later. Nothing is for nothing.
>
> A lot of these brothers are Muslims, but we do try not to put that on the front line because unfortunately we're still living in a society that is not just racially divided, but also very religiously divided.
>
> I think a lot of that though we try not to put on the frontline, because one of the things that starts to happen, and it's kind of unspoken, but we all know it, we don't want the media to latch on and say what they see inside, and play on people's fears about the Muslims. Because they really tried to play on people's fears after that 9/11 thing. From all I know, everyone I've spoken to from the Ummah, Muslim communities in the prisons, they went through all their books during this time period, and they took thousands of books out of their libraries. And it was based on this witch hunt about Muslim prisoners being extremists.[61]
>
> Now, I am an extremist, but I'm not the extremist in their definition. But they would line me up to be an extremist according to them, because I'm a revolutionary. So, if you're a revolutionary I think you are an extremist (laughs). And that's just something we don't want to happen, because we do have a lot of these brothers and sisters who are revolutionaries. We believe in a different form of government. And

---

61. Gregory Sisk and Michael Heise, "Muslims and Religious Liberty in the Era of 9/11: Empirical Evidence from the Federal Courts," *Cornell Law Faculty Publications*, November 1, 2012, https://scholarship.law.cornell.edu/facpub/430.

we don't want them to try to latch it on with some bogus claim about Sharia law or something, that [we] don't even believe in. So this is kind of some of the fears within the Muslim community inside the prisons of trying not to let that go too far.

Given the state of surveillance and demonization of Islam in the modern world, and in the era of chattel slavery, it is hard to argue that Mike's concerns are misguided. The repression he has faced for organizing over the years mirrors that of the slaveocracy: the demonization of religious practice; the denial of educational materials; and the state's desire to maintain disunity among oppressed peoples. While 9/11 represented a new demonization of Muslims, these dialectics of repression and resistance go back for centuries, and Mike understands it as a protracted struggle.

VIII. SPIRITUAL GUIDANCE FOR AN ABOLITIONIST FUTURE

Abolitionists possess a spirituality that calls upon the oppressed, as Marx said, "to give up their illusions about their condition" through a process that decimates "a condition that requires illusions."[62] From the vantage point of a state that could produce and justify chattel slavery or the largest penal complex in history, abolition spirituality can only be seen as heretical and terroristic.

These judgements can only possibly make sense through the aforementioned "moral sanction" of an "inverted world,"[63] since only in a realm where slavery, rape, murder, torture, maiming, and family separation constitute order and have legal sanction can one understand the spiritual rage produced to overcome that sanction or the spiritual caretaking necessary to survive it.

That stands in stark contrast with Trotsky's maxim regarding religion: "He who believes in another world is not capable of concentrating all his passion on the transformation of this one."[64] Kate Clifford Larson speaks to religion as "moral sanction" in her understanding of Tubman's abolition spirituality. "Black evangelicals," she

---

62. Karl Marx, "A Contribution to the Critique of Hegel's Philosophy of Right," Marxist Internet Archive, 1843, https://www.marxists.org/archive/marx/works/1843/critique-hpr/intro.htm.

63. Karl Marx, "A Contribution to the Critique of Hegel's Philosophy of Right," Marxist Internet Archive, 1843, https://www.marxists.org/archive/marx/works/1843/critique-hpr/intro.htm.

64. Leon Trotsky, "The Tasks of Communist Education," Marxist Internet Archive, December 1922, https://www.marxists.org/history/international/comintern/sections/britain/periodicals/communist_review/1923/7/com_ed.htm.

writes, "rejected the white version of the Bible; they believed that God intended to set them free, delivering them in '*this* world.'"[65]

Confronting that inverted world and its systems of control and repression requires both material and spiritual force. It calls for the creation of a broader basis of kinship and solidarity, which seeks to not only confront the systems of division and dominance instilled by the ruling class, but provide support, organization, and healing along the way. Methods of communication and propaganda that subvert and extend beyond legal sanction are necessary. At times rigid discipline and secrecy are necessary. Other moments require a revolutionary call to action.

These struggles necessitate spiritual connections between the freedom dreams of ancestors and the struggles of future generations, building intergenerational movements towards universal emancipation. In abolitionist struggles across the African diaspora what mattered was not which God rebels prayed to but that rebels believed their cause was righteous on a moral level and was supported by sources of spiritual power that would come to their aid in their fight.

As one of the primary functions of their current organizing, Jailhouse Lawyer Speak members serve as advocates for agreements to end hostilities among rival factions within prisons. These agreements serve as one of the most powerful prisoner-led processes towards unification as an organized force against a system which oppresses them. While not ostensibly based on a syncretism of spirituality, syncretization is a negotiation process, not unlike the one necessary to bring different factions of prisoners into alliance with one another. In that way, the processes to put these agreements into place might mirror what Helen Timothy Pyne referred to as spiritual calls in the modern context, "after four hundred years, to reverse the fragmentation, to reconnect the branches to the tree."[66]

REFERENCES

Aptheker, Herbert. *American Negro Slave Revolts*. New ed. New York: International Publishers, 1970.

Beyond. "Beyond Prisons—Episode 11: Jailhouse Lawyers Speak." Shadowproof, August 10, 2017. https://shadowproof.com/2017/08/10/beyond-prisons-episode-11-jailhouse-lawyers-speak/.

Cabral, Amilcar. "The Weapon of Theory." Marxist Internet Archive, 1966. https://www.marxists.org/subject/africa/cabral/1966/weapon-theory.htm.

65. Larson, *Bound for the Promised Land*, 47.

66. Helen Pyne Timothy, "(Re)Membering African Religion and Spirituality in the African Diaspora," *Journal of Haitian Studies* 8, no. 1 (2002): 134–49, 148.

Childs, Dennis. *Slaves of the State: Black Incarceration from the Chain Gang to the Penitentiary*. Minneapolis: University of Minnesota Press, 2015.

Davis, Angela Y. *The Angela Y. Davis Reader*. Edited by Joy James. *Blackwell Readers*. Malden: Blackwell, 1998.

Deren, Maya. *Divine Horsemen: The Living Gods of Haiti*. Documentext ed. New Paltz: McPherson & Company, 2004.

Du Bois, W. E. B. *Black Reconstruction in America*. New York: Touchstone, 1995.

Dubois, Laurent. "Vodou and History." *Comparative Studies in Society and History* 43, no. 1 (January 2001): 92–100.

Freehling, William W. *Prelude to Civil War: The Nullification Controversy in South Carolina, 1816–1836*. New York: Harper & Row, 1966.

Garnet, Henry. "An Address to the Slaves of the United States of America." *Electronic Texts in American Studies*, August 16, 1848. https://digitalcommons.unl.edu/etas/8.

Gomez, Michael A. *Exchanging Our Country Marks: The Transformation of African Identities in the Colonial and Antebellum South*. Chapel Hill: University of North Carolina Press, 1998.

Gray, Thomas, and Nat Turner. "The Confessions of Nat Turner." *Zea E-Books in American Studies*, January 1, 1831. https://digitalcommons.unl.edu/zeaamericanstudies/11.

Hartman, Saidiya. *Lose Your Mother: A Journey Along the Atlantic Slave Route*. First edition. New York: Farrar, Straus and Giroux, 2008.

James, C.L.R. *The Black Jacobins; Toussaint L'Ouverture and the San Domingo Revolution*. 2d ed., rev. New York: Vintage Books, 1963.

Larson, Kate Clifford. *Bound for the Promised Land: Harriet Tubman, Portrait of an American Hero*. 1st ed. New York: Ballantine, 2004.

Marx, Karl. "A Contribution to the Critique of Hegel's Philosophy of Right." *Marxist Internet Archive*, 1843. https://www.marxists.org/archive/marx/works/1843/critique-hpr/intro.htm.

Rawick, George P. *From Sundown to Sunup: The Making of the Black Community*. Westport, Conn: Greenwood, 1971.

Robinson, Cedric J. *Black Marxism: The Making of the Black Radical Tradition*. Chapel Hill: The University of North Carolina Press, 2020.

———. *Black Movements in America. Revolutionary Thought/Radical Movements*. New York: Routledge, 1997.

Shiffrin, Steven H. "The Rhetoric of Black Violence in the Antebellum Period: Henry Highland Garnet." *Journal of Black Studies* 2, no. 1 (1971): 45–56.

Sisk, Gregory, and Michael Heise. "Muslims and Religious Liberty in the Era of 9/11: Empirical Evidence from the Federal Courts." *Cornell Law Faculty Publications*, November 1, 2012. https://scholarship.law.cornell.edu/facpub/430.

Stuckey, Sterling. *Slave Culture: Nationalist Theory and the Foundations of Black America*. New York: Oxford University Press, 1987.

Timothy, Helen Pyne. "(Re)Membering African Religion and Spirituality in the African Diaspora." *Journal of Haitian Studies* 8, no. 1 (2002): 134–49.

Trotsky, Leon. "The Tasks of Communist Education." Marxist Internet Archive, December 1922. https://www.marxists.org/history/international/comintern/sections/britain/periodicals/communist_review/1923/7/com_ed.htm.

Ware, Jared. "'I'm for Disruption': Interview with Prison Strike Organizer from Jailhouse Lawyers Speak." *Abolition* (blog), August 20, 2018. https://abolitionjournal.org/im-for-disruption-interview-with-prison-strike-organizer-from-jailhouse-lawyers-speak/.

———. "Interview: South Carolina Prisoners Challenge Narrative Around Violence." Shadowproof, May 3, 2018. https://shadowproof.com/2018/05/03/interview-south-carolina-prisoners-challenge-narrative-around-violence-lee-correctional-institution/.

SECTION II: TESTIMONY

SPIRITUAL ABOLITION (OR SOMETHING LIKE THAT)

Fatima Shabazz

I

"I looked at the traitor and terrorizer with unlimited, undeniable contempt." So, for those who are unfamiliar with me, my name is Fatima Malika Shabazz. I am an activist, advocate, CEO/President of Fatima Speaks LLC and a member of several activist organizations including Black and Pink. The opening quote is from John Brown, a white and possibly the first white abolitionist to take up aggressive arms in the cause of abolishing slavery. I bring him to the fore because aside from his raid at Harpers Ferry before he was finally caught and hanged, his religious zeal had already become legendary, or at least that's what the history books say. The question however, is can the concepts of spirituality and the desire to abolish a corrupt carceral system coexist? Think about that for a moment.

In an altruistic society they can, but it would seem to only if you are wealthy and can afford the benefits of white privilege. This allows you to back out of the real boots on the ground type of fighting against a group of people who clearly have a skewed way of thinking when it come to the abolishment of a system designed for the degradation of a subset of its people.

However, as an African American trans woman, the concept of spirituality is not foreign to me. Culturally African American families are among the most religious and spiritual people to be found. However, as a formerly incarcerated individual I found it hard then as I do now to reconcile the obtaining of spiritual peace with the urge to violently destroy a system that all but destroyed me. See, I believe that the carceral system has to be smashed into dust through physical revolution, much like John Brown. I too am tired of the marches, protests, and legislative bullshit that no one in power in the system really adhere to.

I believe revolution of this kind is of an explosive nature born out of instantaneous acts of rebellion, and I do not see the spirituality in those actions, or at least I didn't, but as I remember my passages of scripture, God often turned humble men into warriors for freedom, as I remember my African cultural roots Queen Nzingha fought and took back the respect and the kingdoms her brother had lost, and though a warrior woman she was not savage but spiritual in the truest sense. Yet as we move into 2021, I can't help but wonder where spirituality has been these last four years while the so-called commander in chief spewed hatred and vitriol from the most powerful seat in the land. Think about that for a moment, then ask yourself, what is the state of your own spirit?

II

Had 2020 not been such a tumultuous year where would you be spiritually? In times of actual or perceived crises, people turn to their faith, whatever it is. But if you look closely at systems of belief, you will find that regardless of what people's religious doctrine says about other systems of belief we invariably find that at the root of it all we are more alike than unalike. So, imagine for a moment that our likenesses were rooted in the same belief that the carceral state was such a demoralizing system of abuse that it must be dismantled at any cost. That would give you the makings of a conversation about moral revolution and spiritual abolition.

Seeds of liberation that are planted in a field of discontent are often harvested by the scythe of anger and frustration. Believe it or not this is a spiritual awakening, an awakening that towers above bullshit rhetoric like a monolith to spiritual and intellectual freedom. As someone who has survived and even more so thrived in a dysfunctional carceral system, I am saying that it is imperative that acknowledging the need to abolish systemic morays and habits take precedence in your mind, otherwise you end up falling victim to the same shit as everyone else in your surroundings, rather than your spirit being clear and ready for the abolition fight you will have every day from the moment that you realize something must be done to correct the problem

So, the next question would logically be, how do you accomplish this? The logical, or let me say "MY" logical answer is: "Don't start me to lying." I have no idea how to make that happen, the one thing I do know is you have to divest yourself of bullshit people, people who only serve to drain you of energy and drag you down. If you allow this negative energy to rest on your shoulders you also invite that same energy to crush you into ineffectiveness and possibly into oblivion, in any fight to abolish anything, there will ALWAYS be those who oppose what you do and stand or, that does not change in the case of spiritual abolition, especially in this country's carceral system. The system could not exist in its present form without the ability to degenerate and demoralize its captors.

This demoralization is not limited to strip and cell searches, nor is it limited to the language used against you, I say against you because the language is not meant to uplift and fulfill you but to do exactly the opposite. Language can be used in many forms and words have more power than guns. To say that the pen is mightier than the sword is not an overstatement; so placed in the context of spiritual abolition, negative verbiage is used as a weapon to demoralize the spirit as well as the mind, thus destroying the whole person. We must be careful to not only use language that bolsters the spirit but to also not allow contrary language to destroy the spirit otherwise spiritual abolition becomes a contradiction in terms.

Spiritual abolition does not require a holier than thou approach, it simply requires that you recognize the power of spirit to move, inspire and to motivate, to quote the great Maya Angelou, people will forget your name, people will forget how you look, but they will never forget how you make them feel. Bear this in mind as you travel on your spiritual journey.

With Love and Purpose,
Fatima Malika Shabazz

A PRAYER OF ABOLITION

Rev. Jason Lydon

It has been nearly two decades, but when I close my eyes, I can still find myself lying on my top bunk at the fifth prison I was incarcerated in, surrounded by sleeping, snoring, and restless men, all desperately wanting to be elsewhere. Many were likely dreaming of the life they once lived, or a new life they longed to get out to. Others were having nightmares about accidentally walking off the yard in the wrong direction, resulting in a bullet from a racist guard, or maybe getting picked up and then given a longer sentence in a higher security prison, never to breathe fresh air again. A few night owls were in the TV room, watching late night shows because when the sun came up, they headed back to bed to sleep the rest of their bid away. It was during these days that I rediscovered prayer. It was in the heartbreaking solitude of an open, massive room filled with concrete cubicles, steel lockers, metal bunk beds, and heavy breathers that I found a renewed commitment to connecting with the divine.

I had prayed many times before. I come from an Irish Catholic family, was raised by two parents who went to seminary school (and two other parents who did not), attended a progressive Lutheran summer camp, and was very active in my Unitarian Universalist (UU) church starting at age nine. Words of prayer, especially grace at dinner time, had always been a fundamental aspect of my life. Before becoming a UU, I would practice the Lord's prayer when I went to sleep at night. I can still hear the echoes in the Holy Trinity Church sanctuary from all the parishioners speaking in unison, "Lord, have mercy," while Pastor Moline led the congregation in the prayers of the people each Sunday morning.

As a nontheistic Unitarian Universalist, it can be a unique challenge to effectively communicate what I understand the divine to be and what role I understand prayer to play in the universe. There are two crucial quotes that guide my thinking about prayer. The first is from ecofeminist theologian, Ivone Gebara: "Prayer is our personal and collective preparation for acting in solidarity and respect, for awakening feelings of tenderness and compassion for persons and for all living things."[1] The second is from Unitarian minister, John Haynes Holmes: "Prayer is attention unfolding into intention. It is purpose,

---

1. Ivone Gebara, *Longing for Running Water: Ecofeminism and Liberation* (Minneapolis, MN: Augsburg Fortress Publishers, 1999), 117.

resolution, dedication. Which brings us face to face with the greatest of all spiritual discoveries—that if our prayers are to be answered we must answer them ourselves; that we are already answering our prayers in the mere expression of the desire that they be fulfilled."[2] The practice of prayer, then, is the practice of connecting and acting. This connection is internal, interpersonal, and intertwined with all that exists. Similarly, the action prayer calls for is action for our own selves, others, and all of existence. Prayer is quiet and raucous; righteous and humble. Prayer is intentional, thoughtful, and rooted in the power of what might be. Just as abolition is. Prayer is relational, resistant to oppression, and lifted up through love. Just as abolition is. For me, I do not pray for abolition, the movement for abolition is the prayer. Every letter we send, each overpriced phone call, each visit, and every moment we get closer to collective liberation—these moments are the prayer I connect most deeply to.

In his book, *Thinking Prayer: Theology and Spirituality Amid the Crises of Modernity*, Andrew Prevot offers new ways of engaging with prayer in critical movement building ways. In the introduction he proposes some helpful definitions that have been grounding for me: "If theology, then, can be defined as thinking prayer, *spirituality* can be defined analogously as *living prayer*: that is, as that way of life which prays and as that practice of prayer which lives. . . And spirituality is, therefore, nothing other than prayer without ceasing. It is prayer spread across the many works and habits of each day."[3] With Prevot's definition of spirituality as the living out of prayer, we can understand that our shared work towards abolition is both a collective spiritual practice and a common prayer.

The practice of prayer is most easily seen and heard with words, even if we understand actions to be prayer as well. In the church that I serve in Chicago, we use spoken prayer/meditation each Sunday to connect more deeply with one another. Since returning to prayer on my prison bunk, I have always started my prayer practice with gratitude. Unsurprisingly, it was not always easy to begin with gratitude when I was stuck inside concrete buildings, particularly during the weeks I was in solitary confinement. That difficulty, though, became an invitation to take time to be grateful for that which I often overlooked. At night, I would close my eyes and practice paying attention to my body as my abdomen went up and down with each breath. I would try to tune out the noises around me, while also being thankful that each person around me was also breathing. Laying there, I would turn my mind to my gratitude for the letters I received, for the food cooked and shared by other prisoners, for the friendships I made,

---

2. Clarence Russell Skinner, *A Free Pulpit in Action* (Freeport, NY: Books for Libraries Press, 1971), 98.

3. Andrew Prevot, *Thinking Prayer: Theology and Spirituality amid the Crises of Modernity* (South Bend, IN: University of Notre Dame Press, 2015), 17.

for time outside when it happened, and for the anti-war movement I felt part of even as I was stuck behind bars. In a space that was so violent and scary, taking time to be grateful felt like a subversion of power. Prisoners are so often treated as less than human, and to take a moment to be grateful for other prisoners, to be attentive to my humanness and connection to the world—this was part of my resistance to being dehumanized. To be grateful was to feel powerful. To practice gratitude in the face of violence was to commit to connecting with others around me and resisting the violence of the prison system itself. My prayer was for myself and lived within my own heart, though each prayer was part of the collective faith and spiritual practice swirling around in that concrete cage.

I appreciate connecting with written prayers that people have been using for generations. I know that our visions of abolition are about generational struggles for liberation and will take longer to realize than any of us would like. Knowing that, I am sustained by the knowledge that there have been so many who struggled long before us who are ancestors now. Some of these ancestors are recent and are people we once embraced in the warmth of our arms. Others live in the stories we are told by grandparents or mentors. There are those ancestors who we will never know of but who made it possible for us to be where we are today. One of my practices to stay connected to ancestors is to read words from Ancient Near East poets in the form of the Psalms. For thousands of years, people have been singing, reading, memorizing, critiquing, and, yes, praying these words. The Psalms are complicated, and this essay is not intended to be a profound exegetical engagement with any text. I will, though, highlight a specific Psalm that I have prayed and adapted many times. Given that these texts were passed along to others for generations by spoken word, before being written down, I enjoy taking plenty of liberty with reimagining what the words can transform into overtime, while maintaining its intended meaning.

Psalm 146 is among what scholars call the Hallelujah Psalms. Beginning with praise of God feels very similar to beginning in gratitude. While I do not believe in an otherworldly deity that gets involved in the affairs of humanity, I do believe deeply in the interconnectedness of all existence. When I read of God in this Psalm, I understand my belief to be similar to the conception of God in this prayerful song. There is constant translation at work here, from ancient Hebrew to modern English, from theistic to nontheistic, from thousands of years ago to the present. The translation need not diminish the beauty of the connection or the power of the prayer. Instead, the deeper engagement creates something that is both ancient and given new life in this moment.

It is worth noting that this Psalm is one of many places in the Hebrew and Greek Bible when liberation or care for prisoners is lifted up and oppressive power is chided. Over the centuries, the references to prisoners throughout these texts are often spoken about by clergy as metaphorical. It is rare that I will suggest anyone take Biblical text literally, though our abolitionist movement gains some strength when we offer reminders that not only are the prisoners in these sacred texts literal captives, multiple books within the Bible are themselves prison literature, written by incarcerated authors.

After the hallelujahs, this Psalm implores listeners, or those joining in the prayer, not to put their trust in leaders who cannot bring about salvation. In my abolitionist spiritual practice, I hear this as a reminder to stay away from racist and carceral-expanding reforms, much like Mariame Kaba's list of police reforms we must always oppose.[4] It is our prayerful responsibility to avoid claiming false victories, either for ourselves or for our movement. We must avoid falling in with campaigns that will lead to us having to abolish something else later. While abolition is certainly a creative process, we need to be cautious and intentional about what we are creating. Just as the princes in the Psalm simply return to the earth and their plans come out with no freedom, the same is true for the false promise of reform. The prayer is for more. The prayer is for a salvation that comes not from false promises, but from the beauty of collective action rooted in love and liberation.

The Psalmist continues with celebrations of God's power. Again, my theology and the author's theology diverge here. However, if I choose to understand God here as the interconnectedness of all existence, and I understand abolition as a prayerful practice of meeting the needs of that collective existence, then God becomes love, or life, or us. Thus, it is love and our collective power that creates and uncreates all things. It is life and our actions that join the cause of the oppressed and ensure all bellies are filled. It is through atoms vibrating, children crying, and ocean waves crashing that we love the righteous, lift up those who are bowed down, care for those who have been othered, and upset those with unjust power. Through this prayer and with one another, it is us who set the prisoners free. Love and liberation reign, hallelujah!

To pray this Psalm is not to relinquish responsibility to act. The prayer is our grounding and sustaining faith in the face of seemingly insurmountable odds. The anti-Blackness, white supremacy, queer antagonism, colonialism, and overwhelming violence of carceral structures are pervasive and powerful in their extreme as well as banal functionality. To pray is to remember that we are bigger than any one body and that our singular bodies are essential. Depending on how we pray, though, our prayers are not immune to the same systems of

---

4. Mariame Kaba, "Police 'Reforms' You Should Always Oppose," *Truthout*, December 7, 2014, https://truthout.org/articles/police-reforms-you-should-always-oppose.

violence that uphold the prison industrial complex. Womanist theologian M. Shawn Copeland, writing on the Catholic Church in the United States during the 19th Century, underlines the culpability of the Church in the forwarding of anti-Blackness:

> Anti-black logics were so pervasive and so restrictive, so precise and so pleasurable that they overrode the exercise of potentially legitimate authority, seized and displaced Divine Authority, thereby totalizing and fetishizing whiteness and white human beings. In the process, anti-black logics repressed demands of conscience, obscured morality, and eclipsed ethics to induce authority and authorities to kneel before the racialized idol of whiteness. In an even more perilous, totalizing move, these authorities attempted to bleach and domesticate the Divine, to make over the Divine in their image and likeness.[5]

In order for a prayer to be authentically abolitionist and deserving of a collective answering, it must be a prayer that centers Black life, Black spirituality, and Black creativity. This abolitionist prayer must also be theologically diverse, queer, disability-inclusive, anticapitalist, and created by people on both sides of the concrete walls. Like all prayers, these prayers we create will look different in our differing communities and will offer a multitude of answers that we can honor and challenge together.

As I said my prayers on my bunk, I tried to imagine love surrounding all beings. I tried, so hard, to imagine a love that would hold the guards accountable for their violence. I prayed and often found no clear answers. I continue to seek answers to those prayers and the countless other prayers I have said since then. While so many prayers have not yet found answers, so many others have. I no longer have nightmares about solitary confinement. My cellie from that time is on this side of the wall now. Black and Pink came into existence with the work of so very many people, and tens of thousands of LGBTQ/ HIV+ prisoners across the United States have connected with each other and with people on the outside to strengthen the movement for abolition as well as get support for the very personal needs of surviving the day-to-day life of incarceration. These are answered prayers, answered by the divinity of relationship, the power of love that destroys suffering. Far too many prayers have not been answered. Far too much suffering continues. Despair comes and I find my solution in a return to prayer, a return to gratitude, and a return to the power

---

5. M. Shawn Copeland, "White Supremacy and Anti-black Logics in the Making of U.S. Catholicism," in Vincent W. Lloyd and Andrew Prevot, eds., *Anti-Blackness and Christian Ethics* (Maryknoll, NY: Orbis Books, 2017).

of communities that refuse to back down. Abolition is the prayer I pray because I know we will, one day, answer it with a fullness that transforms us all.

REFERENCES

Copleland, M. Shawn. "White Supremacy and Anti-black Logics in the Making of U.S. Catholicism," in Vincent W. Lloyd and Andrew Prevot, eds., *Anti-Blackness and Christian Ethics*. Maryknoll, NY: Orbis Books, 2017.

Gebara, Ivone. *Longing for Running Water: Ecofeminism and Liberation*. Minneapolis, MN: Augsburg Fortress Publishers, 1999.

Kaba, Mariame. "Police 'Reforms' You Should Always Oppose," *Truthout*, December 7, 2014, https://truthout.org/articles/police-reforms-you-should-always-oppose.

Prevot, Andrew. *Thinking Prayer: Theology and Spirituality amid the Crises of Modernity*. South Bend, IN: University of Notre Dame Press, 2015.

Skinner, Clarence Russell. *A Free Pulpit in Action*. Freeport, NY: Books for Libraries Press, 1971.

REFLECTIONS ON SPIRITUAL LIFE AND ABOLITION

Michael Cox

I attended my first Buddhist group while I was incarcerated at NCCI-Gardner, a medium security prison located in rural Massachusetts. Each Sunday at 1pm, a small group of prisoners filed into a sunlit room with the scent of sandalwood wafting in the air. The volunteer chaplain would look each of us directly in the eye and greet us, in stark contrast to the dehumanizing treatment we received from guards. We would then grab a *zafu*, or meditation cushion, and prepare for our regular routine of silent meditation, chanting, and to listen to a *Dharma* talk, or sermon.

The topic was *metta*, or love, with an emphasis on loving oneself. Our chaplain described this as foundational to loving others. Throughout the talk I felt like I was melting into my *zafu*, fidgeting constantly, as if she could see directly into my heart. As the talk concluded, we were offered an opportunity to engage in a classical meditation practice to methodically cultivate *metta*. For the first time I heard words to describe the language of the heart.

I attended the group for the next three years because I knew I had stumbled upon something precious. My commitment to a daily meditation practice was steadfast. Up to this point in my life my practice was probably the only thing I committed to with genuine devotion. I gradually became more present and responded to routine tensions in prison life with new and more effective ways. I laughed more. My mind was sharper. My heart was more tender.

As a young boy my experience in the church left me with too many unanswered questions. I grew up in a Born-Again Baptist Church, but I never considered myself a religious person. My questions were often met with impatience but sometimes hostility. By contrast, Buddhism encouraged intensive inquiry into life, truth, and our relationship to all things. This was a perfect fit for my overactive imagination and critical skepticism.

Setting out on a genuine spiritual or abolitionist path necessarily brings us into confrontation with deeply held beliefs and uncomfortable truths. Both paths invite us to see clearly the truth of things. Not as we'd like them to be but *just* as they are. Rarely are we asked to tread in familiar waters, rather, we're asked to dive deep and explore unknown, unfamiliar, and sometimes scary places. White comrades may need to digest the uncomfortable reality of white supremacy, reckon with the daily harm each of us cause, or identify how best to support liberatory work.

Both are a philosophy and a practice. Their end goal: liberation. Practitioners are offered tools to decolonize ourselves and our communities. Simultaneously, we are encouraged to cultivate—internally and externally—qualities like generosity, love, and wisdom. What is beautiful about both paths is that they are both pragmatic, not dogmatic. In non-proscriptive ways, they invite us to create a world that values life and joy over dehumanization. In the same way we are encouraged to cultivate the conditions that allow health, care, and love to thrive, particularly for the most marginalized among us like Black, Indigenous, POC, LGBTQI+, and poor people.

Our inner realm, intentions, and thoughts are the forerunner of all things. Greed and punitiveness exist in our minds which manifest in our actions and—by extension—within the structures of society. The colonization of North America was motivated by these ailments which paved the way for the genocide of Indigenous peoples, the enslavement of Black people, and an uncanny thirst for extracting natural resources through the exploitation of labor. Of course, the pretext for all of this is capitalism, an economic and political system in which a country's trade and industry are controlled by private owners for profit, rather than by the state. We are called upon to begin the work of decolonizing our hearts and minds from the conditioning we were born into. This is the beginning of a spiritual life. This is the beginning of a life with abolitionist values.

As Bikkhu Bodhi wrote about setting out on a spiritual path, he could easily be speaking about an abolitionist one:

> The search for a spiritual path is born out of suffering. It does not start with lights and ecstasy, but with the hardtacks of pain, disappointment, and confusion. However, for suffering to give birth to a genuine spiritual search, it must amount to more than something passively received from without. It has to trigger an inner realization, a perception which pierces through the facile complacency of our usual encounter with the world to glimpse the insecurity perpetually gaping underfoot. When this insight dawns, even if only momentarily, it can precipitate a profound personal crisis. It overturns accustomed goals and values, mocks our routine preoccupations, leaves old enjoyments stubbornly unsatisfying.[1]

---

1. Bhikkhu Bodhi, *The Noble Eightfold Path: Way to the End of Suffering* (Onalaska, WA: Pariyatti Publishing, 1994).

Embarking on a spiritual journey is not too unlike stepping onto the abolitionist path. We often begin with a sense of curiosity and sustain ourselves on borrowed faith, perhaps from people like the Dalai Lama or Angela Davis. Eventually we cultivate our own faith that initially flickers but grows steadier. As our ability to listen deeply and to speak sharpens, we will trust our own instincts more and make space for others to be their own leaders. Eventually, if not already, we will become a spark of faith for others. As we journey into the unknown, we will encounter the 10,000 joys and 10,000 sorrows inherent in this work. To prepare for these moments, we must do this work in community and avoid working in silos.

Being in community and having a mentor, whether with a *sangha* or a coalition, will help us make course corrections as needed. As we explore uncomfortable and unfamiliar places, whether they be internal, interpersonal, or structural, we can easily become riddled with guilt, paralyzed by fear, or consumed by the grief inherent in this work. Just as the prison mediation teacher expounded: loving ourselves is foundational. Self-care is required. Without joy, the practice and path will no longer feed us. They become bone dry.

As we draw from both theory and practice, perhaps reading seminal pieces like *In This Very Life* by Sayadaw U Pandita or joining a local coalition to decriminalize sex work, our resolve for liberation grows. Some of us are more inclined toward academia than showing up in the streets. When asked whether theory or practice is supreme, Bhikkhu Bodhi succinctly elevates the path over theory, "The path claims primacy because it is precisely this that brings the teaching to life. The path translates the [teaching] from a collection of abstract formulas into a continually unfolding disclosure of truth. It gives an outlet from the problem of suffering with which the teaching starts. And it makes the teaching's goal, liberation [. . .], accessible to us in our own experience, where alone it takes on authentic meaning."

Our training—whether spiritual, political, or both—is deeply rooted in notions of liberation, freedom, and breaking our fetters. How best to achieve that goal? What is the next right move? How can we become more free? If we are to truly liberate our minds and communities these questions must be living questions, constantly re-evaluated, and never far from the front of our minds. While there are many vehicles to address these questions, love is one path to achieve all of these lofty but necessary goals.

Buddhism became a touchstone for powerful courage as I began to abide more in love than in fear. I remember when a guard perpetuated an injustice in our housing unit. I stood up to him and explained why his actions were wrong. That didn't stop me from being placed in solitary confinement for addressing the situation, but it is certainly something I would not have mustered the courage to do before beginning a regular meditation practice. While in solitary I replayed the incident over and over. It was okay to speak out against harm even if it was commonplace and normalized. Love manifests in different, sometimes unexpected ways.

Like most spiritual traditions, Buddhism has a strong thesis about love. The classical Buddhist teaching of the Brahma Viharas offer a multifaceted way of thinking about love. In short, the scriptures tell us that love is a sense of universal friendliness toward all living beings without reservation. It is a deep wish that all beings be well. When this energy encounters suffering, we call it *karuna*, or compassion. Does the heart not quiver when we read about a transgender woman hauled off to prison for engaging in survival sex work? When love encounters the happiness of another, we call it *mudita* or sympathetic joy. Do we not feel joy when we see a father step out from the prison gates and his child rushes to embrace him? To balance these three manifestations of love we call on *upekkha*, or balance, to anchor us from drifting away on a pink cloud.

It would be a fatal mistake to buy into the fantasy that we can incarcerate someone out of love in order to protect society at-large or to prevent harm from happening. To do so would be to completely ignore the inherent suffering caused by organized abandonment and incarceration. The prison is a source of so much suffering rooted in transphobia, anti-Blackness, and the unchecked pursuit of capitalism. Incarcerated people are ripped from their family and community. While incarcerated, they experience untold instances of sexual, physical, and emotional violence. Many are forced into solitary confinement, small cells devoid of any meaningful contact or personal possessions for extended periods of time. Others never make it out alive.

What happens when the power of love and wisdom turn toward the prison?

Love demands we break down prison walls and return our people back to their communities with resources for healing and material well-being. Wisdom tells us that by all metrics the prison is a failed social control experiment. Wisdom and love invite us to conduct a root cause analysis. They call upon all of us, for the sake of humanity, to transform the structures of society that perpetuate a culture of punitiveness and depravity and to care for our neighbors.

Indeed, the state seems to invest endless resources into the vast infrastructure and social conditioning that allows the prison industrial complex to thrive whereby millions of humans are ripped from their homes, caged, and subjected to unspeakable conditions. We would all be better served if we reversed the devastating policies of organized abandonment by investing in reparations, transformative justice, healing, housing, education, and healthcare inclusive of treatment on demand. This is the path.

Much like my early experiences in the church, society will signal in implicit and explicit ways to not question the underpinnings of this social structure. Our country has gone to great lengths to paper over social and economic inequities and pointing out the sloppiness of it is considered rude. Rather than challenge the status quo, we are expected to internalize the difficulty of navigating a senseless system as a personal failure. Like any genuine spiritual path, prison abolition invites us to seek the truth and to begin transformative work.

After I was released from prison, I was often conflicted between pursuing an abolitionist path or a spiritual one, perhaps to work at a meditation center or to take robes. After many years of grappling with this conflict, I signed up for a three-month silent meditation retreat at Insight Meditation Society. For many, it is a profound experience to silently meditate in a supportive environment. While in the depths of this retreat, I realized that there is no distinction between building an abolitionist world and walking a path with heart. I had created a false binary. When the retreat ended, I made a personal vow to fuse these parallel paths into one.

Spiritual and political awakenings can be pivotal moments for practitioners. Whether they are waking up to the mess of things, coming to terms with how we show up in the world, or allowing the possibility of liberation to permeate our bones, we can rarely return to our prior state of complacency. We are often spurred on to dive deeper, to love more fiercely, and to dedicate more of ourselves to freedom dreaming. "No longer can we continue to drift complacently through life, driven blindly by our hunger for sense pleasures and by the pressure of prevailing social norms. A deeper reality beckons us; we had heard the call of a more stable, more authentic happiness, and until we arrive at our destination, we cannot rest content."

REFERENCES

Bodhi, Bhikkhu. *The Noble Eightfold Path: Way to the End of Suffering*. Onalaska, WA: Pariyatti Publishing, 1994.

SECTION III: BLACK SPIRITUAL STUDY

IS, WAS, AND IS TO COME: FREEDOM DREAMWORLD DISPATCHES

Andrew Krinks

What impedes our paths to a world made new? What keeps the transformations entailed in "abolition" out of reach? Certainly, deeply pervasive material conditions of racial capitalist, patriarchal exploitation, dispossession, violence, and carceral captivity block our way. In the face of such impediments, the work of abolition is, in part, the collective work of dismantling, of tearing down, of clearing paths so that others may pass on through to the other side. Abolition also entails creating a world in which people share collective access to and control over the social goods that make flourishing and safety possible and thereby make carceral institutions obsolete.[1] But the work of abolition consists of more than the labor of rearranging materialities alone. Transformative abolitionist organizing, educating, and healing begins by inviting us to artfully imagine and envision the worlds for which we are fighting, because, as Robin D.G. Kelley puts it, "the map to a new world is in the imagination."[2]

Abolition, in other words, requires freedom dreamwork.

Dreams are often associated with escape, with unreality, with naïve otherworldliness. What does an activity as seemingly immaterial as dreaming or imagining have to do with the concreteness of abolition, of a world made materially new? Contrary to what the term might seem to imply, dreaming as a practice for creating a more just world has a long history originating in Black radical and Indigenous practices of survival and self-determination in the face of white racial capitalism and settler colonialism. Indeed, because it is, in the end, "another world" that abolition fights for, freedom dreamwork that transcends the conceptual and material boundaries of the present order of things is a necessary tool for helping us all get there. When confronted with the violently imposed limitations

---

1. As Ruth Wilson Gilmore famously argues, "Abolition is about presence, not absence. It's about building life-affirming institutions." (Keynote Conversation, Making and Unmaking Mass Incarceration Conference, University of Mississippi, Oxford, MS, December 5, 2019.) For a foundational account of what it means to make carceral institutions obsolete, see: Angela Y. Davis, *Are Prisons Obsolete?* (New York, NY: Seven Stories Press, 2003).

2. Robin D.G. Kelley, *Freedom Dreams: The Black Radical Imagination* (Boston, MA: Beacon Press, 2008), 2.

of the present order, freedom dreams are a means not of mindless escape, but of buoying our capacity to believe that something new can in fact break into the present, and of becoming attentive to what that something might look and feel like—and, indeed, what it already has looked and felt like. In the words of Indigenous scholar Dian Million, "Dreaming . . . is the effort to make sense of relations in the worlds we live, dreaming and empathizing intensely our relations with past and present and the future without boundaries of linear time. Dreaming is a communicative sacred activity."[3]

Entrenched as we are today in struggles against the seemingly unassailable forces of what bell hooks calls imperialist white -supremacist capitalist patriarchy, dispatches from the beyond in our midst, from the freedom dream worlds among us, have the power to nourish us for the hard work of discerning how—and believing that— "the present form of this world" is neither natural nor permanent, but is instead, somehow, "passing away."[4] Imperialist white-supremacist capitalist patriarchy and the carceral cages it creates, sustain themselves in part on the basis of the idea that they are natural—that they reflect the world as it always has been and always will be. But they have not always been, and so need not always be. Propelled by the dreams of freedom fighters before us, abolitionist freedom dreaming disrupts the lie that the present order is inevitable, pressing us instead toward living faith in the realizability of the as-yet-unreal world we all deserve.

Practices that orient us to the actual possibility of a world beyond the present order constitute spiritual practices: they embody the hopeful refusal to accept the deadly material conditions of the present, insisting that radically different life-giving realities and arrangements are possible in our lifetime, and are already present in our midst, even if only partially. Freedom dreamwork discerns traces of those alternate realities in our past, present, and future. Practices rooted in an abolitionist imagination also constitute spiritual practices in the sense that they often draw both explicitly and implicitly from aspects of the rituality, sociality, singing, folk traditions, theologies, and philosophical frames of various religious and spiritual traditions. In the end, whether or note those who labor to forge means of life out of conditions of death do so by way of a conscious spirituality or specific spiritual or religious tradition, the work of believing in and struggling

---

3. Quoted in Lena Palacios, "With Immediate Cause: Intense Dreaming as World-Making," in Abolition Collective, eds., *Abolishing Carceral Society: Abolition: A Journal of Insurgent Politics*, (Brooklyn, NY: Common Notions, 2018), 59. See: Dian Million, "Intense Dreaming: Theories, Narratives, and Our Search for Home," *American Indian Quarterly* 35, no. 3 (2011): 314-315.

4. bell hooks, *The Will to Change: Men, Masculinity, and Love* (New York, NY: Atria Books, 2004), 17; 1 Corinthians 7.31. New Revised Standard Version. All subsequent biblical references come from this translation.

to birth a new world in the shell of the old may be understood as a work of sacred proportion.[5]

The movement for a world without police and prisons—a movement largely led, like abolitionist movements before it, by Black women—is often accused, usually with racial and gendered overtones, of being dangerously out of touch with reality. If so-called "reality" means economies of scarcity built on exploitation and dispossession, cultures of supremacy that value some by devaluing others, politics of organized abandonment that deliberately disenfranchise entire populations, and systems of organized violence that create the illusion of "safety" for a few through the caging and endangerment of many, then yes, abolitionists are out of touch with "reality."[6] Deliberately unaligned with a death-making order, refusing to accept the way things are as the way things must be, abolitionist freedom dreaming is ultimately less naïve, escapist, and otherworldly than it is anotherworldly: it discerns the present order as a distortion of the natural and sacred order of things, organizes collective transcendence and transformation of that order, and reconfigures what it means to live together by preparing and building—here and now, piece by piece—a new world in the wreckage of the old. Abolitionist freedom dreams—and the movements led by Black, Indigenous, and other people of color that catalyze and enflesh them—constitute a transformative refusal to conform to the deadly patterns of the racial capitalist, settler colonial, carceral world.[7]

The spiritual practice of abolitionist freedom dreamwork also requires reckoning with the fact that the capitalist-colonial-carceral order that abolition seeks to transcend and transform is a religious project, too. Serving and protecting the pseudo-sacred social order of patriarchal whiteness and private property by exiling those who trespass against it to carceral hell, cops and cages perform a mythological,

---

5. Peter Maurin of the Catholic Worker movement regularly argued that "The Catholic Worker believes in creating a new society within the shell of the old with the philosophy of the new, which is not a new philosophy but a very old philosophy, a philosophy so old that it looks like new." Peter Maurin, "What the Catholic Worker Believes," https://www.catholicworker.org/petermaurin/easy-essays.html. For a compelling meditation on abolition as "sacred work," see Laura McTighe, "Abolition is sacred work," *The Immanent Frame*, January 28, 2021, https://tif.ssrc.org/2021/01/28/abolition-is-sacred-work/.

6. On "organized abandonment" and "organized violence," see: Ruth Wilson Gilmore and Craig Gilmore, "Beyond Bratton," in Jordan T. Camp and Christina Heatherton, eds., *Policing the Planet: Why the Policing Crisis Led to Black Lives Matter* (London: Verso Books, 2016).

7. Romans 12.2. This also echoes the spirit of Mary Hooks' and Southerners on New Ground's movement "mandate" for Black people, which includes the invitation to "be willing to be transformed in the service of the work." See: https://southernersonnewground.org/themandate/.

salvific function for the order they uphold.[8] The death-dealing religiosity of European-American carceral, capitalist, and colonial systems may tempt some to view a rigorously secularist or atheistic abolitionism that rejects any trace of spiritual thought or practice as our only hope. And understandably so. But liberating spiritualities and religiosities have, for centuries, permeated freedom movements—including the long slavery, prison, and police abolition and Black freedom movements in the United States that remain alive and well in the present.[9] While carcerality pursues an exclusive, illusory transcendence—heaven for a few—by confining and dealing death to many, abolition pursues a world attuned to the abundance of natural and sacred order in which individual and collective wellbeing does not require anyone's harm or elimination.[10] Whether incorporating formal religious practices and beliefs or not, the work of transcending the world as it is in order to transform it into the world as it could be entails a kind of hope and faith that exceeds the raw, scientific calculus of rearranging political and economic materialities alone.

Recognizing that abolitionist transformations take place somewhere between the possible and the impossible, the real and the imagined, and over great expanses of time, the dispatches that follow traverse freedom dream geographies in which an inspirited abolition "is, was, and is to come."[11] Through shared rituals of prayer, song, and sacred reading under conditions of death, through vigil, communion, protest, and public grieving in the wake of state violence, through incantations for the earth consuming carceral machinery, through recollection of prison labor and prison rebellion, through imperfect struggles to establish police oversight and redirect funds from cops and cages to public goods, through neighborhood potlucks and fragmented accountability processes, through cursing at cops and

---

8. This is a central component of the argument I make in my forthcoming book, *White Property, Black Trespass: The Religion of Mass Criminalization* (New York, NY: New York University Press, 2024).

9. Vincent Harding, *There is a River: The Black Struggle for Freedom in America* (New York: NY: Harcourt Brace Jovanovich, 1981); Joshua Dubler and Vincent Lloyd, *Break Every Yoke: Religion, Justice, and the Abolition of Prisons* (New York, NY: Oxford University Press, 2020); Reina Sultan, "Say Your Prayers, Conservatives! Prison Abolitionists Are Reclaiming Faith," *Truthout*, July 26, 2021, https://truthout.org/articles/say-your-prayers-conservatives-prison-abolitionists-are-reclaiming-faith/.

10. For more on "exclusive transcendence" as an expression of whiteness, see: Robert E. Birt, "The Bad Faith of Whiteness," in *What White Looks Like: African-American Philosophers on the Whiteness Question*, ed. George Yancy (New York, NY: Routledge, 2004).

11. Revelation 1.8. Some Christian monastic traditions, including the Cistercians, conclude the chanting of Psalms and other prayers with the following doxology: "Praise the Father, the Son and Holy Spirit. The God, who is who, was and is to come. At the end of the ages."

shouting at lifeless concrete walls, another world reveals itself, even if only "dimly."[12] Abolition requires material negation and creation, but it also demands faith in the collectively realizable possibility of material worlds beyond our own. What has it been like and what will it be like to imagine and live such worlds into existence? Where is abolition forging fire that the darkness around us cannot overcome?[13] Might we understand the faith that catalyzes abolitionist transformation as a faith of both spiritual and political proportions? Might we discern—and practice—abolitionist freedom dreamwork as a work of (the) spirit that is "making all things new"?[14]

The real and imagined dispatches that follow do not intend to be exhaustive, nor to represent all possible pathways through sacred abolition geographies. They are merely mine, dreamed both alone and together with my people, narrated both implicitly and explicitly from the Christian tradition to which I belong. And yet, though they are mine, they are also not mine alone. The world-making traditions of abolition and freedom dreaming come from the struggles of peoples organizing themselves to survive the destructive forces of heteropatriarchal whiteness and private property—forces that I have inherited and that vie for my religious devotion and political allegiance. Convinced that the invitation to cling to my racial, gender, and class inheritances as a means of salvation is in fact an invitation to my own spiritual death, and believing, as Black radical feminists and freedom fighters have taught us for at least the last century, that nobody is free until everybody is free, I channel the tradition of abolitionist freedom dreaming as one small means of pursuing my own spiritual and political transformation, as well as that of the world around me.

More than anything, the dispatches that follow are intended as a spiritual and political invitation to the reader to dream your own, both as an individual and together with your people. Where do you discern the transcendent and transformative spirit of abolition in your midst? Where does the sacred work of abolition manifest in your—and our—past, present, and future? How might your courageous freedom dreaming make a home worthy of those who came before and those who will come after? The new world that abolitionist freedom dreaming seeks to realize takes shape not all at once, but in piecemeal, partial, small-scale, mundane, incomplete, and imperfect acts and orientations that forge something greater than the sum of their parts. Utterly finite, and yet utterly transcendent,

---

12. 1 Corinthians 13.12.

13. John 1.5.

14. Revelation 21.5.

perhaps abolition is at once a horizon and the ground beneath our feet.[15]

* * *

THE EARTH RECLAIMS AN ABANDONED PRISON IN WEST NASHVILLE.
IMAGE COURTESY OF THE AUTHOR.

Ten miles west of downtown—out where industrial warehouses litter the road at the edge of green fields, hills, the Cumberland River— there is a razor wire fence holding no one captive. The emptied guard towers watch no bodies, no souls. No metal clinks or slams in the squat rows of empty cellblocks. The grass is waist high in this, the world of which we dream, for which we fight. Half-dreaming when I drive past it, I mistake the parking blocks stacked near the abandoned administration building for rows of raised beds, a community gar-den. My eyes deceive me. My mind sees clearly. Another mile down the road, past the mini airport, past more industrial headquarters, behind more razor wire, concrete, and steel, nestled inside a beauti-ful bend in the river, 748 men sit in cages on 132 acres of flood plain. Ten of us—insiders and outsiders—sit in a circle to read, share, and pray. This is a spiritual community not of this world, and yet very much fragmented by it. For two hours, we dwell together, aspiring to an unreal togetherness. We both obtain and fail to obtain it. Carceral walls and cages are not built for such communality, but we do the best we can. The razor wire fencing enclosing us does not untangle

15. On abolition as a horizon, see: Mariame Kaba, "Toward the Horizon of Abolition," in Mariame Kaba, *We Do This 'Til We Free Us: Abolitionist Organizing and Transforming Justice* (Chicago, IL: Haymarket Books, 2021).

when we're together, but perhaps the path to a world without carceral cages is forged in part through the mundane collectivity of gathering to read, pray, and simply be together. We're reading a book of letters written during the Holocaust. "Which was worse," someone asks, "the Holocaust or slavery?" After some discussion, the answer comes back: "Yes." When the time comes for evening prayer, one insider asks another: "Do you think we're slaves in here?" No one answers as we close our books and put them aside. We know the answer.

Halfway through the liturgy, there sits the soon-to-be mother of God, intense. She voices anticipation for another world, maybe someday ours: "My soul proclaims the greatness of the Lord / my Spirit rejoices in God my savior." *For he has looked with favor on his lowly servant*, we respond.

> He has shown the strength of his arm,
> *he has scattered the proud in their conceit.*
> He has cast down the mighty from their thrones,
> *and has lifted up the lowly.*
> He has filled the hungry with good things,
> *and the rich he has sent away empty.*
> He has come to the help of Israel,
> *for he has remembered his promise of mercy,*
> The promise he made to our fathers,
> *to Abraham and his children forever.*
> Glory to the Father, and to the Son, and to the Holy Spirit:
> *as it was in the beginning, is now, and will be forever. Amen.*[16]

A corrections officer saunters past the room and peers in the window, then keeps walking. We keep praying—for members of our group who have gone elsewhere, for those without food and shelter, for those who need medical care but have no access to it, for those on death row, for the hearts of those in charge, and for all our intentions. "Peace and stuff," we say, embracing, and depart, some of us to cars, some of us to cages. The sky blazes purple over the fences and hills. When we reach our cars, it fades.

Driving out of the prison parking lot, I've never seen anything like it: the dewy fields of June dusk outside the walls flicker to the hills with a million fireflies. Back on down the road, I pull over at the obsolete razor wire fence and get out of my car. That dark emptied gaol is filled with them—neon green-yellow flame flashing. And the darkness does not overcome it.[17] Now, but not yet. Time of decay, work of transition.

---

16. *The Book of Common Prayer and Administration of the Sacraments and Other Rites and Ceremonies of the Church: Together with the Psalter or Psalms of David According to the Use of the Episcopal Church* (New York, NY: Seabury Press, 1979), 119.

17. John 1.5.

***

Eight o'clock at night on November 6, 2018. Election day, a day that what would become a wave of progressive ballot defeats. On a third-floor loft on Rosa Parks Boulevard in North Nashville, organizers and volunteers are gathering, tired, nervous, excited. In the center of the room, a makeshift altar with a photo of Jocques Clemmons, murdered by the Metro Nashville Police Department (MNPD) on February 10, 2017. Next to it, a photo of Daniel Hambrick, murdered by the MNPD on July 26, 2018. Someone lights a candle between the images. Dan Dan's mother, Vickie Hambrick, sits somber, surrounded by her family. Jocques' mother, Sheila Clemmons Lee—who some call the "soul force" at the center of this grassroots effort to forge a community oversight board with subpoena power—hardly leaves Miss Vickie's side the entire night.

MISS SHEILA (BOTTOM CENTER LEFT) AND MISS VICKIE (BOTTOM CENTER RIGHT) EMBRACE AS THEY CELEBRATE THE COMMUNITY OVERSIGHT BOARD VICTORY. IMAGE COURTESY OF THE AUTHOR.

It's been months, years—no, decades—of many hands on the freedom plow. TVs are showing one right-wing victory after another. And then they call our name: Amendment 1, the ballot initiative to institute a community oversight board to attempt to hold the police department accountable for its violence—134,135 votes for, 94,055 votes against. A burst of screams shift shape into melody and groove: the DJ blasts McFadden & Whitehead's "Ain't No Stoppin' Us Now" and the room is jubilant, dancing. At the center of a joyous circle, Miss Sheila and Miss Vickie embrace and pump their fists in the air.

Ain't no stoppin' us now!
We're on the move!
Ain't no stoppin' us now!
We've got the groove![8]

This didn't come easy. On November 23, 1973, a Metro officer shot and killed nineteen-year-old Ronald Lee Joyce as he ran from the police after allegedly breaking into an abandoned house to play dice. Community members called for the resignation of the police chief and the creation of a civilian review board. On both fronts, the city ignored them.[19] In October 2016, forty-three years later, despite a public image of a much gentler, more progressive police department, a coalition of community groups led by community organization Gideon's Army published a massive report detailing racially disparate outcomes in MNPD traffic stops and searches.[20] Despite clear evidence that echoed what Black Nashvillians had been saying for decades, MNPD denied the accusation of any racial profiling every chance they got, even calling the authors of the report "morally disingenuous."[21] Three short months later, MNPD cop Joshua Lippert chased and killed Jocques Clemmons while he ran for his life after a traffic stop in East Nashville. He was thirty-one, a father, brother, and son. Local organizers gathered around the Clemmons Lee family and formed the Justice for Jocques coalition, which demanded the firing of Officer Lippert and a civilian oversight board with subpoena power, among other things. Miss Sheila and a dedicated group of others—mostly other Black women—engaged in a months-long sit-in outside the East Precinct demanding they fire the man who murdered her son. The District Attorney opted not to bring any charges against Officer Lippert.

Fed up with willful governmental obfuscation and inaction, local leaders in the Movement for Black Lives seized control of a Metro Council meeting where their righteous grief and holy anger took its

18. McFadden & Whitehead, "Ain't No Stoppin' Us Now" (1979).

19. David Plazas, "Nashville police killed a black man, public wanted oversight board – 45 years ago," *The Tennessean*, August 15, 2018, https://www.tennessean.com/story/opinion/columnists/david-plazas/2018/08/15/daniel-hambrick-nashville-police-briley-oversight-board/986717002.

20. Gideon's Army, *Driving While Black: A Report on Racial Profiling in Metro Nashville Police Department Traffic Stops* (October 2017), https://drivingwhileblacknashville.files.wordpress.com/2016/10/driving-while-black-gideons-army.pdf.

21. Joey Garrison, "Nashville police chief slams racial profiling report as 'morally disingenuous,'" *The Tennessean*, March 7, 2017, https://www.tennessean.com/story/news/2017/03/07/nashville-police-chief-slams-racial-profiling-report-morally-disingenuous/98856754/.

rightful place on the chamber floor.[22] Emerging from those and other business-as-usual-disruptive demands for justice, the Community Oversight Now coalition was born. Agile, deft, resilient, and led by Black women, some of whom (including Miss Sheila and organizer Gicola Lane) had lost family members to police violence in Nashville, the coalition put in the work to follow through on local efforts dating back to at least 1973 to form a community oversight board. Those who came before dreamed dreams of a world without police officers chasing and murdering Black men. An impossible dream, it has long seemed, and one that will not become reality through community oversight alone. And yet, forty-five years later, nourished by faith that those freedom dreamers planted and sowed, faith in a world not yet seen, we walk a waking dreamscape and start to step into the real.[23]

And then it happened all over again. A year and a half after MNPD killed Jocques, in July 2018, white MNPD officer Andrew Delke chased, then stopped, planted his feet, aimed, and shot Daniel Hambrick in the back of the head as he, like Jocques, ran for his life. According to the District Attorney, Delke "did not know the identity of the man he was chasing."[24] Dan Dan was twenty-five. So was Delke. I was collecting signatures for the community oversight effort with another organizer when they heard that another Black man had just been shot by the police. When I drove to the police tape perimeter at Jo Johnston and Fisk Street, there were two women from the neighborhood pacing back and forth. One of them lost her son to gun violence a few years back. She heard the shots that killed Dan Dan ring out from her apartment. "God is not happy about what's going on down here," she kept saying. I agreed.

Two days later, I watched Miss Vickie weep before a crowd of people in Watkins Park, a hundred feet from where Delke murdered her son. "I gotta fight for my son because they shot him like he was a dog," she shouted. "My child is not a dog. He was a human being!"[25] As the memorial came to an end, some of Dan Dan's young family

22. Steven Hale, "Clemmons Protestors Seize Control of Metro Council Meeting, *Nashville Scene*, February 22, 2018, https://www.nashvillescene.com/news/pith-in-the-wind/article/20852881/clemmons-protesters-seize-control-of-metro-council-meeting.

23. Hebrews 11.1-3.

24. Adam Tamburin, Natalie Allison, and Anita Wadhwani, "Prosecutors file homicide charge against officer in Daniel Hambrick's death," *The Tennessean*, September 27, 2018, https://www.tennessean.com/story/news/crime/2018/09/27/nashville-police-shooting-daniel-hambrick-andrew-delke-charge-denied-homicide/1441834002/.

25. Adam Tamburin and Natalie Allison, "Man shot by Nashville police remembered for caring spirit before protest blocks streets," *The Tennessean*, July 28, 2018, https://www.tennessean.com/story/news/2018/07/28/nashville-police-shooting-daniel-hambrick-andrew-delke-tn-officer-involved-shooting/857788002/.

members and friends moved into the street in formation behind one of Dan Dan's cousins who rapped for a camera held by a man walking backwards down the middle of the road. As more people joined—family, friends, residents of John Henry Hale homes—the video memorial soon morphed into a full-scale march. The green-vested Neon Guard safety team followed and hemmed them in on all sides. People need space to grieve and rage, and sometimes that space is the middle of the road. Holy anger guarded by public pastoral care. By the time the march reached Jo Johnston and 16th Ave. N., a small army of unmarked police cars materialized out of thin air—they had been lying in wait out of view the whole time—and surrounded the group, their sirens yelping, their speaker boxes emitting unintelligible muffle. I ran down Henry Hale and cut over on Pearl Street in time to see the group entering the busy intersection at 16th and Charlotte—defiant, unphased, nothing to lose. "No justice, no peace!" they screamed. "Fuck the police!"

MNPD MARKS A WIDE PERIMETER AFTER CHASING AND KILLING DANIEL HAMBRICK. IMAGE COURTESY OF THE AUTHOR.

The security footage from Martin Luther King high school shows Dan Dan in full sprint in one frame, and flattened in the next. He laid there for two full minutes, his head torn open, when another officer arrived and placed the body of Vickie's only son in handcuffs. In the middle of Charlotte Pike, I hear his brother ask a cop in his squad car, "Why'd y'all kill Dan Dan? Huh?!" He repeats himself, louder. Employees at the Burger King are standing in the parking lot next to customers filming the action with their cell phones.

Behind them, I see smoke rise—a century and a half back.

The old Tennessee State Penitentiary: built in 1831, demolished in 1898. A place of confinement, a place of wealth accumulated through captive labor, and therefore a place of fire. In September 1845, the Tennessee State Legislature voted to use people caged at the penitentiary to dig from quarries on the edge of town the stone that would be used to erect the new State Capitol Building. Marching westward down Charlotte with Dan Dan's people, we can see its tower and spire up past the highway where dozens of patrol cars flash their blue lights and block the on-ramps. It's a house built on convict labor, and a house built on slave labor: in the spring of 1846, Nashville stone Mason A.G. Payne loaned fifteen enslaved Africans for $18 a month to the state to dig through the dense limestone atop the hill upon which the capitol stands at the end of the road blocked by the family and friends of yet another Black man killed by the state.[26] "Are we slaves in here?" my friend, the "convict," asks from the penitentiary descended from this one. Standing here in the middle of a stretch of road that connects the labor of the imprisoned and the labor of the enslaved, a road literally built by enslaved Africans in 1804, the answer couldn't be clearer.[27]

"Oh shit, something's on fire!" I think I hear someone in the Burger King parking lot shout, pointing behind the store. The black cloud thickens and proliferates. Out in the street, a squad car presses slowly into the legs of a young Black woman standing her ground, her arms raised up, connecting dots between past and present, smoke and street.

Who were the people caged inside the thick stone walls behind the Burger King 150 years ago? By and large, they were men—Black and white, enslaved, formerly enslaved, and "free"—who offended against whiteness, property, and their owners.[28] Words like "larceny," "robbery," and "horse stealing" fill the penitentiary's record books.[29] In a racial capitalist social order, the rule of racialized property produces "criminals" out of those dispossessed by it. And then, it often turns out, those same "criminals"—exploited labor—produce property from which they are ultimately excluded. So "convicts" forced to labor within the walls of the original Tennessee State Penitentiary allegedly

26. Thomas Broderick IV, "They moved the earth: The slaves who built the Tennessee State Capitol," *Vanderbilt Undergraduate Research Journal* 4, no. 1 (Spring 2008).

27. The owner of the enslaved African peoples who built this particular road was James Robertson, co-settler of Nashville. Ridley Wills II, *Nashville Streets & their Stories* (Franklin, TN: Plumbline Media, 2012), 25.

28. For more on the relationship between whiteness and property, see: Cheryl I. Harris, "Whiteness as Property," *Harvard Law Review* 106, no. 8 (June 1993): 1707–91.

29. "Inmates of the Tennessee State Penitentiary, 1851-1870," https://sos.tn.gov/products/tsla/inmates-tennessee-state-penitentiary-1851-1870.

set fire to furniture workshops there in 1855. Again, in 1876, inmates allegedly set fire to a wagon workshop inside the walls, which was followed a few months later by three hundred prisoners attempting escape. We can call this excarceral transcendence.[30] Leased convicts allegedly set fires again in 1881, 1884, and 1890, and in the Tennessee State Prison in 1902 and 1960.[31] The destiny of an institution built for the purpose of disappearing and exploiting those discarded by racial capitalism can only be fire, even if now only just proleptically— now (and then) but not yet. Standing in the middle of Charlotte Pike, a few of us hold the sacred line against the force that killed Dan Dan in order to protect the crowd of family and friends gathered to mourn that murder and say "fuck you" to those who did it. In the all too real invisible smoke shadow of one burning institution of carceral death, Dan Dan's people defy the agents of another.

After the protest and a tense standoff—public grief facing down the cause of that grief—at the site of Dan Dan's murder, I sit on a ledge with Miss Sheila. It's been a year and a half since Lippert took her son's life. And here she is standing alongside another mother walking the same path she has. I ask how she and her husband Mark have been holding up. They get by with God's help, she said— wouldn't be here without it. "I didn't understand at first," Sheila says, "but now I do: Jocques was a sacrifice. God is using his death in the fight for justice. He died so others don't have to." Some sacrifices are mere appeasements, means of satisfying some abstract principle of debt or justice that relinquish us from any further responsibility. But not Jocques: his is the kind of "sacrifice" that catalyzes, that moves forward, that makes his mother bold and brave in the face of so much bullshit, helping us "believe," as the people say, "that we will win," even when the enemy seems bent on destruction. Sheila's belief, and the belief she's helping instill in the rest of us, is the belief that "the present form of this world"—the world that killed Jocques and Dan Dan—is neither natural nor permanent, but is instead, somehow, "passing away."[32] Jocques isn't here anymore. And yet, in another sense, he is, Miss Sheila likes to say, especially on days like this one, and even more so in days to come. The soul force of Sheila's faith enables her to discern and declare her son's presence among those fighting for the world she and her son always deserved, the world of which so many before her have dreamed. With the great pain and struggle of mothers wailing in the park, of family facing down cops in the middle of the road, of public grief channeled into public power,

---

30. On the notion of the "excarceral," see: Peter Linebaugh, *The London Hanged: Crime and Civil Society in the Eighteenth Century*, 2nd ed (London and New York: Verso, 2006), 23.

31. Tristan Call, "'The Splendid Gifts of God to the South': Struggles for Control on Tennessee Plantations," Ph.D. Dissertation (Vanderbilt University, 2020).

32. 1 Corinthians 7.31.

the dream of that "hoped for," not-yet-seen world starts to take on flesh in our midst, a prayer becoming its own answer.[33]

Three months before the Tennessee State Legislature voted to use convict labor to excavate raw materials to construct their new capitol building in 1845, the killer of Native Americans and enslaver of Africans, Andrew Jackson, died at his mansion in Nashville. A century and a half later, Nashville's chapter of the Fraternal Order of Police (FOP) does its work from its headquarters at the Andrew Jackson Lodge. Acting on the basis that the deaths of two Black men and the trauma endured by their families and thousands of others are justified, Nashville's FOP spent half a million dollars to proliferate bald-faced falsifications on the airwaves about the fight for a community oversight board. They surveilled and sought to intimidate the Black organizers spearheading the community oversight effort. They criminalized the men they killed even after their deaths.[34] They lied and lied and lied.

And it wasn't enough. Money and lies often win. But sometimes people-power-moving spirit carves a new—even if imperfect—reality out of the heavy stone of impossibility. Sometimes the mothers of Black men murdered by the police get to sing:

> There's been so many things that's held us down
> But now it looks like things are finally comin' around
> I know we've got a long, long way to go
> And where we'll end up, I don't know
> But we won't let nothin' hold us back
> We're putting ourselves together
> We're polishing up our act!
> If you felt we've been held down before
> I know you'll refuse to be held down anymore!
> Don't you let nothing, nothing
> Stand in your way!
> I want y'all to listen, listen
> To every word I say, every word I say!
> Ain't no stoppin' us now!
> We're on the move!
> Ain't no stoppin' us now!
> We've got the groove![35]

33. Hebrews 11.1.

34. Steven Hale, "Police Union Website Targets Daniel Hambrick," *Nashville Scene* (February 19, 2019), https://www.nashvillescene.com/news/pith-in-the-wind/article/21048001/police-union-website-targets-daniel-hambrick.

35. McFadden & Whitehead, "Ain't No Stoppin' Us Now" (1979).

* * *

A BARBED WIRE FENCE IN WEST NASHVILLE. IMAGE COURTESY OF THE AUTHOR.

"No Trespassing | Metro Nashville Government Property." Someone recently used their finger to mark out two clean diagonal lines—a defiant "x"—across the dusty sign. A rusted chain and lock winds through the gate of the tall chain-link fence lined at its top with old barbed wire. A small strand of weathered blue tarp is caught in a barb, and waves like a sad flag in the wind. Behind the fence, 150 Chevy Impalas, give or take, sit no-longer-used, dirty, dented, lined up closely in long rows. The words "Nashville's Guardians" are still legible in faded blue type across a few of the trunks. In some places, grass grows up to their windows, a number of which are broken in. When I walk along the side toward the rear fence of the lot, I hear quick rustling from inside. Some animal—a fox, I think—has made a home of one of the cars, a new world in the shell of the old. It wasn't easy to find this place—unmarked industrial roads leading behind a waste processing plant in West Nashville. They would rather us not see, perhaps out of embarrassment.

It's been twelve years now since they murdered Jocques. Dan Dan has been gone nearly ten. It was around that time, and especially in the years following the formation of the community oversight board, that officers started leaving the force. Reports about racially disparate stops and searches, lawsuits, complaints of a culture of racism, sexism, and fear within the department, public hearings about the good-old-boy chief and his eventual resignation, cell phone footage of cops harassing residents of Cayce Homes, mismanagement of funds, calls to defund, and the list of reasons why officers started to retire early goes on and on. The oversight board did not end police violence—far from it. But it did create the conditions for, and contribute momentum to, subsequent struggles to build a city freed from the inherent violence of policing and surveillance by ending the mass looting of public dollars that was making it inevitable year after year. More and more residents slowly but steadily realized that the police weren't reducing crime rates, weren't keeping them safe. Folks in historically divested communities were fed up with violence in their neighborhoods, with gunfire piercing their windows, with a perpetual lack of resources for longtime residents being displaced left and right by settler colonial gentrification. The police were constantly driving around all hours of the day, pulling people over. Helicopters buzzed and rattled windows day and night. So why didn't the violence stop? When the police couldn't answer that question anymore, residents organized themselves to do something about it.

A new world comes not from above but from below. It started with the former gang members turned violence interrupters who weaved together relationship and accountability in a way the cops never could.[36] Then it was the neighborhood accountability and emergency response meetings, neighborhood-based safety and de-escalation training, piecemeal building of communication infrastructure, and regular get-to-know-your-neighbors potlucks. In the wake of these assemblies, organizers launched a "call your neighbors, not the police" campaign. As residents learned, it's one thing to call for a reduction or end to ineffective and traumatic hyperpolicing in predominantly Black and low-income communities, but another to put in the work to make that policing irrelevant. Obsolescence by replacement.

Standing with my fingers in the chain link fence, a blue jay lands on the busted spotlight of the cruiser in front of me. I freeze. We stare. Filled with a mixture of awe and dread, I wonder what he's thinking. *Is he standing his ground, telling me to get lost? Is he protecting baby birds from a potential intruder? Is he about to fly in my direction?* Bird calls sound from a distance, then get louder, and the blue jay breaks his attention, flitting his head around. The calls get louder and a moment later three cardinals swoop in to reclaim what appears to be *their* territory, not his. One cardinal perched on the spotlight, chest puffed proud, two on the roof lights no longer flashing. The blue jay nowhere to be found.

At a Metro budget hearing back in May 2016, an elder from our neighborhood, Miss Dorothy, took to the podium and told it like it was. "Two years ago, we had fourteen—*fourteen!*—murders in our neighborhood," she spoke firmly, looking into the eyes of each council member. "I'm here to tell you that we had only one murder in our

<hr>

36. See: Steven Hale, "How Gideon's Army Is Making Peace in North Nashville," https://www.nashvillescene.com/news/cover-story/article/21074753/how-gideons-army-is-making-peace-in-north-nashville.

neighborhood last year!" Some of the council members started clapping, but she cut them off. "No, no, no! What are you clapping for?" she chided them. "You didn't do that! We did that! The police you still paying to chase our kids and grandkids around didn't do that—we did that! The developers you still trying to pay to kick people like me outta there didn't do that—we did that!" A hush from the chambers, hollers from the gallery—the sound of an old order passing away, a new one being born, half-formed figures crawling out of a valley of dry bones.[37]

It was impossible to imagine this a decade or two ago. Policing, for the vast majority of people in Nashville, and in the United States more broadly, had for so long been a sacred cornerstone of the order of things. To publicly dream of its withering away was thus a kind of sacrilege. But the belief of people like Miss Sheila and Miss Vickie and Miss Dorothy—the belief, born of pain, that the life-upending violence of what "was" need not remain what "is" and what "will be"—chipped away at an edifice so many presumed to be permanent.

In the face of an ever-growing mass of residents and organizations rejecting and disrupting business as it had been, and with so many officers gone, the city could no longer justify funding the police department like it used to. By the next budget cycle, funding for MNPD had been reduced by $6 million. By the next, another $5 million. By the next, their budget had been cut nearly in half. But the fight—a knockdown, drag-out, highly organized tooth-and-nail fight—wasn't just a fight to defund the police, as if the police alone were the problem. It was a fight to redistribute funds towards people's basic quality of life in the poorest parts of the city: new playgrounds, basketball courts, arts centers, and community gardens, increased funding for public schools and teachers, accessible and reliable transportation, quality affordable housing, the elimination of tax breaks for luxury development, expanded living wage job opportunities and worker-owned cooperative enterprises, community-based alternatives to juvenile and eventually adult incarceration, the eradication of money bail, dismantling and redistributing the power of the city's housing authority, and the development of resident-managed community land trusts in the most historically divested districts in the city.

But old worlds die hard. The freedom fighters whose belief in another world helped forge the paths we now walk taught us that the new world they dreamed of comes only through organized struggle, struggle in which victory and defeat often intertwine so subtly that it can be difficult to discern where one ends and the other begins. In the wake of the MNPD's dwindling, with fewer police around, people who felt they had no choice but to rely on them before often felt helpless and got stuck whenever violence erupted on the block or people stole stuff from their backyard. Organizers and activists had

37. Ezekiel 37:1-14.

been calling on the department for decades to stop overpolicing predominantly Black and poor communities. And then, amazingly, they did. No more answered calls for service, no more patrols, no more cameras fixed to telephone poles. A passive-aggressive consent to a long arc of decline. *Fine, see how that works out for you,* we could hear them say. Things got worse for a few years, but with time, community safety, accountability, and crisis response formations strengthened and spread, and many residents in historically divested parts of town took a new, collective sense of ownership and pride in their neighborhoods.

It hasn't been easy, but perhaps nothing good is. About a year ago, I got a text message. "Someone was shot on our street." That used to happen with more regularity a decade ago, but it's rarer now. I hurried home and pulled up at the same time as a firetruck. They unraveled the hose and washed blood toward the curb, down to the drain. My neighbor tells me a young Black man was walking down the sidewalk when a car pulled up. Fifteen loud pops. Multiple bullets in his leg. He lied in the street screaming. They wrapped towels and old t-shirts around his leg to slow the bleeding until the ambulance arrived. The shots that missed him hit our house. Six, seven, eight, nine bullets lodged in blue siding. I found a single bullet sitting in a pile of broken glass on the windowsill behind our living room couch.

A SINGLE BULLET SITS IN A PILE OF BROKEN GLASS ON THE WINDOWSILL BEHIND OUR LIVING ROOM COUCH. IMAGE COURTESY OF THE AUTHOR.

The police never showed—a cause for both concern and relief. Another neighbor called our sub-district's community safety and accountability reps. Thirty minutes later, they arrived, interviewed and provided some care and presence for the neighbors who saw it happen, then paced around on the sidewalk making calls for the next hour. The next morning, the violence interrupters walked the neighborhood checking in with folks. A week later, the accountability team figured out who was responsible and what had happened. It was an old beef recently revived. A small group of them confronted the man responsible in his friend's living room, explained to him all that would happen next, then escorted him to the fellowship hall at Greater Heights Missionary Baptist down the street where the pastor and other safety and accountability folks were setting up metal chairs in a circle. The young man he shot wasn't ready to face him yet, but he gave directives on what he wanted to happen—get him to own up to what he did, and commit to taking responsibility for "making shit right," including with medical costs. The process was months long, extremely messy, and painstakingly difficult. The man responsible for the shooting did not cooperate at first, and even disappeared for a few weeks. Eventually, the process reached as reasonable a conclusion as was possible given the conflict. The relationship was not repaired, but a recompense agreement was signed, and folks are moving on. The young man is off his crutches, but still walking with a limp.

The police became obsolete not because they chose to, but because communities made vulnerable by the death-dealing principalities of racial capitalism and the policing that protects it forged their own means of safety in a world bent on their destruction. For some, the struggle of the last decade and more has been a struggle specifically for a world without police. For others, the struggle of the last decade has been a struggle with no objective other than survival: to enter a world in which it is possible to keep on living. Where these two dimensions of the same struggle converge, something at once ad hoc and organized—something very much imperfect and incomplete—continues to emerge. Catalyzed by radical faith that another world—or even just another day—is possible, carried along by the living prayers of those whose lost loved ones accompany us in spirit, this struggle is, was, and will be a sacred one.

At the far back corner of the dusty lot caging the old cop cars, Japanese honeysuckle winds in and out of the fencing: a wall of green dotted with white and yellow protrusion, fragrant, a scent that reminds me of childhood. The squad car backed into the corner of the lot is being eaten alive by the thing. It has pierced the rusted floorboards, snakes up the steering column, and tangles in the wires of the monitors on the dash, a holy, living vine. In the shell of an old world, a new one takes root. Today, more than a decade after the department began to deteriorate in public view, this is still no utopia we live in. People still hurt each other, reconciliation often remains out of reach, vultures still hover, and stray blue lights still chase young folks down back streets from time to time. But in some places—perhaps eventually most places—beyond what we once thought possible, something verdant prevails.

Six months ago, after coordinated pressure from a coalition of community organizations, a newly elected Metro council member proposed a bill that would repurpose a portion of these unused squad cars, making them available at reduced cost on installment plans to low-income community members who have survived violence, and even to people with criminal records. The ordinance passed by a narrow margin. That it passed at all would have been unthinkable a decade ago. Sitting on our porch with our eight-year-old the other day, the young man whose blood they sprayed into the gutter last year drove by in an old Chevy Impala, his elbow in the window, and waved.

* * *

"Next," the corrections officer calls out. I walk through the metal detector in my socks, then turn a full 360 degrees in front of the second metal detector, a vertical pole with little flashing lights, flipping the bottom of each foot up to face it directly. Put your finger on the scanner. "Scanner's ready." Step up and face radiation. "Scanner starting." I imagine my cells shifting shape as the machine moves me slowly left to right. Shoes back on, key, invisible stamp. From there, I count them: fourteen heavy steel and razor-wire-fence doors—opened and closed from some invisible beyond—to reach the room where my new friends on death row sit in a circle, smiling. They are, in most but not all cases, guilty of immense harm. And they rise from their plastic chairs to hug me one by one. I came to ask them about spirituality in confinement directed toward death.[38]

I have learned that if you listen, you can hear these inanimate walls and cages talk. They exercise a kind of agency, even. They shift, shape, and alter the life they contain. "What does this institution want you to know in your body?" I ask these men condemned to die. "How does it tell you? How do you hear it?"

The men translate what the rest of us perceive only dimly. "They want me to know that they have this body," Don said.[39]

"How does it tell you that?" I ask.

"I have to walk through eight locked doors to get from here [open gathering room] to my cell," Don responded.

Kurt elaborated: "*They* tell you when you can do everything."

38. I have also written about the following conversations here: Andrew Krinks, "Soulful Resistance: Theological Body Knowledge on Tennessee's Death Row," *The Other Journal* 23: The Body Issue (2014). Some of the following quotes also appear in the above essay.

39. For their protection, I use pseudonyms for all of the men quoted in what follows, with the exception of Don, who was executed by the state of Tennessee in 2019.

"What they tell [my body] is 'control,'" Paul added. "They tell me how long I can visit with my family and how often."

"There's very little that remains yours in here. They have me captured. I know they want to kill me," Thomas made clear. "I know these things—they're obvious. They may have me physically, but I'm never gonna let them have my mind."

These walls and cages are creatures of death: they victimize those who were already victimized, and who then, trapped by their trauma and pain, victimized others in turn. But to render Don, Kurt, Paul, Thomas, Jacob, and the rest of the men something as simple as either passive victims or monstrous offenders would be imprecise. They, too, shapeshift, altering the death-world around them.

"What do you want this institution to know?" I ask. "How do you tell it? And how does it hear it?"

Kurt tightens his body, sits forward in his chair, and points in the direction of the nearest wall. "I am not who you try to make me to be!" he exclaims intensely. Respecting the space carved out by Kurt's vehemence, the others quietly nod in agreement.

"How exactly do you communicate this message?" I ask.

"I smile, shake hands," he responds, "ask guards how they're doing. I pay people respect; tell them I'm praying for them."

Paul elaborates: "You tell 'em by acting like a human, by being civil, being intelligent."

"After a while," Don added, "when they see all the hugging, and we shake their hands every day, we're breaking down preconceived barriers."

That was October 2012. A year later, the attorney general for the state of Tennessee requests execution dates for ten prisoners on the state's death row—almost twice as many men as the state has executed since 1976. Don's name is on the list. When I see him two weeks after the attorney general's request, I ask him how he's feeling. "They think they know when my life will end," he says. "But only God knows that." We sit in a circle—men on death row and their friends—and take turns praying for the dismantling and undoing of death in all its forms. I sit next to Kurt. When it's his turn to pray, he grips my hand so tightly it starts to turn purple. He's literally shouting, a corrections officer standing in the corner of the room, imploring God to stop the state's march toward the death of men sitting among us.

Don's date—and others'—eventually came and went by way of legal challenges and delays. Five and a half years later—May 16, 2019—we drive again past the razor wire fence holding no one captive, past the mini airport, past the industrial headquarters. At the ad hoc checkpoint past the prison entrance, a sweating, walking weapon of a man puts a piece of yellow tape on our windshield to mark us as against the death penalty. "Y'all have fun," he says, pointing us further down the road. Past another checkpoint, past the mounted patrolmen, we park in a field hemmed in by rolling green hills. They tower over the pile of concrete and fencing that tries but fails to impress us like those hills—earthen shoulders—do.

We stand with Don's friends, his congregants, his family, inside a large fence in a field, praying, singing, remembering, mourning lives ended too soon—his wife's, his, others'. Soon, we will take communion. First, traditional bread and juice, then, jailhouse communion: cookies and punch. We are here despite pleas for clemency from hundreds, thousands, including his own stepdaughter who, after decades of all-consuming hatred for the man who killed her mother, after unleashing her rage upon him in person, was surprised to find release, and the beginnings of reconciliation. But the demonic death machine was too much. "After a prayerful and deliberate consideration of Don Johnson's request for clemency, and after a thorough review of the case," the faithfully Christian governor Bill Lee announced, "I am upholding the sentence of the State of Tennessee and will not be intervening."[40]

In the field outside the prison, Don's friend and former chaplain Jeannie steps forward, begins to speak, and then stops, holding her finger to her lips until her bearing, momentarily daunted by the weight of this moment, returns. The five years she spent in that building, she says, were the most sacred, transformative, and traumatic years of her life. Don was one of the ones who convinced her, against all reasonable judgment, to become chaplain in the first place. It's because of relationships with people like Don, she often says, that she went in a death penalty abolitionist and came out a prison abolitionist, an abolitionist of systems that define those they cage as monsters, when in fact it is the cages themselves that are monstrous. "We are called not just to visit the prisoner; we are called to set captives free, and in doing that, we find our freedom," she says, the buzzing sounds of the institution trying but failing to drown her out. "My prayer tonight is for God to damn these systems and send them back to hell where they belong."

"How do you visualize the future?" I asked Don and his brothers when we sat in a circle together six and a half years ago.

"One day, I will leave here," Don said, "either up [pointing upward] or through the front door."

Out in the field, at about 7:40 p.m., our brother Chris, once caged inside those same walls, steps forward to offer a benediction. He invites us to look not down but up, into the sky, as he blesses our brother Don. Across the circle, I see Lisa, friend of Don and so many

---

40. Adam Tamburin, "Gov. Bill Lee denies clemency for Donnie Edward Johnson; execution set for Thursday," *The Tennessean*, May 14, 2019, https://www.tennessean.com/story/news/crime/2019/05/14/tennessee-execution-donnie-johnson-clemency-bill-lee/1094175001/.

others on death row, somehow smiling, her face lifted toward a 'v' of geese passing above us. A few moments later, a handful of people start moving around quickly, touching the shoulder of the person next to them, holding their phones. Someone steps forward.

"Don Johnson was declared dead at 7:37."

Journalists in the witness room outside the execution chamber report that, before the State of Tennessee took his life, Don echoed the words of Jesus on the cross—"I commend my life into your hands"— before commending his final two minutes of breath to song:

> No more crying there, we are going to see the king,
> No more dying there, we are going to see the king.[41]

When we walk across the field to our cars, the sky is a subtle orange, clouds hovering low just above the earth's darkening shoulders— the color of fire turned to embers, smoldering. Driving away, in my rearview mirror, the lights of the prison recede until those beautiful hills swallow the place whole. Looking back again, only aerial embers remain.

Dear God, may it be so.

THE HILLS SWALLOW THE PRISON WHOLE. IMAGE COURTESY OF THE AUTHOR.

---

41. Adam Tamburin, Katherine Burgess, Yihyun Jeong, and Mariah Timms, "Tennessee executes Donnie Edward Johnson by lethal injection," *The Tennessean*, May 16, 2019, https://www.tennessean.com/story/news/crime/2019/05/16/execution-donnie-johnson-tennessee-leathl-injection/3668943002/. Don's words echoed those of Jesus in Luke 23.46. The hymn Don sang is "Soon and Very Soon." He also sang "They Will Know We Are Christians."

Another mile on down the road, the emptied prison. I can't take my eyes off the freedom dream world beyond that futile fence, fixed forever in my mind. A pale blue steel door pressed open against the adjacent concrete wall, yawning wide. Another door, half-tilted, busted off its hinge. Large piles of dirt next to half-demolished cell blocks. I think I see someone bent over next to a wheelbarrow, digging.

Now but not yet. Fully awake but dreaming.

An hour later, I watch from my car as my partner Lindsey holds a box of pizza and talks to a man sitting on a bench by the Cumberland River at 1st and Broadway. When she tells him where the pizza came from—that a man named Don was executed tonight, that he skipped his last meal, and asked that people pool their resources to feed unhoused folks instead—he takes his hat off "in disbelief and reverence," as she puts it, and partakes of the "third communion of the night." The absent becomes present. This world becomes another.

The governor, faithful Christian, "prayed." The outcome of his prayer was death.

Don, condemned to that death, prayed too. And the people, by loaves and fishes, under overpasses, on the steps of churches, on benches by the river, were nourished. In the dark wake of death, the subtle firefly flicker of a world made new.

REFERENCES

Birt, Robert E. "The Bad Faith of Whiteness," in *What White Looks Like: African-American Philosophers on the Whiteness Question*. ed. George Yancy. New York, NY: Routledge, 2004.

Broderick IV, Thomas. "They moved the earth: The slaves who built the Tennessee State Capitol," *Vanderbilt Undergraduate Research Journal* 4, no. 1 (Spring 2008).

Call, Tristan. "'The Splendid Gifts of God to the South': Struggles for Control on Tennessee Plantations," Ph.D. Dissertation. Vanderbilt University, 2020.

Davis, Angela Y. *Are Prisons Obsolete?* New York, NY: Seven Stories Press, 2003.

Dubler, Joshua and Vincent Lloyd. *Break Every Yoke: Religion, Justice, and the Abolition of Prisons*. New York, NY: Oxford University Press, 2020.

Garrison, Joey. "Nashville police chief slams racial profiling report as 'morally disingenuous,'" *The Tennessean*, March 7, 2017, https://www.

tennessean.com/story/news/2017/03/07/nashville-police-chief-slams-ra-cial-profiling-report-morally-disingenuous/98856754/.

Gideon's Army, *Driving While Black: A Report on Racial Profiling in Metro Nashville Police Department Traffic Stops* (October 2017), https://drivingwhileblacknashville.files.wordpress.com/2016/10/driving-while-black-gideons-army.pdf.

Gilmore, Ruth Wilson and Craig Gilmore. "Beyond Bratton," in Jordan T. Camp and Christina Heatherton, eds., *Policing the Planet: Why the Policing Crisis Led to Black Lives Matter.* London: Verso Books, 2016.

Gilmore, Ruth Wilson. Keynote Conversation, Making and Unmaking Mass Incarceration Conference, University of Mississippi, Oxford, MS, December 5, 2019.

Hale, Steven. "Clemmons Protestors Seize Control of Metro Council Meeting, *Nashville Scene*, February 22, 2018, https://www.nashvillescene.com/news/pith-in-the-wind/article/20852881/clemmons-protesters-seize-control-of-metro-council-meeting.

Hale, Steven. "How Gideon's Army Is Making Peace in North Nashville," https://www.nashvillescene.com/news/cover-story/article/21074753/how-gideons-army-is-making-peace-in-north-nashville.

Hale, Steven. "Police Union Website Targets Daniel Hambrick," *Nashville Scene* (February 19, 2019), https://www.nashvillescene.com/news/pith-in-the-wind/article/21048001/police-union-website-targets-daniel-hambrick.

Harding, Vincent. *There is a River: The Black Struggle for Freedom in America.* New York: NY: Harcourt Brace Jovanovich, 1981.

Harris, Cheryl I. "Whiteness as Property," *Harvard Law Review* 106, no. 8 (June 1993): 1707–91.

hooks, bell. *The Will to Change: Men, Masculinity, and Love.* New York, NY: Atria Books, 2004.

"Inmates of the Tennessee State Penitentiary, 1851-1870," https://sos.tn.gov/products/tsla/inmates-tennessee-state-penitentiary-1851-1870.

Kaba, Mariame. "Toward the Horizon of Abolition," in Mariame Kaba, *We Do This 'Til We Free Us: Abolitionist Organizing and Transforming Justice.* Chicago, IL: Haymarket Books, 2021.

Kelley, Robin D.G. *Freedom Dreams: The Black Radical Imagination.* Boston, MA: Beacon Press, 2008.

Krinks, Andrew. "Soulful Resistance: Theological Body Knowledge on Tennessee's Death Row," *The Other Journal* 23: The Body Issue (2014).

Krinks, Andrew. *White Property, Black Trespass: The Religion of Mass Criminalization.* New York, NY: New York University Press, 2024.

Linebaugh, Peter. *The London Hanged: Crime and Civil Society in the Eighteenth Century,* 2nd ed. London and New York: Verso, 2006.

Maurin, Peter. "What the Catholic Worker Believes," https://www.catholicworker.org/petermaurin/easy-essays.html.

McTighe, Laura. "Abolition is sacred work," *The Immanent*

Frame, January 28, 2021, https://tif.ssrc.org/2021/01/28/abolition-is-sacred-work/.

Million, Dian. "Intense Dreaming: Theories, Narratives, and Our Search for Home," *American Indian Quarterly* 35, no. 3 (2011): 314-315.

Palacios, Lena. "With Immediate Cause: Intense Dreaming as World-Making," in Abolition Collective, eds., *Abolishing Carceral Society, Abolition: A Journal of Insurgent Politics*. Brooklyn, NY: Common Notions, 2018.

Plazas, David. "Nashville police killed a black man, public wanted oversight board – 45 years ago," *The Tennessean*, August 15, 2018, https://www.tennessean.com/story/opinion/columnists/david-plazas/2018/08/15/daniel-hambrick-nashville-police-briley-oversight-board/986717002.

Sultan, Reina. "Say Your Prayers, Conservatives! Prison Abolitionists Are Reclaiming Faith," *Truthout*, July 26, 2021, https://truthout.org/articles/say-your-prayers-conservatives-prison-abolitionists-are-reclaiming-faith/.

Tamburin, Adam. "Gov. Bill Lee denies clemency for Donnie Edward Johnson; execution set for Thursday," *The Tennessean*, May 14, 2019, https://www.tennessean.com/story/news/crime/2019/05/14/tennessee-execution-donnie-johnson-clemency-bill-lee/1094175001/.

Tamburin, Adam and Natalie Allison. "Man shot by Nashville police remembered for caring spirit before protest blocks streets," *The Tennessean*, July 28, 2018, https://www.tennessean.com/story/news/2018/07/28/nashville-police-shooting-daniel-hambrick-andrew-delke-tn-officer-involved-shooting/857788002/.

Tamburin, Adam, Natalie Allison, and Anita Wadhwani. "Prosecutors file homicide charge against officer in Daniel Hambrick's death," *The Tennessean*, September 27, 2018, https://www.tennessean.com/story/news/crime/2018/09/27/nashville-police-shooting-daniel-hambrick-andrew-delke-charge-denied-homicide/1441834002/.

Tamburin, Adam, Katherine Burgess, Yihyun Jeong, and Mariah Timms, "Tennessee executes Donnie Edward Johnson by lethal injection," *The Tennessean*, May 16, 2019, https://www.tennessean.com/story/news/crime/2019/05/16/execution-donnie-johnson-tennessee-leathl-injection/3668943002/.

The Book of Common Prayer and Administration of the Sacraments and Other Rites and Ceremonies of the Church: Together with the Psalter or Psalms of David According to the Use of the Episcopal Church. New York, NY: Seabury Press, 1979.

Wills II, Ridley. *Nashville Streets & their Stories*. Franklin, TN: Plumbline Media, 2012.

THE ABOLITION OF HELL: ABOLITIONIST INTERPRETATIONS OF JESUS' DESCENT INTO HELL

Hannah Bowman

He destroyed Hell when He descended into it.
He put it into an uproar even as it tasted of His flesh. . . .
Hell was in an uproar because it was done away with.
It was in an uproar because it is mocked.
It was in an uproar, for it is destroyed.
It is in an uproar, for it is annihilated. . . .
Christ is Risen, and life is liberated![1]

The "harrowing of hell" refers to the ancient Christian tradition, referenced in the Apostles' Creed, of Christ's descent into hell, or the realm of the dead, in the time between his death on the cross and his resurrection. This essay investigates what an abolitionist reading of this Christian doctrine offers to the movement and to Christian thought.

An abolitionist reading of the descent into hell reframes the central mystery of the Christian faith—the symbolic narrative of Christ's death and resurrection—as a picture of, and insistent demand for, freeing all prisoners in this world now. The practice of abolition, as goal and process, is sanctified and given spiritual meaning as a way of making a divine transformation of the entire cosmos visible. Specific aspects of abolitionist thought and praxis—such as ending carceral structures, solidarity with prisoners, liberation from coercion, and reconciliation into community[2]—illuminate and are illuminated by the narrative of Jesus' descent into hell.

Additionally, an abolitionist reading of the descent into hell imposes onto it a conception of universal salvation based on solidarity. All people imprisoned, separated, or punished in "hell" will be liberated from coercion and reconciled to community. The basis for such salvation of all people is Jesus' presence in hell with them. Jesus'

---

1. From "St. John Chrysostom's Easter Sermon," accessed 25 March 2020.

2. This list is drawn from Fay Knopp et al., "Nine Perspectives for Prison Abolitionists," in Knopp et al., *Instead of Prisons: A Handbook for Abolitionists* (Syracuse, NY: Prison Research Action Education Project, 1976).

descent into hell supports a theology and practice of solidarity that ultimately envisions reconciliation as arising from solidarity in the depths of imprisonment. Such solidarity builds communities of reconciliation which then make liberation possible.

The interpretation of Jesus' descent into hell as an act of solidarity with those condemned and forsaken by God features prominently in the work of Catholic theologian Hans Urs von Balthasar. It is also present in German Reformed theologian Jürgen Moltmann's understanding of the "Crucified God" and the depths of Jesus' abandonment by the Father on the cross. My argument goes further than Balthasar, who allows for the possibility that some souls may be condemned eternally to hell: I propose that the solidarity inherent in the descent into hell affects universal salvation and the abolition of hell—and, on that basis, reorders secular conceptions of justice in support of prison abolition as well.

In this essay, I will first explore the resonances between the symbols and narratives present in descriptions of Jesus' descent into hell and the realities of prisons and the practice of prison abolition. I will then consider the "universalizing" effect of descriptions of the salvation of Adam and Eve which are central to popular tellings of the descent narrative; explore what it means to interpret the descent into hell as both a past historical event, occurring between Jesus' historical crucifixion and resurrection, and a mythological event outside of historical time which exists eternally in God and anticipates an eschatological future—when God will conquer the powers of evil and "be all in all"[3]; analyze the descent into hell as a sign of Jesus' victory over the cosmic "powers" underlying carceral systems; and engage with Balthasar's interpretation of the descent as an act of solidarity with those in hell. These different interpretive lenses all provide ways of reading the descent into hell as an argument for abolition.

HELL AS PRISON AND THE GOALS OF ABOLITION

My abolitionist interpretation of the descent into hell relies on a long-standing correlation between the concept of "hell" and incarceration.[4]

---

3. 1 Corinthians 15:28, NRSV.

4. See, for example, James Gilligan's *Violence: Reflections on a National Epidemic* (New York: Vintage, 1996), 157, where he writes, "The societies that construct prisons have specifically wanted to make the prisons resemble hell, as much as possible, from their architecture to the relationships between the various groups of people involved in them," and Laurie Throness' book *A Protestant Purgatory: Theological Origins of the Penitentiary Act, 1779* (New York: Routledge, 2016) where the author writes that "deliberations about divine punishment in Hell mirrored temporal considerations of capital punishment and proportion in sentencing" (45).

Two different pictures of hell reflect such a correlation: first, the idea of hell as simply the realm of the dead, where souls are imprisoned; second, the idea of hell as the place or experience of divine punishment.

I want to draw the following connections between the concept of hell and the practice of incarceration: hell can be defined as a symbolic term for any state of being where souls are (1) confined, (2) separated from the love and presence of God,[5] (3) often as punishment for their sinful actions on earth or their failure to grasp salvation through Jesus or the church. This description makes evident the correlation between the condemnation to hell and the condemnation to imprisonment (and the consequent banishing from community) as punishment for a crime. Even if hell is interpreted simply as the realm of the dead, the souls within it are still understood to be confined (incarcerated) and separated (banished) from the life-giving love of God. If hell is understood as an expression of divine punishment as well—as depicted in popular descriptions of hell and its torments like Dante's *Inferno*—the correlation with retributive, torturous imprisonment is even more obvious. Insofar as hell is defined by coercion/confinement, separation, and retribution, it is to some degree related to any societal and state interventions reliant upon those practices: in other words, all those interventions that make up the wider carceral state beyond the literal prison.[6]

Prison abolition is the struggle against all such practices of coercion, separation, and retribution, epitomized in the practice of incarceration. Abolition is both an ideal—the end of incarceration and related practices—and a process—the practice of solidarity with prisoners and empowerment of communities to keep themselves safe without prisons.[7] The dual goal of abolition is liberation, "the least amount of coercion and intervention in a person's life," and reconciliation, "restor[ing] both the criminal and the victim to full humanity, to lives of integrity and dignity in the community"

---

5. The *Catechism of the Catholic Church* describes the dead as "deprived of the vision of God." *Catechism of the Catholic Church*, sec. 633, accessed 18 April 2019.

6. A seminal resource on the widening of the carceral state is the book *Prison by Any Other Name: The Harmful Consequences of Popular Reforms* by Maya Schenwar and Victoria Law (New Press, 2020).

7. Discussion of abolition as both goal and process is found in the transcribed interview "Perspectives on Critical Resistance," in *Abolition Now!: Ten Years of Strategy and Struggle against the Prison Industrial Complex*, ed. CR10 Publications Collective (Oakland, CA: AK Press, 2008). Activist Rose Braz says in this discussion, for example, that "abolition defines both the end goal we seek and the way we do our work today" (11).

whenever harm is done.[8] Liberation and reconciliation are closely linked; the goal of abolition is to build "caring communities" that provide for restoration and support, and thereby make freedom from coercion a reality for all people.[9]

Hell has had an important ethical function in Christianity as one way of expressing God's judgment against the injustices of the world—just as the carceral system claims to provide "justice" in human communities. Similar to the way abolition reframes justice as the dual pursuit of liberation and reconciliation, recent Christian thought has also begun to reemphasize the conception of divine justice as ultimately tied to reconciliation and the restoration of right relationships with God.[10]

The earliest conceptions of hell, especially in connection with the references to Christ's descent into it, envision it as a more-or-less neutral realm of the dead, where souls are not necessarily punished but imprisoned after death. This concept, known by the Hebrew term "Sheol" or the Greek term "Hades," is the "location" associated with Christ's descent in the earliest accounts. Gradually, however, hell came to take on more of a deliberately punitive character, derived from Jesus' statements about the torments of "Gehenna" for the wicked, a place where "the fire never goes out"[11] and where "there will be weeping and gnashing of teeth"[12] (e.g. Matthew 5:22–30, Mark 9:43–47, Luke 12:5).[13] By the patristic era, the concept of hell as the place of the condemnation of the reprobate was well-established, with the torments of the damned discussed in writings of theologians from Justin Martyr and Tertullian to John Chrysostom and Augustine of Hippo, who (per Balthasar) first

8. Knopp et al., "Nine Perspectives." The authors write: "Abolitionists believe reconciliation, not punishment, is a proper response to criminal acts. . . .The abolitionist response [to harm] seeks to restore both the criminal and the victim to full humanity, to lives of integrity and dignity in the community. Abolitionists advocate the least amount of coercion and intervention in an individual's life and the maximum amount of care and services to all people in the society." This expresses the duality of liberation and reconciliation, each of which requires the other.

9. Knopp et al., "Nine Perspectives."

10. See Christopher D. Marshall, *Beyond Retribution: A New Testament Vision for Justice, Crime, and Punishment* (Grand Rapids, MI: William B. Eerdmans, 2001), Howard Zehr, *Changing Lenses: Restorative Justice for Our Times* (Harrisonburg, VA: Herald Press, 2015), and Dominique DuBois Gilliard, *Rethinking Incarceration: Advocating for Justice that Restores* (Downers Grove, IL: InterVarsity Press, 2018).

11. Mark 9:47, NRSV.

12. Matthew 13:42, NRSV.

13. Archibald L.H.M. van Wieringen, "Descent into the Netherworld: A Biblical Perspective," in *The Apostles' Creed: 'He Descended into Hell,'* ed. Wieringen and Marcel Sarot (Leiden: Brill, 2018), 9–32; see especially the discussion of Gehenna on page 29. See also Hans Urs von Balthasar's discussion of this phenomenon—Sheol becoming hell—in *Mysterium Paschale: The Mystery of Easter* (San Francisco: Ignatius Press, 1990), 161.

clearly identify the torments of hell with "the loss of the grace and vision of God."[14] Centuries later, Thomas Aquinas further developed the geography of hell by describing it as containing four realms which differ in the presence of grace and the "pain of sense" (torments experienced by the souls in hell) but are united in the absence of the vision of God;[15] Dante further subdivided hell into nine circles of increasing punishments suited to particular types of sin.

Even when hell started being conceived as the locus of divine punishment, ambiguity about its nature nonetheless remained. Christians' opinions differed, and still differ, on whether hell is eternal or whether all will eventually be saved; whether hell is a place to which God coercively condemns or assigns people (as in the doctrine of "double predestination"); or whether people condemn themselves to hell by refusing God in an exercise of their free will. The most famous and perhaps most influential of the patristic debates on hell was the conflict between Origen, who propounded a doctrine of the eventual restoration of all to God,[16] and Augustine, who insisted that hell and its punishments were eternal on the basis of God's fidelity to the promises of reward and punishment God made: "by Himself [God] confirmeth His threats. . . as His promise is true, so is His threat sure."[17] In modern times, Balthasar, among others, argued that individuals condemn themselves to hell—God does not condemn them but "the man who irrevocably refuses love condemns himself"[18] —and depicted hell as a state of spiritual, rather than physical, suffering experienced by those who have rejected God and know themselves to be separated from God.[19] Balthasar also argued that we can hope that hell is in fact empty.[20] More recently, Eastern Orthodox theologian David Bentley Hart has similarly argued that all will eventually be saved from hell, on the basis of patristic sources.[21]

---

14. Hans Urs von Balthasar, *Dare We Hope That All Men Be Saved? With a Short Discourse on Hell* (San Francisco: Ignatius Press, 1988), 49–50. Augustine, however, also insists that spirits after death suffer pain, forever, in the same way as people do in life (Paul J.J. van Geest, "Augustine's Certainty in Speaking about Hell and His Reserve in Explaining Christ's Descent into Hell," in *The Apostles' Creed: 'He Descended into Hell,'* 37–38).

15. Harm J.M.J. Goris, "Thomas Aquinas on Christ's Descent into Hell," in *The Apostles' Creed: 'He Descended into Hell,'* 95–96.

16. van Geest, "Augustine's Certainty in Speaking About Hell," 33.

17. Quoted in van Geest, "Augustine's Certainty in Speaking about Hell," 35. See also Balthasar's discussion of the development of the doctrine of hell particularly by Augustine, in *Dare We Hope All Men Be Saved?*, 47–72.

18. Balthasar, *Dare We Hope That All Men Be Saved?*, 165.

19. Balthasar, *Dare We Hope That All Men Be Saved?*, 51–58.

20. Balthasar, *Dare We Hope That All Men Be Saved?*, 14–17.

21. David Bentley Hart, *That All Shall Be Saved: Heaven, Hell, and Universal Salvation* (New Haven: Yale University Press, 2019).

Abolition offers a new perspective to the ongoing theological question of universal salvation versus condemnation to eternal torment in hell. The duality of liberation and reconciliation expressed by abolitionist activists and practitioners of "transformative justice" provides a new perspective on the traditional concept of salvation, while the symbol of Jesus in hell widens the traditional recipients of salvation to include anyone who has suffered any sort of condemnation, punishment, or bondage. Taken together, the insights of prison abolition in conjunction with the narrative of Christ's descent into hell offer a new lens on the question of whether we "dare hope that all may be saved."

TRADITIONAL UNDERSTANDINGS OF
THE DESCENT INTO HELL

If the concept of hell remains contested in Christian thought, the nature and purpose of Christ's descent into hell is even more ambiguous. The New Testament basis for the doctrine of the descent into hell is based primarily on two brief references:

> Therefore it is said, 'When [Jesus] ascended on high he made captivity itself a captive; he gave gifts to his people.' (When it says, 'He ascended,' what does it mean but that he had also descended into the lower parts of the earth?)[22]

> [Jesus] was put to death in the flesh, but made alive in the spirit, in which also he went and made a proclamation to the spirits in prison, who in former times did not obey, when God waited patiently in the days of Noah, during the building of the ark, in which a few, that is, eight persons, were saved through water.[23]

The meaning of "he had also descended" and "also he went and made a proclamation to the spirits in prison" have been subject to much interpretation. A useful example is the *Catechism of the Catholic Church*, which defines the descent into hell as an element of Jesus' true subjection to death: "This was the first meaning given in the apostolic preaching to Christ's descent into hell: that Jesus, like all men, experienced death and in his soul joined the others in the realm of the dead. But he descended there as Savior, proclaiming the Good

---

22. Ephesians 4:9, NRSV.
23. 1 Peter 3:18–20, NRSV.

News to the spirits imprisoned there."[24] Catholic teaching about the descent into hell affirms that "the descent into hell brings the Gospel message of salvation to complete fulfillment" as Jesus' "redemptive work [is spread] to all men [sic] of all times and places."[25]

Abolitionist imagery of liberating prisoners is already present to some extent in the traditional Catholic dogma of the descent into hell. The purpose of Jesus' descent into hell is in liberating the dead from the realm in which they are imprisoned and "deprived of the vision of God."[26] Upon his rising from the dead (when he "ascended" per Ephesians 4:8), Jesus holds "the keys of hell and of death"[27] to unlock hell and free the dead into eternal life.

Traditional interpretations of the descent into hell place limits on an abolitionist interpretation of it. Official Catholic doctrine does not allow for Jesus' descent to go to the furthest depths of hell or to proclaim release to *all* prisoners: "Jesus did not descend into hell to deliver the damned, nor to destroy the hell of damnation, but to free the just who had gone before him."[28]

But broadening our view from this example of the official Catholic doctrine of the descent reveals ongoing ambiguity in the Christian tradition over which conception of hell Jesus descended into. The earliest understanding of the descent into hell may have taken it primarily as proof that Jesus had truly died, entering an unspecified realm of the dead where he preached to at least some of the dead.[29] Patristic theologians differed on the "scope of redemption"[30] in Jesus' preaching to the dead. Augustine suggested the harrowing of the "temporary dwelling place" of Hades/Sheol did not destroy the permanent hell/Gehenna while others such as Clement and Cyril of Alexandria suggested that all the dead were liberated by Christ's descent, so that only the devil was left.[31] Aquinas, with his fourfold hell, restricted Jesus' descent to only one level, "the limbo of the fathers," a particularly mild circle of hell where those virtuous people who lived before Jesus' time resided.[32] Early liturgical texts emphasize the harrowing of hell as an act of victory over death,[33] while other theologians across

---

24. *Catechism*, 632.

25. *Catechism*, 634, 635.

26. *Catechism*, 633.

27. Revelation 1:18, KJV.

28. *Catechism*, 633.

29. *Catechism*, 632.

30. See Marcel Sarot, "The Scope of Redemption on Finding Meaning In Christ's Descent into Hell" in *The Apostles' Creed: 'He Descended Into Hell,'* 185–206.

31. van Geest, "Augustine's Certainty in Speaking About Hell," 43, 45.

32. Goris, "Thomas Aquinas on Christ's Descent into Hell," 109.

33. Gerard A.M. Rouwhorst, "The Descent of Christ into the Underworld in Early Christian Liturgy," in *The Apostles' Creed: 'He Descended into Hell,'* 55.

centuries and traditions have interpreted the descent as Jesus sharing in some experience of divine punishment or condemnation, from Aquinas himself,[34] to John Calvin,[35] to Moltmann and Balthasar.

Ambiguity over the nature of the descent into hell throughout Christian history makes it a symbol well-suited to creative reinterpretation in support of liberatory truth. An abolitionist reading of the descent into hell cannot be satisfied with restricting the freeing of prisoners only to "the just who had [died] before Jesus." I am reminded of the distinctions drawn in discussions of prison reform between "non-violent" offenders who should be freed and "violent criminals" whom we would prefer to leave banished behind bars.[36] Prison abolition demands that no one be seen as disposable,[37] and that, in the context of the "prison" of hell, Jesus' redemptive work in fact be offered to "all men [sic] of all times and places": before and after Jesus' death and resurrection and regardless of the reason for the soul's condemnation. Below, I will offer possible interpretations of the descent into hell as offering liberation for *all* people under any sort of punitive coercion, on the basis of reconciliation derived from divine solidarity even with the dead in hell.

THE SUGGESTION OF UNIVERSAL LIBERATION

I read the descent into hell as a narrative of universal liberation based on three elements of its later interpretation: 1) the imagery of breaking chains and rescuing Adam and Eve, understood as the prototypical "sinners," in non-canonical descriptions of the descent into hell such as that in the fifth-century Gospel of Nicodemus; 2) the theological understanding of the descent into hell as an event standing outside of time, which offers a basis for its application in supporting the abolition of carceral systems *now;* and 3) the interpretation of the descent into hell as victory over the powers of death at work in every instantiation of our current carceral system.

Jesus' descent into hell became a popular topic for later Christian texts and sermons in the patristic and medieval periods. A far fuller picture of what Christ did in hell than any in the New Testament is

---

34. Goris, "Thomas Aquinas on Christ's Descent into Hell," 113.

35. *Institutes of the Christian Religion,* Book II, Chapter 16, Section 10. Accessed 6 October 2022.

36. See John Pfaff, *Locked In: The True Causes of Mass Incarceration—and How to Achieve Real Reform* (New York: Basic Books, 2017) or Marie Gottschalk, *Caught: The Prison State and the Lockdown of American Politics* (Princeton, NJ: Princeton University Press, 2016) for a discussion of the weaknesses of this reformist dynamic.

37. This is a common abolitionist refrain, popularized by Bryan Stevenson in *Just Mercy* (New York: Spiegel & Grau, 2014).

found in the Gospel of Nicodemus, which presents a picture of the state of popular piety surrounding the descent into hell at the time of its (probably fifth-century) writing.[38] Its concrete imagery of Jesus' descent into hell presents it with the character of a divine rescue mission for the prisoners, as Jesus breaks open the gates of hell, "the fetters which before could not be broken,"[39] and draws Adam and others out of hell,[40] leaving the "prince of hell" to lament the loss of his prisoners: "He will set at liberty all those whom I hold in prison under unbelief, and bound with the fetters of their sins, and will conduct them to everlasting life.. . . . He has broken down our prisons from top to bottom, dismissed all the captives, released all who were bound."[41]

The vivid imagery in the Gospel of Nicodemus presents Jesus' descent into hell as a symbol of prison abolition in its most concrete form: Jesus breaks down doors and chains and draws the prisoners out of captivity. Hell is not destroyed in this telling—in fact, it is not even necessarily emptied—but the motif of liberation for prisoners is evident. Jesus does not simply "[make] a proclamation to the spirits in prison,"[42] but literally frees those in bondage.

The abolitionist imagery continues in popular conceptions of the descent into hell in the medieval period, even as Christian doctrine simultaneously reified the conception of hell as a place of eternal punishment. Alongside Aquinas' categorization and Dante's descriptions of hell's various levels and torments, medieval tellings of the descent narrative frame it with the great drama of a divine prison break. In the Anglo-Saxon poem "The Dream of the Rood," Jesus brings a "vast host of souls" from hell into God's kingdom.[43] An Anglo-Saxon sermon on the harrowing of hell builds "dramatic action" specifically around Jesus' invasion to rescue the prisoners: "[And then he] completely broke the gates of hell and their brass bolts;"[44] the redeemed from hell respond to Jesus, saying "Now ascend, Lord Saviour Christ, now you have robbed hell."[45]

Just as the Gospel of Nicodemus emphasizes Jesus' liberation of those in hell beginning with Adam the prototypical man, this Anglo-Saxon sermon relates the response of Eve the prototypical woman,

38. Rouwhorst, "The Descent of Christ into the Underworld in Early Christian Liturgy," 56.

39. *Gospel of Nicodemus* 16:18, 16:13, in *The Lost Books of the Bible* (New York: Testament Books/Random House, 1979), 84.

40. *Gospel of Nicodemus* 19:1–3, 19:12, in *The Lost Books of the Bible*, 86–7.

41. *Gospel of Nicodemus* 15:20, 18:4, in *The Lost Books of the Bible*, 83, 85.

42. 1 Peter 3:19, NRSV.

43. "The Dream of the Rood," trans. Jonathan Glenn, accessed 18 April 2019,

44. Brandon W. Hawk, *Preaching Apocrypha in Anglo-Saxon England* (Toronto: University of Toronto Press, 2018), 167.

45. Hawk, *Preaching Apocrypha*, 168.

placed in juxtaposition with the Virgin Mary as she begs for liberation: "I implore you now, Lord, by your servant Saint Mary. . . have mercy on me, most wretched of all women, and my Maker pity me, and deliver me from the bonds of this death."[46] The relevant features of this prayer are the (abolitionist) language of deliverance from bondage, but also Eve's self-identification as the "most wretched of all women." The imagery of the salvation of Eve the prototypical sinner (as of Adam) cuts against the traditional interpretation that Jesus freed only "the *just* who had gone before him."[47]

My point here is *not* to suggest a hierarchy of sin (despite the language of "most wretched" used by the medieval author). The importance of Adam and Eve's inclusion in the imagery of the harrowing of hell lies in the traditional Christian understanding of them as the prototypical sinners. They are "most wretched" not because they are the worst sinners but rather because they symbolize the original sin or inherent sin of all humanity.[48] The salvation of Adam and Eve (a popular image for icons of the resurrection and patristic homilies[49]) symbolically represents the salvation of all humanity: "for as in Adam all die, even so in Christ shall all be made alive."[50] Theologically, Jesus' descent into hell presents the undoing of the curse of original sin which is, according to traditional Christian theology, an unavoidable part of the human condition. Jesus refers to the myth of the fall of humankind that gave rise to original sin when he says to Adam, in the telling of the Gospel of Nicodemus, "Come to me, all ye my saints, who were created in my image, who were *condemned by the tree of forbidden fruit*, and by the devil and death. Live now by the wood of my cross."[51] Jesus' rescue of Adam and Eve implies the righting of the sinful human condition and the liberation and reconciliation of all human sinners.

This interpretive move is where abolitionist politics and universalist theology meet. Jesus' descent into hell offers an image of liberating captives, but abolition requires more than the liberation of *some*.

---

46. Hawk, *Preaching Apocrypha*, 168.

47. *Catechism*, 633.

48. A discussion of the "worst" sinners inevitably brings to mind Dante's hierarchical conception of hell and his naming of Judas Iscariot as the most-damned traitor (*Inferno*, Canto 34). Dante, in line with traditional Catholic teaching, places Adam and Eve in what Aquinas called "the limbo of the fathers." But the placement of Adam and Eve in limbo does not address their centrality, in this alternate tradition, as the originators of human sin, prefiguring all future sin within their original transgression.

49. See Rouwhorst, "The Descent of Christ to the Underworld in Early Christian Liturgy"; "From an Ancient Homily for Holy Saturday," accessed 22 April 2019; and St. Augustine's Holy Saturday homily, in Stephen Mark Holmes, *The Fathers on the Sunday Gospels* (Collegeville, MN: Liturgical Press, 2012), 127.

50. 1 Corinthians 15:22, KJV.

51. *Gospel of Nicodemus* 19:2, in *The Lost Books of the Bible*, 86. Emphasis mine.

To read the descent into hell as an abolitionist symbol imposes onto the narrative an understanding that the liberation Jesus brings to hell comes to *all* the captives held there.

Balthasar's perspective of hell as an inner or spiritual state of suffering[52] allows us to truly call this liberation the abolition of hell. If hell is interpreted simply as a place (the land of the dead, commonly symbolized as the "lower parts of the earth"[53]), then Jesus' rescue mission depicts its emptying, but not necessarily its destruction—it is a picture of liberation for prisoners, but not necessarily of abolition of carceral structures. But if hell is located primarily in the experience of those suffering in it, then their rescue from hell could truly be said to be its abolition, as it would have no existence beyond them. In this way, the liberation of those condemned can also be identified with Jesus' destruction of death and hell.[54] (I will discuss further implications of the concept of Jesus' victory over the powers of death below.) The freeing of the prisoners in hell is the destruction of the prison of hell itself.

In this case, reconciliation, rather than liberation, may be a better aspect of the concept of salvation to emphasize, as the rescue depicted would not be from externally imposed punishment but from the interior suffering of isolation: suffering which can be addressed by reconciliation to community with God. What Jesus promises Adam in the telling of the Gospel of Nicodemus is that he will "live now."[55] Here connections arise again with abolition understood not only as a political goal of ending carceral systems but as an ongoing communal effort to produce justice by building "caring communities." Liberation and reconciliation depend upon each other.[56] Given that the concept of hell functions in part as an ethical symbol to express the judgment of God against the injustice of the world, any "abolition" of hell which takes seriously the question of injustice requires a recognition that God's justice is ultimately expressed not through divine "redemptive violence"[57] but through restorative justice and reconciliation in caring community.[58]

52. Balthasar, *Dare We Hope That All Men Be Saved?*, 51–58.

53. Ephesians 4:9, NRSV.

54. John Chrysostom describes that destruction this way: "Let no one fear death, for the Death of our Savior has set us free. He has destroyed it by enduring it. He destroyed Hell when He descended into it. He put it into an uproar even as it tasted of His flesh." See "St. John Chrysostom's Easter Sermon."

55. *Gospel of Nicodemus* 19:2, in *The Lost Books of the Bible*, 86.

56. Knopp et al., "Nine Perspectives."

57. See Ched Myers and Elaine Enns, *Ambassadors of Reconciliation: New Testament Reflections on Restorative Justice and Peacemaking*, volume 1 (Maryknoll, NY: Orbis Books, 2009), 94.

58. See Zehr, *Changing Lenses*, Gilliard, *Rethinking Incarceration*, and Marshall, *Beyond Retribution*, for further discussion of the interpretation of God's justice as restorative rather than retributive.

My interpretation that the descent into hell liberated all the souls condemned to hell, and thus perhaps "abolished" hell itself, is admittedly outside the traditional and historic understandings of the descent. These understandings usually restricted Jesus' liberating work either only to the just or only those "elected" by God for salvation—a position which can be read as consistent with the telling in the Gospel of Nicodemus, where those freed by Jesus are identified as "[his] saints"[59]—or only to those who have died before Jesus.[60] This latter *temporal* restriction deserves additional consideration. It derives support from the scriptural texts cited above as 1 Peter 3:19 says, Jesus "made a proclamation to the spirits in prison, who *in former times* did not obey." The implication of this passage is that when Jesus descended into hell, the only inhabitants to whom he came were those who had died before him in history (and perhaps he came only to the righteous dead among those).

To address this question of who was "already" in hell when Jesus arrived there, I would suggest that an alternative understanding of how divine action relates to historical time can situate the crucifixion of Jesus and the descent into hell as events which participate in eternity and are therefore not bound to a linear view of history. This is a common theme in devotional and theological writings about the crucifixion. Robert Farrar Capon, for example, writes of perceiving the crucifixion from both the "historical, horizontal" perspective and the "immediate, vertical" perspective—"the images of the Lamb slain from the foundation of the world and of the eternal Great High Priest and Victim taking away all sins, at all times, all at once, in one Mystery of Heavenly Intercession"—which he attributes to God's eternal vision.[61] Capon uses the symbolic language of the Book of Revelation here, which identifies Jesus as "the Lamb slain from the foundation of the world"[62] in the midst of its imagery of the end times, thereby identifying the death of Jesus as an event occurring somehow at the beginning and the end of the world as well as at a particular time in history. Using this language, Capon is attempting to visualize how God's work of atonement might look to God, outside of time and history. The crucifixion of Jesus is a historical event at a particular time and place, but according to Christian theology also effects an atonement applicable to all times and places, and, as

---

59. *Gospel of Nicodemus*, 19:1, in *The Lost Books of the Bible*, 86.

60. *Catechism*, 633.

61. Robert Farrar Capon, *Between Noon and Three: Romance, Law, and the Outrage of Grace* (Grand Rapids, MI: Eerdmans, 1997), 218. See also Fleming Rutledge's interpretation of Rev. 13:8 in *The Crucifixion: Understanding the Death of Jesus Christ* (Grand Rapids, MI: Eerdmans, 2015), 299.

62. Revelation 13:8, KJV.

Capon suggests here, God "sees" it occurring eternally as well as at an appointed time in history. Moltmann suggests that the crucifixion in some sense occurs *within* God as well as within history. He writes of the crucifixion and death of Jesus, and thus his descent into hell, as an eternal event within God: "The cross is at the centre of the Trinity. This is brought out by tradition, when it takes up the Book of Revelation's image of 'the Lamb who was slain from the foundation of the world.' . . . Before the world was, the sacrifice was already in God. No Trinity is conceivable without the Lamb, without the sacrifice of love, without the crucified Son. For he is the slaughtered Lamb glorified in eternity."[63] Adrienne von Speyr similarly describes the Cross as "'atemporal,' because all the sins from the past and future are gathered on the Son, who is 'made sin.' In this sense the Cross is the zero hour."[64]

The idea of the crucifixion as an eternal event is common, but it is rarely used to suggest that the descent into hell accomplished liberation for all souls in hell from any time in history, present, or future. My point in using these examples is to support my abolitionist reading that Jesus liberated everyone in hell past, present, and future.

Such atemporality also suggests the interplay of eschatological and historical time which is essential to the abolitionist project of reading the eschatological promise of freedom for prisoners as a call for abolition *now*. If Jesus descended into hell at the (historical) time of his crucifixion, and yet his crucifixion, descent, and resurrection comprise the "first fruits" of the promised salvation at the end of time,[65] how does this affect our social imagination of how we should structure our communities in the time between Jesus' historical death and the eschaton, the end of history?

Thus the descent in some sense brackets the current time so that the ultimate liberation of all at the end of time can be understood as already being in progress ever since the historical moment of the descent. In this way, the image of the descent into hell helps situate current political and practical efforts toward abolition as "participation" in the divine act of eschatological, cosmic liberation that is in progress.[66]

A helpful conception of history for illustrating the concept of "abolition as participation in eschatological liberation" may be found

63. Jürgen Moltmann, *The Trinity and the Kingdom: The Doctrine of God* (San Francisco: Harper and Row, 1981), 83.

64. von Speyr, quoted in Riyako Hikota, "And Still We Wait; Hans Urs von Balthasar's Theology of Holy Saturday and its Implications for Christian Suffering and Discipleship" (Ph.D. diss., University of Edinburgh, 2015), 20.

65. See 1 Corinthians 15:20–28.

66. I owe this idea of "participation" to Fleming Rutledge's discussion of apocalyptic theology in *Advent: The Once and Future Coming of Jesus Christ* (Grand Rapids, MI: Eerdmans, 2018), 27.

in dialogue with Giorgio Agamben's description of "messianic time," which he calls "the time that time takes to come to an end."[67] Agamben's messianic time offers a helpful critique of a strict separation between the current, historical reality and the eschaton, the traditional theological term for the end of time or the new age to come at the end of the world. He sees the current age as being in a sort of middle space between time and eschaton: "the time that time takes to come to an end." Ultimately, Agamben ascribes no concrete political content to messianic time.[68] My own argument defines the current age less in terms of the ending of the current, historical reality than in terms of the beginning of the eschatological "age to come." What effects does the future promise of liberation in the eschaton have on how we live and act *now*? Rather than defining messianic time as "the time that time takes to come to an end," I am more interested (in terms influenced by Agamben) in understanding the present age as the middle space which is "the time that the eschaton takes to begin": imagining the present as a proleptic participation in ultimate liberation. The present age *is already* the beginning of the "age to come." This concept of time provides a framework for seeing and supporting concrete acts of abolition as part of the promised, complete cosmic liberation at the end of time, already happening "ahead of schedule" in our world today. The way we live and act now within the present day *should* reflect politically the ongoing cosmic liberation undergirding reality—liberation that will be finally accomplished at the end of time but that is already beginning. Cosmic liberation, such as that accomplished by Jesus in hell, is not restricted to some "final judgment" of the world when God will make all things right but is always already occurring in acts of freedom-making happening here and now.[69]

---

67. Giorgio Agamben, *The Time That Remains: A Commentary on the Letter to the Romans* (Stanford: Stanford University Press, 2005), 67.

68. Thanks to Lyle Enright for helpful conversation on Agamben.

69. Radical Orthodox theologian John Milbank makes a similar claim for the political relevance to the present age of the coming reign of God and for the priority over the secular of the Church (understood in Augustinian terms as the "city of God" and as a, or perhaps *the*, political reality (Milbank, *Theology and Social Theory: Beyond Secular Reason* (Malden, MA: Blackwell Publishing, 2006), 410–413); in an example relevant to the topic of prisons, he suggests that the Church, during the present day, should not "punish" but rather "suffer. . . the consequences of sin, beyond considerations of desert and non-desert" (*Theology and Social Theory*, 428). He sees the Church as a non-retributive political reality which rightly re-forms the secular into an image closer to that of the coming reign of God. Unlike Milbank, however, I do not associate proleptic participation in the eschaton with the Church as a particular institution or community, but rather with all political practices of liberation that characterize the coming reign of God—the practices exemplified in the narrative of the descent into hell and characterized by solidarity with prisoners and all acts toward liberation—wherever they arise.

The reign of God at the end of history is not something we can move towards incrementally—instead it maintains its character as something "qualitatively and not quantitatively otherwise than our present situation."[70] However, it *is* something already accomplished in which we can take part in this world now. Abolition is one concrete sign of its already-accomplished nature in which we participate.

CARCERAL STRUCTURES AND THE POWER OF DEATH

Developing an abolitionist reading of the symbol of the descent into hell requires more than simply extending its reach across time and history. Abolition is not restricted to only freeing prisoners in literal chains but includes the dismantling of all systems of coercion and control, including all forms of "policing, punishment, surveillance, and exile."[71] Other theological perspectives on Jesus' descent into hell express its applicability to the broader problem of carceral systems.

The narrative of the descent into hell expresses Jesus' victory over the powers of death and hell, and his corresponding power to liberate the dead. A useful conceptualization of this power is provided by Lee Griffith, in his abolitionist reading of Ephesians 4:8–9, who identifies the descent into hell with the declaration of Jesus' victory over those powers of death which are at work also in every form of captivity and prisons.[72] Griffith draws on the biblical conception of "spirits and the demonic" to characterize the essential nature of violence, even when that violence, as in carceral systems, is justified as necessary for "public safety": "Everywhere violence appears, no matter what the motivations and justifications, it is inevitably and tediously the same. Paul shows the inadequacies of our modern mythos when he speaks of the 'spirit' and the 'power' that surround realities such as violence . . . . The problem is that prisons are *identical in spirit* to the violence and murder that they pretend to combat . . . In the biblical understanding, the spirit of the prison is the spirit of death."[73]

Thus, Jesus' victory over death takes on abolitionist overtones of victory over captivity as well.[74] For Griffith it functions as the consummation of his earlier proclamation of "release to the captives."[75]

70. David Congdon, personal communication, 28 September 2018.

71. Andrea J. Ritchie, interview with Sonali Kolhatkar, "An Abolitionist Makes a Case for 'No More Police,'" *Yes Magazine*, 3 October 2022.

72. Griffith, *Fall of the Prison*, 109.

73. Griffith, *Fall of the Prison*, 104–106.

74. Griffith writes in *Fall of the Prison*: "When Jesus' proclamation of liberty is viewed in the light of the resurrection, it can be said that Christ led captivity captive or that he captured captivity (Eph. 4:8)," 110.

75. Luke 4:18, NRSV.

In Jesus' defeat of death the power of God "unmasks . . . and renders . . . visible" the powers of death and bondage that underlie any system of imprisonment.[76] Griffith identifies Jesus' proclamation of liberty to captives as "[pointing] toward the resurrection itself,"[77] which the New Testament consistently identifies with victory over the power or spirit of death (e.g. Colossians 2:15, 1 Corinthians 15:20–27). Correlatively, the descent into hell—understood, by Griffith-like patristic authors,[78] as Christ's proclamation of victory over the powers of hell—points back toward liberation from anything "identical in spirit" to death.

Griffith's conceptualization of a "spirit of death" at work in prisons offers a possible lens on the applicability of the concept of the descent into hell to the multifaceted and expansive carceral system. The spirit of the prison, which is the spirit of death, is at work in every intervention which banishes, coerces, or controls those defined as "criminal" by the dominant powers. Theologically, hell is to some degree present in any instantiation of the "spirit of death," so there is a correlation between hell and aspects of the prison-industrial complex. Jesus' descent into hell symbolizes victory over the spirit of death in whatever form it occurs. This particularly includes the divine "unmasking and rendering visible"[79] of the powers of coercion and control at play in systems that claim to be supportive, including prison "alternatives" such as home confinement and electronic monitoring, probation and parole, mandatory drug treatment, sex-offense registries, and the child welfare system.[80] Perhaps it is especially in these forms of containment and surveillance, which do not immediately invoke visible comparisons to a traditional "hell" like literal cages do, where the naming of the powers of death at work in them, and the corresponding religious promise of victory over those powers, is most needed.

Taken together, my interpretation develops the symbol of the descent into hell along abolitionist and universalist lines. The imagery of the freeing of prisoners can be seen (through its application to Adam and Eve) to apply to all people in their varying degrees of bondage. The theological understanding of what Jesus accomplished is extended to apply to all people who might be understood to be condemned to hell throughout history, while simultaneously suggesting a practical basis for imagining abolitionist work in the present as participation in a future cosmic or eschatological liberation. Meanwhile,

---

76. Griffith, Fall of the Prison, 109.

77. Griffith, Fall of the Prison, 107.

78. See Rouwhorst, "Christ's Descent to the Underworld in Early Christian Liturgy," 61.

79. Griffith, Fall of the Prison, 109.

80. This list of examples is drawn from Schenwar and Law, Prison By Any Other Name.

the symbol of Jesus' victory over the power of death presents divine opposition to every coercive and destructive aspect of the entire carceral system.

VICTORY THROUGH SOLIDARITY

Traditional pictures of the descent into hell offer an image of liberation, but modern abolitionists may be uncomfortable by the extent to which these narratives depend on images of conquest and liberation from the outside. After all, the medieval term "harrowing" derives from the Old English "herian, [which] means 'to harry, to make a war raid.'"[81]

Prison abolition is closely tied to struggles for racial, class, and gender equity. Angela Y. Davis reminds us that "[i]mprisonment is associated with the racialization of those most likely to be punished. It is associated with their class and, as we have seen, gender structures the punishment system as well."[82] In work towards abolition, she writes, "[a]lternatives that fail to address racism, male dominance, homophobia, class bias, and other structures of domination will not, in the final analysis, lead to decarceration and will not advance the goal of abolition."[83]

Christians and their good intentions have been responsible for some of the worst forms of imprisonment. For example, well-intentioned Quakers introduced solitary confinement in the development of the penitentiary in Philadelphia, out of a desire to "[emphasize] the reformation of prisoners through the nurturing of penitence."[84] It is natural for abolitionists to be uncomfortable adopting the harrowing of hell as an abolitionist image insofar as it suggests liberation is something that comes to prisoners from an outside authority, re-establishing exactly a "structure of domination" contrary to abolitionist goals. How do we address the question of positionality raised by this symbolic narrative of the descent into hell? How can the descent into hell avoid becoming a domination of it?

The interpretation of the descent represented in modern times by Balthasar offers one possible way forward. For Balthasar, the descent into hell is not Jesus' conquest of it, but rather his solidarity in "being with the dead."[85] "This ultimate solidarity is the final point and the goal of that first 'descent,' so clearly described in the Scriptures, into a 'lower world' . . . . In order to assume the entire penalty imposed upon

---

81. Rutledge, *Crucifixion*, 410.

82. Angela Y. Davis, *Are Prisons Obsolete?* (New York: Seven Stories Press, 2003), Kindle, location 1456.

83. Davis, *Are Prisons Obsolete?*, Kindle, location 1407.

84. Griffith, *The Fall of the Prison*, 174.

85. Balthasar, *Mysterium Paschale*, 150.

sinners, Christ willed not only to die, but to go down, in his soul, *ad infernum* [into hell]."[86] For Balthasar, contra the Catholic *Catechism*, Christ truly descended to all the dead not as a conqueror but as a fellow sufferer. He describes Christ's descent as to "Sheol," the land of the dead, "understood in the classic Old Testament sense, putting between parentheses the speculations of later Judaism . . . about the difference of destiny which distinguishes men by way of reward and penalty after death."[87] (Here he returns to the earliest understandings of the descent and denies the distinction made in the *Catechism* between the "hell of damnation" and the experience of "the just who had died before [Jesus]."[88]) He emphasizes Christ's solidarity with all the dead, and, in fact, his experience of the "second death" along with sinners, writing, "this [experience of spiritual death or abandonment] constitutes the logical consequence of what we have said about a substitutory 'being with the dead' and permits an understanding of how Sheol, or the Old Testament Hades, can pass theologically into the New Testament Hell."[89] For Balthasar, Jesus' experience of hell "has no need to be anything other than what is implied by a real solidarity with the inhabitants of Sheol that no redemptive light has brightened. For all redemptive light comes uniquely from the one who was in solidarity until the end,"[90] and "The Redeemer showed himself . . . as the only one who, going beyond the general experience of death, was able to measure the depths of that abyss."[91] The fullness of what we call hell is experienced by Christ.

This view of the descent into hell can offer our abolitionist interpretation the insight that every effort towards liberation begins in solidarity. For Balthasar, Jesus' solidarity with the dead is what accomplishes their liberation. Balthasar quotes early-church theologian Irenaeus on this point: "only what has been endured is healed and saved."[92] Because Christ has descended in solidarity to the deepest abyss, he is able to overcome it for all. Von Speyr puts it this way: "At the place where the Son believed himself to be most abandoned by the Father, the abandonment is used to *break open the prison of abandonment, Hell,* and to admit the Son, along with the redeemed world, into the Heaven of the Father."[93]

---

86. Balthasar, *Mysterium Paschale*, 164.

87. Balthasar, *Mysterium Paschale*, 161.

88. *Catechism*, 633. See also the discussion of Christ's descent to the hell of the damned in *Mysterium Paschale*, 176.

89. Balthasar, *Mysterium Paschale*, 171. Balthasar goes so far as to say, strikingly, in *Mysterium Paschale*: "Hell in the New Testament sense is a function of the Christ event" (172).

90. Balthasar, *Mysterium Paschale*, 172.

91. Balthasar, *Mysterium Paschale*, 168.

92. Balthasar, *Mysterium Paschale*, 165.

93. Speyr quoted in Hikota, "Still We Wait," 24, emphasis mine.

Balthasar is not alone in expressing this conception of solidarity in forsakenness as the source of liberation. Moltmann offers a similar idea: "The Father . . . sends his Son through all the abysses and hells of Godforsakenness, of the divine curse and final judgment,"[94] and concludes, in the words of Christopher D. Marshall, that "Jesus' own sufferings exhausted and destroyed the torments of hell."[95] Anglican theologian Fleming Rutledge expresses Christ's forsakenness this way:

> If we say that Jesus Christ descended into hell, perhaps we mean most of all *the hell of the perpetrators*—not just those who are in Sheol because they died, not just those who are in Limbo awaiting the Conqueror, but those who are in Gehenna under a sentence of everlasting condemnation.[96]

The paradox of the descent into hell is that Jesus' conquest of the powers of death and hell comes by being subjected to them, suffering alongside those who suffer, even those who suffer the ultimate imprisonment of damnation in hell.

The implications of this conception of Jesus' solidarity support the practice of abolition both as a current ongoing process of solidarity and an ideal of liberation. Balthasar suggests that the role of Christians is to follow Jesus into this solidarity, in the striking phrase, "being dead with the dead God."[97] Griffith makes the converse point, emphasizing the overtones of rescue in the phrase "visit the prisoner" in Matthew 25:31–46. "The Greek term *opiskeptomai* connotes more than spending time with people. The same term is used most often to refer to the divine activity of redeeming and freeing and caring for people. . . . In Luke 1:68, for example, we read that God 'has visited us and accomplished redemption.'"[98] For Griffith, accompaniment and visitation is intended by the New Testament authors to stand in for liberation: visiting prisoners for companionship misses the point unless this solidarity also leads to their redemption into freedom.

This tension is precisely what I see in the dialectic presented by the descent into hell. Is Jesus' descent one of victorious conquest— but conquest over powers of death and captivity—aimed at ultimate liberation? Or is it one of submission and accompaniment even in the deepest depths? Does accompaniment alone offer a starting point

---

94. Moltmann, *Trinity*, 82.

95. Moltmann, quoted in Marshall, *Beyond Retribution*, 187.

96. Rutledge, *Crucifixion*, 453. Her excellent treatment of the descent into hell in *The Crucifixion* leads her to an (almost) universalist conclusion, based on her understanding that Jesus descends to the place of condemnation of those who are actually guilty of doing the most grievous harm.

97. Balthasar, *Mysterium Paschale*, 181.

98. Griffith, *The Fall of the Prison*, 117.

for liberation, or must it be understood in the framework of broader success in ending incarceration? These questions present a theological framing of an ongoing practical tension in prison ministry and prisoner support. Solidarity and accompaniment can be on their own a form of profound liberation, and all abolitionist work must start with accompaniment of those most marginalized. Because abolition is not only a goal but a process, the practice of solidarity—"being dead with the dead God"[99]—*is* in itself an abolitionist act. But the ongoing process of prisoner solidarity derives its power from the long-range goal or ideal of the abolition of all imprisonment.[100] Meanwhile, for Christians the hope of abolition is in fact the overthrow of all powers of death, including prisons and all carceral structures, and concrete freedom for prisoners accomplished by God.[101]

Riyako Hikota, an interpreter of Balthasar, offers a helpful perspective on this tension:

> We will attempt to deal with the question by connecting the in-betweenness of Holy Saturday [when Christ is in hell] and the in-betweenness of Christian existence, which is located between suffering and victory. What we would like to do in the end is to reflect on the meaning of suffering in Christian life by emphasizing the fundamentally 'in-between' state of the Christian represented by Christ in Hell on Holy Saturday, and thus attempt to affirm the victory that is *hidden but already present* without explaining away the concrete reality of suffering.[102]

This is the reality for all prisoners in this world (and all who suffer under coercive control) and for those who accompany them—they share the state of Christ in hell on Holy Saturday, so while their suffering persists as long as they are imprisoned, God's victory over suffering and imprisonment is "hidden but already present" in the reality of divine solidarity with them. Perhaps this conception of liberation as something "hidden but already present" even within the prison provides a way of thinking about abolition as a project that

---

99. Balthasar, *Mysterium Paschale*, 181.

100. Knopp et al., "Nine Perspectives."

101. This tension of solidarity and hope was driven home to me in my own volunteer work from 2016 to 2020 as a chaplain in the Los Angeles County Jails. While our ministry understands Jesus to be already present in solidarity with those incarcerated in the jails, so that we are not bringing anything to the prisoners but rather exploring the divine comfort and hope already present in and with them, we also rely on the ultimate hope of the liberation of all, which gives us perseverance to accompany those who still wait for their freedom.

102. Hikota, "Still We Wait," 63. Emphasis mine.

transcends the binary between free and unfree. Abolition means working toward an end to prisons and carceral systems, but it also means recognizing, making visible, and nurturing the freedom that is "hidden but already present" within communities even under various forms of coercion and control. In the perspective of abolitionist handbook *Instead of Prisons*, this is expressed as a recognition that "abolitionists are 'allies' of prisoners rather than traditional helpers" and that "abolitionists realize that empowerment of prisoners and ex-prisoners is crucial to prison system change."[103] Building collectively upon the hidden-but-present freedom of those who are incarcerated or under carceral control is the strongest basis for abolitionist praxis. In Christian terms, this collective action can be understood to be founded on divine solidarity with those who suffer any form of bondage.

The symbol of the descent into hell does not offer a picture of salvation only as liberation or freedom from captivity, but also as an entrance into renewed life and reconciliation. The perspective offered by the centrality of the concept of solidarity in the narrative of the descent into hell is that the strongest (or, in fact, only) basis for such reconciliation in "caring communities"[104] is solidarity (in "hell") with those who suffer and are marginalized. One theological implication occurs in dialogue with the claim that those in hell suffer separation from God due to their own rejection of God's love offered to them.[105] Jesus' solidarity, in such a case, means that he is suffering separation from God alongside those who have rejected God. This deconstructs the concept of hell as an experience of separation, as even in the depths of separation God (as Jesus) is nonetheless *present* in solidarity.[106]

In practical terms, the theme of solidarity present in the descent narrative suggests that authentic allyship with those most affected

---

103. Knopp et al., "Nine Perspectives."

104. Knopp et al., "Nine Perspectives."

105. See Balthasar, *Dare We Hope That All Men Be Saved?*, 51-58, 165.

106. Feminist theologians such as Rebecca Ann Parker and Rita Nakashima Brock have criticized theologies that valorize suffering, emphasizing instead the power of "Presence" in healing. See, e.g., Parker and Brock, *Proverbs of Ashes: Violence, Redemptive Suffering, and the Search for What Saves Us* (Boston: Beacon Press, 2015), 110. I am suggesting here not a conception of suffering as redemptive, but instead understanding Jesus' suffering or forsakenness in terms of presence or solidarity with those who suffer. While I do not believe this would address all objections of theologians such as Parker and Brock to my emphasis on Jesus' suffering and god-forsakenness here, I maintain that the idea that solidarity is sometimes (although by no means always!) enacted through fellow-suffering merits continued consideration and exploration. In particular, here the emphasis on Jesus' suffering is a necessary corrective to the domination/conquest themes in traditional portrayals of the descent into hell.

by unjust systems is the starting point not only for the work towards liberation, but also for the work towards reconciliation.[107] What arises from solidarity in suffering is in fact renewed and reconciled life in communities. The growth of new life in Christ, born from Jesus' solidarity with the dead and damned, correlates to the practical continuum of building safer communities, from organizing prisoners within prisons to restorative and transformative justice programs inside and outside carceral spaces. Safety is born from the depths of organizing in solidarity with those communities most impacted by carceral structures just as, in Christian terms, new life is born from solidarity with those suffering under the power of death.

When we recognize Jesus as present in solidarity with all those who suffer oppression, then the collective effort towards liberation and reconciliation—in which all of us, in our varying degrees of bondage, work together to free ourselves and build caring,.non-carceral communities—becomes an alternate image of Jesus' ultimate victory over captivity through his suffering it. Such an image offers an interpretation of the descent narrative that perhaps transcends the troubling particularity of Jesus' role as divine liberator for non-Christians.

CONCLUSIONS: TOWARDS THE SALVATION OF ALL

The descent into hell offers an illustration on a cosmic scale of what abolition can look like. The descent into hell shows a picture of a cosmos and history oriented ultimately toward the liberation of all those in any type of bondage and the destruction of carceral systems. At the same time, an abolitionist analysis of the descent into hell brings the idea of liberating all prisoners into the central mystery of the Christian story. It therefore sits uncomfortably with every traditional attempt to restrict salvation. The descent into hell is a picture of liberation which derives from solidarity. Liberation and reconciliation cannot be withheld from even those in the deepest recesses of hell because God, in Jesus, is already present with them. John Chrysostom writes: "Hell took a body and discovered God."[108] The story of the descent into hell is the story of God's solidarity with the damned, those in "the prison of abandonment, hell."[109] The movements of liberation and solidarity become one and the same, as it is God's very presence among the dead that effects the glorious liberation imagined by the early Christians in their pictures of the "harrowing of hell." If, as C.S.

---

107. This concept/phrasing comes from Knopp, "Nine Perspectives."

108. "St. John Chrysostom's Easter Sermon."

109. Speyr quoted in Hikota, "Still We Wait," 24.

Lewis claims, "the doors of hell are locked on the *inside*,"[110] then Jesus has entered the prison of hell in order to break down those doors from within.

In this essay, I have reinterpreted the descent into hell theologically to support two intertwined conclusions: first, to justify a systematic doctrine of universal salvation, accomplished by Christ through his liberative fellow-suffering with those in hell; and second, to demand political action to abolish prisons and all carceral structures in this world in light of their ultimate, eschatological abolition. To put it personally: I am a universalist because I am an abolitionist, and I am an abolitionist because I am a universalist.

These theological and political claims inform each other. Jesus' liberation of "spirits in prison"[111] and victory over the powers of death (and, per Griffith, captivity) provides a model and ultimate hope for liberation of all people under coercive control and victory against the carceral state in all its forms, while the ongoing project of abolitionist opposition to the prison-industrial complex forces a reading of that victory as something not fully accomplished independent of our participation in the fight. Jesus' solidarity with those in hell forms a basis for a politics based in solidarity, while the abolitionist emphasis on solidarity *requires* a theology of divine self-emptying by which Jesus truly stands alongside the dead in resistance grounded in true solidarity. Jesus' divine presence in and with those who suffer and promise of new life for those in hell illustrates the transformation possible in community justice aimed at reconciliation, while practical efforts toward reconciliation make concrete the promise of new life in community central to Christian doctrinal claims.

I have presented a view of universal salvation above in particularly Christian terms, but the theological and political claims of my reading of the descent into hell have even broader consequences. Through its connection to prison abolition, the descent-into-hell narrative becomes not only a Christian myth but also a demand for universal compassion beyond even the boundaries of Christian belief or identity. Prison abolition makes concrete in the current age the promise of universal liberation. Abolition pushes the Christian promise of universal salvation beyond the realm of theological claims, by making it visible in the realm of the secular in the image of a political commitment to liberation for *all*.

By engaging with the correlated images of theological universalism and prison abolition, I believe we can rediscover the true and liberating heart of the Christian faith, where it coincides with the principles of abolition: no one is beyond the reach of God or of human

---

110. C.S. Lewis, *The Complete C.S. Lewis Signature Classics* (San Francisco: Harper One, 2002), 626.

111. See 1 Peter 3:19.

compassion, and no one should be—or, according to my theological claims, *can* be—banished from the divine community or our own earthly communities. This paradigm shift allows us to proclaim with confidence, in the theological and the political spheres: bondage is broken, and prisoners are set free.

REFERENCES

Abolition Now!: Ten Years of Strategy and Struggle against the Prison Industrial Complex. Edited by CR10 Publications Collective. Oakland, CA: AK Press, 2008.

Agamben, Giorgio. *The Time That Remains: A Commentary on the Letter to the Romans.* Stanford, CA: Stanford University Press, 2005.

Balthasar, Hans Urs von. *Dare We Hope That All Men Be Saved? With a Short Discourse on Hell,* trans. David Kipp and Lothar Krauth. San Francisco: Ignatius Press, 1988.

Balthasar, Hans Urs von. *Mysterium Paschale: The Mystery of Easter,* trans. Aidan Nichols. San Francisco: Ignatius Press, 1990.

Calvin, John. Institutes of the Christian Religion. Accessed 6 October 2022. https://www.ccel.org/ccel/calvin/institutes.iv.xvii.html.

Catechism of the Catholic Church, accessed 18 April 2019, https://www.vatican.va/archive/ENG0015/P1R.HTM.

Capon, Robert Farrar. *Between Noon and Three: Romance, Law, and the Outrage of Grace.* Grand Rapids, MI: Eerdmans, 1997.

Davis, Angela Y. *Are Prisons Obsolete?* New York: Seven Stories Press, 2003.

"From an Ancient Homily for Holy Saturday," accessed 22 April 2019, http://www.vatican.va/spirit/documents/spirit_20010414_omelia-sabato-santo_en.html;

Geest, Paul J.J. van. "Augustine's Certainty in Speaking about Hell and His Reserve in Explaining Christ's Descent into Hell," in *The Apostles' Creed: 'He Descended into Hell,'* ed. Archibald L.H.M van Wieringen and Marcel Sarot. Leiden: Brill, 2018.

Gilliard, Dominique DuBois. *Rethinking Incarceration: Advocating for Justice that Restores.* Downers Grove, IL: InterVarsity Press, 2018.

Gilligan, James. *Violence: Reflections on a National Epidemic.* New York: Vintage, 1996.

Goris, Harm J.M.J. "Thomas Aquinas on Christ's Descent into Hell," in *The Apostles' Creed: 'He Descended into Hell,'* ed. Archibald L.H.M van Wieringen and Marcel Sarot. Leiden: Brill, 2018.

Gottschalk, Marie. *Caught: The Prison State and the Lockdown of American Politics.* Princeton, NJ: Princeton University Press, 2016.

Griffith, Lee. *The Fall of the Prison: Biblical Perspectives on Prison Abolition.* Grand Rapids, MI: Eerdmans, 1993.

Hart, David Bentley. *That All Shall Be Saved: Heaven, Hell, and Universal Salvation*. New Haven: Yale University Press, 2019.

Hawk, Brandon. *Preaching Apocrypha in Anglo-Saxon England*. Toronto: University of Toronto Press, 2018.

Hikota, Riyaku. "And Still We Wait: Hans Urs von Balthasar's Theology of Holy Saturday and its Implications for Christian Suffering and Discipleship." Ph.D. diss., University of Edinburgh, 2015.

Holmes, Stephen Mark. *The Fathers on the Sunday Gospels*. Collegeville, MN: Liturgical Press, 2012.

Hone, William. *Lost Books of the Bible, The*. New York: Testament Books/Random House, 1979.

Knopp, Fay, et al. *Instead of Prisons: A Handbook for Abolitionists*. Syracuse, NY: Prison Research Action Education Project, 1976. https://www.prisonpolicy.org/scans/instead_of_prisons/nine_perspectives.shtml.

Lewis, C.S. *The Complete C.S. Lewis Signature Classics*. San Francisco: Harper One, 2002.

Marshall, Christopher. *Beyond Retribution: A New Testament Vision for Justice, Crime, and Punishment*. Grand Rapids, MI: Eerdmans, 2001.

Milbank, John. *Theology and Social Theory: Beyond Secular Reason*. Malden, MA: Blackwell, 2006.

Moltmann, Jürgen. *The Crucified God*. New York: Harper and Row, 1974.

Moltmann, Jurgen. *The Trinity and the Kingdom: The Doctrine of God*. San Francisco: Harper and Row, 1981.

Myers, Ched and Elaine Enns. *Ambassadors of Reconciliation: New Testament Reflections on Restorative Justice and Peacemaking*. Maryknoll, NY: Orbis Books, 2009.

Parker, Rebecca Ann and Rita Nakashima Brock. *Proverbs of Ashes: Violence, Redemptive Suffering, and the Search for What Saves Us*. Boston: Beacon Press, 2015.

Pfaff, John. *Locked In: The True Causes of Mass Incarceration—and How to Achieve Real Reform*. New York: Basic Books, 2017.

Ritchie, Andrea J. Interview with Sonali Kolhatkar. "An Abolitionist Makes a Case for 'No More Police.'" *Yes Magazine*. 3 October 2022. https://www.yesmagazine.org/social-justice/2022/10/03/police-safety-abolition.

Rouwhorst, Gerard A.M. "The Descent of Christ into the Underworld in Early Christian Liturgy," in *The Apostles' Creed: 'He Descended into Hell,'* ed. Wieringen and Marcel Sarot. Leiden: Brill, 2018.

Rutledge, Fleming. *The Crucifixion: Understanding the Death of Jesus Christ*. Grand Rapids, MI: Eerdmans, 2015.

Sarot, Marcel and Archibald L.H.M van Wieringen, eds. *The Apostles' Creed: 'He Descended into Hell.'* Leiden: Brill, 2018.

"St. John Chrysostom's Easter Sermon," The Easter sermon of John

Chrysostom (circa 400 AD), *Anglicans Online,* accessed 25 March 2020, http://anglicansonline.org/special/Easter/chrysostom_easter.html.

Schenwar, Maya and Victoria Law. *Prison by Any Other Name: The Harmful Consequences of Popular Reforms.* New York: New Press, 2020.

"The Dream of the Rood," trans. Jonathan Glenn, accessed 18 April 2019, https://lightspill.com/poetry/oe/rood.html#text13.

Throness, Laurie. *A Protestant Purgatory: Theological Origins of the Penitentiary Act, 1779.* New York: Routledge, 2016.

Wieringen, Archibald L.H.M. van "Descent into the Netherworld: A Biblical Perspective," in *The Apostles' Creed: 'He Descended into Hell,'* ed. Wieringen and Marcel Sarot. Leiden: Brill, 2018, 9–32.

Zehr, Howard. *Changing Lenses: Restorative Justice for Our Times.* Harrisonburg, VA: Herald Press, 2015.

GOD IS BLACKNESS: MYSTICISM OF THE UNOWNED EARTH

Peter Kline

"Not owning the earth, but walking around gently on it, as it."
—Fred Moten

I

There is a whole genre of so-called "post-metaphysical theology" devoted to the theological deconstruction of "ontotheology," that form of thought that grounds both being as a generic category as well as instances of being (beings) by positing God as the highest and most perfect being. The grounding of beings in God makes the differences among beings "calculable" (to use the Heideggerian / Derridean lingo). Such calculation shows itself most acutely in the table of metaphysical binaries that structure Western metaphysics: male/female, active/passive, spirit/matter, mind/body, light/darkness, oneness/multiplicity, etc. The ontotheological move, or its most common effect, is to establish the priority of the first term of each binary by associating it with the highest being, namely, God. God, accordingly, is coded as masculine, active, spiritual, intellectual, luminous, unified, etc., while all that is not God is coded as feminine, passive, embodied, fleshy, dark, multiple, etc. Usually through various apophatic strategies, post-metaphysical theologies move to deconstruct these binaries by un-thinking God as their ground. Rather than the highest being, God is "beyond being" or "without being." Rather than the most perfect instance of a determinate set of metaphysical differences, God is incalculably withdrawn from all determinate differences as their unfathomable source. Accordingly, or so the theology goes, differences among beings also become incalculable and indeterminate. With the source of beings "considerably prior" (to use Pseudo-Dionysius' language) to any difference among beings, the truth of beings is not representable within any totalizing discourse. The truth of beings is not their enclosure in metaphysical categories but their openness to incalculable mystery, which can be glossed as an openness to openness itself, even though openness can never simply be "itself."

What has tended not to happen in such theologies, however, is the thinking of the deconstruction of ontotheology together with the thought of Blackness, or thinking Blackness as the deconstruction of ontotheology and therefore the possibility of saying "God" against or otherwise than as the grammar of whiteness, which is to say, the ontotheological grammar of sovereignty and ownership. The reasons for this lacuna are multiple, not the least of which is the inability of western thought to register in "blackness" a discourse and practice that interrogates western intellectual production in its most universal ambitions, those of ontology, metaphysics, ethics, and rationality. Blackness is consistently misread and misinterpreted as a parochial matter whose final import is some version of "identity politics." At its best, according to this misreading, Blackness can be given adjunct status relative to the more properly universal concerns of western thought, including western revolutionary thinking. Cedric Robinson directly challenges this misreading in his seminal text, *Black Marxism: The Making of the Black Radical Tradition*,[1] where he argues that the Black Radical Tradition precedes (and therefore exceeds) the traditions of European political radicalism. Black thought and action aims at nothing less than a critique of western civilization itself, including its ontologies and metaphysics. It aims, in other words, at nothing less than a reevaluation of the whole or the universal, which is, of course, also the ambition of theology and philosophy.[2]

Theology and philosophy do not cede their territories easily, however, constructed as they are on what Sylvia Wynter calls "the overrepresentation of Man."[3] Wynter argues that, among all the possible genres of being human and thinking the human, one genre emerges in modernity as "orthodox": the white, bourgeois, propertied, heterosexual, male subject whose condition of possibility is the Black slave or Indigenous "heathen" over and against which proper subjectivity is forged as sovereign. Christianity is deeply implicated in the production and authorization of Man, driven as it by a universal vision of the reconciliation of all peoples and in one God-Man, namely, Jesus Christ. Modernity, for Wynter, names a process whereby the religious figure of the God-Man morphs into a political and then biological figure of normed human subjectivity

---

1. Cedric Robinson, *Black Marxism: The Making of the Black Radical Tradition* (London: University of North Carolina Press, 1983).

2. Key texts within Black Studies that think Blackness and ontology together include Christina Sharpe, *In the Wake: On Blackness and Being* (Durham: Duke University Press, 2016); David Marriott, *Whither Fanon? Studies in the Blackness of Being* (Stanford: Stanford University Press, 2018); Calvin Warren, *Ontological Terror: Blackness, Nihilism, and Emancipation* (Durham: Duke University Press, 2018).

3. Sylvia Wynter, "Unsettling the Coloniality of Being/Power/Truth/Freedom: Towards the Human, After Man, Its Overrepresentation—An Argument," *CR: The New Centennial Review* 3, no. 3 (2003): 257-337.

in relation to which all other subjects are regulated and reproduced along racialized, capitalist logics. Modernity is the story of how God became (white) Man, or, what is the same, the story of how Man emerges as white (a self-possessed, universal, sovereign subject) by becoming God, by recreating the earth in the image of racial capitalism. Any deconstruction of God in the wake of modernity must therefore proceed as a simultaneous deconstruction of Man. What Wynter's analysis highlights is the centrality of race in any such deconstruction. Modernity is synonymous with the emergence of the racialized subject, not simply an unmarked rational subject.[4] Christian theological deconstructions of ontotheology, or of modernity, to the extent that they do not engage this emergence and the material violence that accompanies it, work more to reproduce modernity than to deconstruct it. "Postmodern theology," largely a white discourse, is a site of such reproduction.[5]

One notable exception to the trend within post-metaphysical theologies of ignoring Blackness (that nevertheless proves the rule) is Andrew Prevot's *Thinking Prayer: Theology and Spirituality Amid the Crises of Modernity*.[6] Prevot mobilizes prayer, that "amorous inclination" toward and "volatile interaction"[7] with the freedom of God, against the self-possessed/possessive selfhood of the modern subject. He thinks together "the troubled fate of Western metaphysics" with "various local and global structures of socioeconomic and identity-based violence."[8] Prayer represents and promises a series of "integrated goods"[9] (existential, social, political, aesthetic) that wait to be recovered within and against modernity's reduction of the self to an individuated, calculable object. Prevot dedicates his book "to the millions who have died in slavery,"[10] and it climaxes with a reading of James Cone's reading of slave spirituals/spirituality. Against the overwhelming tendency of academic theologians to regard Black theology and other liberation theologies as nothing more

---

4. In *Race: A Theological Account* (Oxford: Oxford University Press, 2008) J. Kameron Carter demonstrates how the Kantian rational subject—which is the theological subject of modernity—establishes itself as such by marking its inferior others through the category of race.

5. In *A Theology of Failure: Žižek Against Christian Innocence* (New York: Fordham University Press, 2019), Marika Rose helpfully diagnoses "postmodern theology" as an effect of transformations within the modern order of things rather than a break or departure from it. Postmodern theological discourse, emphasizing as it does, fluidity, relationality, and incompletion is possible by virtue of "the relational, processual functioning of empire under late capitalism" (54).

6. Andrew Prevot, *Thinking Prayer: Theology and Spirituality Amid the Crises of Modernity* (Notre Dame: University of Notre Dame Press, 2015).

7. Prevot, *Thinking Prayer*, 2.

8. Prevot, *Thinking Prayer*, 5.

9. Prevot, *Thinking Prayer*, 5.

10. Prevot, *Thinking Prayer*, v.

than "contextual" addendums to a more basic and universal theological tradition, Prevot insists that "Cone helps us to rediscover. . . the meaning of prayer itself and. . . the postmetaphysical and counterviolent form of doxological spirituality that is desperately needed in modernity."[11] Resisting the move to integrate Black theology into non-Black theological discourse, Prevot proposes to make the Black spiritual/theological tradition the "enabling context"[12] of any theological response to modernity: "Christian doxology cannot presently do justice *to itself* unless it becomes *explicitly* informed by the prayerful songs of black people and, thereby, directly contravenes the idolatrous racism of modernity."[13] "Christian doxological spirituality has the potential to become more, and not less, authentically universal by allowing itself to become black."[14] Regarding those post-metaphysical thinkers who otherwise helpfully deconstruct ontotheology, "insofar as they pay very little, if any, attention to the harsh realities of racism and the prayers of black humanity, they effectively permit the antiblack ethos of the modern West to go unchallenged."[15] Prevot goes on to articulate the heart of Cone's theology—encapsulated in the imperative "*become black with God!*"[16]—as a movement of abolition: "to 'become black' means nothing other than to enter into the spirituality of oppressed black people. . . and—as a matter of sheer consistency—to abolish every form of 'white' domination."[17] The Blackness of God is the abolition of whiteness.

Ultimately, however, and here is where the central concern of this essay opens itself, Prevot's post-metaphysical doxological Black theology relies on a *phenomenology* of Blackness. Specifically, it is the slave spirituals that provide Prevot with the positive content of a doxological phenomenology. The phenomena of slave spirituals and their performative, prayerful repetition is the possibility of a Black postmetaphysical theology. Prevot follows here the general drift of twentieth century Catholic phenomenology that moves analogically from aesthetic/liturgical phenomena toward the transcendence of God, or that reads aesthetic/liturgical phenomena as transcendent movement. Accordingly, he reads Cone ultimately in the direction of Catholic Hans Urs Von Balthasar rather than Protestant Karl Barth.[18] Analogy, rather than dialectic, is the logic of Blackness. "God is black"

---

11. Prevot, *Thinking Prayer*, 282.

12. Prevot, *Thinking Prayer*, 282.

13. Prevot, *Thinking Prayer*, 284.

14. Prevot, *Thinking Prayer*, 287.

15. Prevot, *Thinking Prayer*, 283.

16. Prevot, *Thinking Prayer*, 321.

17. Prevot, *Thinking Prayer*, 321.

18. Prevot, *Thinking Prayer*, 296.

indexes an aesthetic phenomenon analogically rooted in and open to the "ever greater"[19] transcendence of God.

Prevot's apophaticism is therefore not the "generalized practice of negation" of "agnostically oriented thinkers."[20] Its apophatics have a definite form, one given in the "aesthetically and discursively textured revelation that takes place in Jesus' life, death, and resurrection."[21] It is a phenomenological apophatics grounded in the "coming-to-presence" of divine revelation in the "sensoriality and linguisticality of human existence."[22] "God comes to meet us through these inescapable existentials, which are therefore not merely givens of worldly being but channels of divine excess that simultaneously disclose and hide a truly divine gift and divine giver."[23] Prayer is the performative response to this coming-to-presence "amid the gruesome history of this world" and "the pain of concrete existence."[24] It is therefore "thinkable not only as doxology but also as apophatic, lamentatious, and petitionary."[25] "There can be no authentic prayer without the trembling silence, the terrifying scream, or the uncanny blending of the two which tears at the fabric of covenantal trust but also perhaps proves its immeasurable endurance."[26]

My interest in this essay, inspired by Prevot, but also moving along a different path, is to ask what it might mean to think theologically from Blackness, which is to say, from the thought of abolition. Any theology forged from the thought of Blackness will be post-metaphysical insofar as slavery is not simply a political or economic institution but an entire onto-theo-metaphysic, one that divinizes sovereignty and ownership. The slave-owning free man—Wynter's "Man"— could be said to bear all those ontological distinctives whose perfect instantiation is the ontotheological God, above all, freedom and self-possession, freedom as self-possession. The abolition of slavery and its afterlives (the multiple ways in which Black bodies continue to be spatialized and temporalized for premature death) therefore calls for the abolition of the ontotheological God and the subject whose perfection he is. This need not simply amount to a denial or repression of God, but may lead, more profoundly, to an unowning of God, inseparable from an unowning of the earth.

Unlike Prevot's Catholic phenomenology of Blackness with its doxological apophatics, this essay approaches Blackness by way of

---

19. Prevot, *Thinking Prayer*, 296.

20. Prevot, *Thinking Prayer*, 331.

21. Prevot, *Thinking Prayer*, 330.

22. Prevot, *Thinking Prayer*, 330.

23. Prevot, *Thinking Prayer*, 330.

24. Prevot, *Thinking Prayer*, 331.

25. Prevot, *Thinking Prayer*, 332.

26. Prevot, *Thinking Prayer*, 331.

Fred Moten's category of "nonperformance," which names a passive-active refusal of subjectivity and consent to the sociality of "flesh." Prevot's theology is grounded on the performance of prayer as the possibility of authentic subjectivity, which makes Blackness legible as access to the coming-to-presence of divine revelation. In contrast, Moten denies that Blackness is phenomenologically legible: "blackness is not a category for ontology or for phenomenological analysis."[27] Blackness "defies narration and phenomenological description."[28] Blackness "will have existed, as it were, only in the absence of the story, as resistance to or abstention from narration."[29] "We have no access."[30] A different sort of apophatics opens itself here, one that affirms not a self-exceeding fulfillment of subjectivity by way of its analogical grounding in transcendence, but rather the annihilation, or abolition, of subjectivity, undergone through a "consent not to be one,"[31] that is, consent not to be a properly individuated subject. Insofar as phenomenology relies on transcendental subjectivity as the site of revelation or coming-to-presence, it cannot, for Moten, escape the confines of individuation and therefore remains within the terms of sovereign calculation: "individuation is the regulation of social life."[32] What the practice of abolition calls for, then, is a "mysticism in the flesh,"[33] an unowning of individuation and subjection and a consent to the flesh of the earth.

To think the abolition or unowning of God from Moten's fleshy mysticism might mean pressing further into James Cone's liberationist affirmation, "God is black," toward a more decolonial-abolitionist affirmation, "God is blackness." The shift from "Black" to "Blackness" would seek to disturb what Delores Williams calls the "androcentric bias" in Black liberation theology that centers "Black experience"[34] and its focus on the masculine subject. Williams prefers "wilderness experience,"[35] which is less about a liberated subject and more about collective, social survival under conditions of duress. The shift also seeks to apply theologically what Moten calls "the paraontological

27. Fred Moten, "Blackness and Nothingness (Mysticism in the Flesh)," *The South Atlantic Quarterly* 112:4 (Fall 2013): 756.

28. Fred Moten, *Stolen Life (consent not to be a single being)* (Durham: Duke University Press, 2018), 246.

29. Moten, *Stolen Life*, 251.

30. Moten, *Stolen Life*, 251.

31. Moten, *Stolen Life*, 242.

32. Moten, *Stolen Life*, 255.

33. Moten, "Blackness and Nothingness (Mysticism in the Flesh)."

34. Delores Williams, *Sisters in the Wilderness: The Challenge of Womanist God-Talk* (New York: Orbis Book, 2013), 141.

35. Williams, *Sisters in the Wilderness*, 141.

distinction between blackness and black people."[36] This distinction functions not primarily as an opening of the claim to Blackness, although it is—"Everyone whom blackness claims, which is to say everyone, can claim blackness"[37]—but as a way of "detach[ing] blackness from the question of (the meaning of) being."[38] Blackness precedes (and therefore exceeds) any ontological mapping or calculation. It disturbs from within every administration of the world. What then would it be to say that blackness precedes (and therefore exceeds) any *theological* mapping or calculation? What would it mean for theology to acknowledge the precedence and priority of Blackness as prior to the *logos* of any possible *theos*? Perhaps it means that theology, against its historical performance of policing the earth, might be given to think, even celebrate, the abolition of whiteness as the unowning of the earth. That is the possibility this essay seeks to open.

II

Moten develops the idea of nonperformance in his essay "Erotics of Fugitivity," which offers a meditation on "Betty's Case." In 1857, Betty, a slave woman from Tennessee, was granted legal freedom by the Supreme Court of Massachusetts. Her legal freedom included her recognition as "a contractual agent with free will"[39] capable of entering into labor contracts. However, immediately upon being granted her freedom, Betty returned to Tennessee and remained with her owners and her family, opting for her sociality in the south rather than her freedom in the north. Her return constitutes a nonperformance of her status as a contractual agent, not because she fails to fulfill an obligation, but because her return exceeds what any contract could anticipate as a performance of freedom. Betty exposes freedom to an "irreducible futurity"[40] not legible or calculable within the law's horizon. "Judges and legislators cannot and will not understand her."[41]

Moten takes Betty's nonperformance of her lawful freedom as an occasion to think of Blackness as the "refusal of normative individuation,"[42] or consent not to be one. Rather than enact or own or display her freedom, Betty disappears into "fugitivity," which is a state of

---

36. Moten, *Stolen Life*, 241.
37. Moten, *Stolen Life*, 159.
38. Moten, "Blackness and Nothingness (Mysticism in the Flesh)," 750.
39. Moten, *Stolen Life*, 246.
40. Moten, *Stolen Life*, 259.
41. Moten, *Stolen Life*, 252.
42. Moten, *Stolen Life*, 266.

"constant escape"[43] *within* the hold of slavery. "Betty submits belonging to a nonperformance that neither exercises self-possessive freedom nor confirms being possessed. In returning, she refuses to perform the terms of the contract she had been forced to enter."[44] "The social life that now we know as Betty is neither slave nor free but fugitive."[45] Such fugitivity is "way over the edge of any kind of knowledge of freedom."[46] It is a "refusal of the solo"[47] and consent to "social entanglement"[48] that renders her incalculable within the metrics of freedom. "The absolute agony of her passion" is "an unspeakble, unrecitable vacation of decision and its metaphysics."[49] Refusing the "arena of competing solo performances" that is the "antisocial sociality"[50] of freedom, Betty's nonperformance occurs not within the possibilities available to a subject but as their "exhaust(ion)."[51]

As exhaust(ion), Betty's nonperformance is not an act of an authentic, self-determining subject. We must be careful "not to misread these disavowals of individual freedom as some transcendent achievement/enactment of absolute freedom but rather to read them as refusal of any such transcendence or abstraction or formalism in the interest of immanence, materiality, and what might be called a certain (il)legal (sur)realism."[52] Betty's fugitivity is surreal because it is unaccountable and unfathomable, even "obscene,"[53] in the terms of a world that cannot think or desire anything but ownership and self-determination. Betty will not take upon herself the freedom to own (herself), to be a self by way of a denial of her entanglement, her flesh. Betty refuses to be "chained to a war for freedom, chained to the war of freedom, to the prosecution of freedom as war, to the necessity, in freedom, that freedom imposes, of the breaking of affective bonds, the disavowal in entanglement, of entanglement."[54] She anticipates a "futurial sociality"[55] not built on the metaphysics of individuals and their contractual relationality. "This is what it is to unown, which is underived from normative agency, which moves neither as act nor enactment, which is consent to entanglement's habitation in

43. Moten, *Stolen Life*, 158.

44. Moten, *Stolen Life*, 264.

45. Moten, *Stolen Life*, 263.

46. Moten, *Stolen Life*, 263.

47. Moten, *Stolen Life*, 252.

48. Moten, *Stolen Life*, 255.

49. Moten, *Stolen Life*, 264.

50. Moten, *Stolen Life*, 255.

51. Moten, *Stolen Life*, 264.

52. Moten, *Stolen Life*, 251.

53. Moten, *Stolen Life*, 247.

54. Moten, *Stolen Life*, 251.

55. Moten, *Stolen Life*, 250.

relationality's void. Consent [not to be one] bespeaks a noncontractual nonrelationality that is underived from individuation."[56]

"[Betty] refuses the individuation that is refused her and claims the monstrosity of obscene social life that is imposed upon/ascribed to her. Tongue-tied, her silence softly speaks anaperformative, degenerative, and regenerative density, in deviance both from and within the grammar and diction of the administered world."[57] This passage follows a general formulation of Blackness around which much of Moten's work circles: "to refuse what is normatively desired and to claim what is normatively disavowed."[58] The double gesture of refusal/claiming constitutes the "essential fugitivity"[59] of Blackness as nonperformance. We are not permitted thereby, however, to claim knowledge of the essence of Blackness, for the structure of refusing the normative and claiming the normatively disavowed means that "blackness has always emerged as nothing other than the richest possible combination of dispersion and permeability in and as the mass improvisation and protection of the very idea of the human."[60] As irreducible improvisation, Blackness is the "kenotic abandon"[61] of a social life with no standpoint or standing.[62] Blackness is "a place out of which emerges neither self-consciousness nor knowledge of the other but an improvisation that proceeds from somewhere on the other side of an unasked question."[63] To claim Blackness is "to live among one's own in dispossession, to live among ones who cannot own, the ones who have nothing and who, in having nothing, have everything. To live, in other words, within the general commonness and openness of *a life* in Deleuze's sense."[64] "What if blackness is the name that has been given to the social field and social life of an illicit alternative capacity to desire? Basically, that is precisely what I think blackness is. I want it to be my constant study. I listen for it everywhere."[65]

All of this is a way of getting at what Moten means by distinguishing Blackness as "absolute nothingness" from Blackness as "relative nothingness." Blackness as relative nothingness measures Blackness opposite the normatively human. As Frank Wilderson

56. Moten, *Stolen Life*, 261.

57. Moten, *Stolen Life*, 252.

58. Moten, *Stolen Life*, 243.

59. Moten, *Stolen Life*, 35.

60. Moten, *Stolen Life*, 159.

61. Moten, "Blackness and Nothingness (Mysticism in the Flesh)," 754.

62. Moten, "Blackness and Nothingness (Mysticism in the Flesh)," 738.

63. Moten, "Blackness and Nothingness (Mysticism in the Flesh)," 756.

64. Moten, "Blackness and Nothingness (Mysticism in the Flesh)," 765.

65. Moten, "Blackness and Nothingness (Mysticism in the Flesh)," 778.

puts it, "a Black [is] the very antithesis of a Human subject."[66] Calvin Warren elaborates: "Blackness cannot lay claim to the capacities that constitute human subjectivity in the world because blackness is a commodity in corporeal form; it is the devastating inverse of onto-logical narcissism—we might call black being 'ontological depriva-tion' in an anti-black world."[67] For Moten, by contrast, Blackness sits not opposite the normatively human in the relative nothingness of ontological deprivation. Blackness moves apposite the normatively human in the *absolute* nothingness of "the unmapped and unmap-pable immanence of undercommon sociality."[68] Such apposition, or placelessness ("blackness is the place that has no place"[69]), situates Blackness "prior to ontology,"[70] that is, prior to the forces—social, political, psychological, historical—that determine who "is" relative to who "is not." Blackness "is ontologically prior to the logistics and regulative power that is supposed to have brought it into existence."[71] In other words, Blackness is not a product of the forces that position Black people outside the category of "the human." Blackness precedes anti-Blackness, even if "blackness will have never been thought when detached from anti-blackness."[72] Anti-Blackness, which is to say, sov-ereignty and its regulatory tactics, is only ever a reactionary attempt to capture or usurp the unregulated priority of Blackness/nothingness. Blackness as absolute nothingness "is present at its own making"[73] as the deviance of fugitive unmaking/unowning. It is therefore not "a property that belongs to blacks,"[74] even though "all the people who are called black are given in and to that presence, which exceeds them."[75]

The priority of Blackness, its "insistent previousness,"[76] is not chronological or historical but "paraontological," which is to say that it names an irreducible or a priori fugitivity that de/struct(ure)s exis-tence. Like Derrida's *différance*, that "non-full, non-simple, structured and differentiating origin of differences,"[77] Blackness is the impossi-

---

66. Frank B. Wilderson, *Red, White, and Black: Cinema and the Structure of U.S. Antagonisms* (Durham: Duke University Press, 2010), 9.

67. Calvin Warren, "Black Mysticism: Fred Moten's Phenomenology of (Black) Spirit," *Zeitschrift für Anglistik und Amerikanistik* 65:2 (June 2017): 223.

68. Moten, "Blackness and Nothingness (Mysticism in the Flesh)," 752.

69. Moten, "Blackness and Nothingness (Mysticism in the Flesh)," 751.

70. Moten, "Blackness and Nothingness (Mysticism in the Flesh)," 739.

71. Moten, "Blackness and Nothingness (Mysticism in the Flesh)," 739.

72. Fred Moten, *Black and Blur (consent not to be a single being)* (Durham: Duke University Press, 2018), viii.

73. Fred Moten, *Stolen Life*, 159.

74. Moten, "Blackness and Nothingness (Mysticism in the Flesh)," 750.

75. Moten, *Stolen Life*, 159.

76. Moten, *Stolen Life*, 245.

77. Moten, *Stolen Life*, 35.

bility of the one, of the singular, isolated, which is to say sovereign, instance. Nothingness, absolute no-thing-ness, is this impossibility. Blackness is nothingness because Blackness voids the means and metrics of sovereign calculation. It a/voids individuation by consenting to its impossibility. "What we're after is a move from the metaphysics of presence, given in the figure of the one, to the physics of presence, given in the transubstantial no-thing-ness, in consent not to be (single), in differential inseparability."[78] Differential inseparability, or "difference without separation"[79] names the irreducible sociality of existence that goes all the way down, even (or perhaps especially) to the quantum level. It names the material, fleshly, undercommon blur that paraontologically precedes, and so torments from within, all claims to be (single). The very assumption of a body, of a bounded individual self, proceeds as an attempted but always impossible subjection of the flesh's differential inseparability, its no-thing-ness. "The experience of subjectivity is the would-be subject's thwarted desire for subjectivity, which we must keep on learning not to want, which we have to keep on practicing not wanting, as if in endless preparation for a recital that, insofar as it never comes, is always surreally present."[80] Blackness only ever arrives as the unowned incompletion of existence, which is to say that it never arrives, or that it is never live. "It goes way back, long before the violent norm, as an impure informality to come."[81]

A word for this ancient, impure informality is "earth," which paraontologically precedes "world" as the precedence of "flesh" to "body." Earth is the sociality of flesh "in its paraontological totality."[82] It "moves against the world . . . [Its] procession is not on the world's calendar . . . It is not in the world's teleology."[83] If whiteness is the violent performance of owning that constitutes the world as body(politic) by way of "the subject's long, developmental nightmare,"[84] culminating in "the modern world as socioecological disaster,"[85] Blackness is the (non)performance or refusal of subjectivity that is "tantamount to the preservation of Earth."[86] Such preservation of "the earthen informality of life"[87] is not about a romantic veneration of "nature"

---

78. Moten, *Stolen Life*, 224.

79. Moten, *Stolen Life*, 244.

80. Moten, *Stolen Life*, 244.

81. Moten, *Stolen Life*, 241.

82. Moten, *Stolen Life*, 243.

83. Stefano Harney and Fred Moten, "Base Faith," *e-flux* 86 (November 2017). https://www.e-flux.com/journal/86/162888/base-faith/

84. Moten, *Stolen Life*, 243.

85. Moten, *Stolen Life*, 243.

86. Moten, *Stolen Life*, 243.

87. Harney and Moten, "Base Faith."

but about "flesh in its irreducible entanglement with (the matter of) earth," which moves against "the separability, the self-imposed loneliness-in-sovereignty, of the concept and its representations (as embodiment or individuation or subject or self or nation or state)":

> It's not about a return to some preconceptual authenticity so much as matter's constant aeration, its constant turning over, its exhaustion and exhaustive sounding, its ascentual and essentially and existentially sensual descent. . . . The earth is on the move. You can't join from the outside. You come up from under, and you fall back into its surf. This is the base without foundation, its dusty, watery disorchestration on the march, bent, on the run. Down where it's greeny, where it's salty, the earth moves against the world under the undercover of blackness. . . [88]

What is given to be thought, then, or given consent, is a (non)phenomenon "which passeth (the) understanding,"[89] namely, "a presence that is more + less than here and now. . . . A presence of flesh rather than a presence of the body."[90] Such mystical consent is given in the movement "from body to flesh, from world to earth. . . where a way is made out of no way into nothing."[91]

III

If traditions of apophatic and post-metaphysical theology (un)locate God as an excess beyond or without or prior to being, it is tempting to view negative theology as kind of ready-made framework for giving Blackness theological status and meaning. If Blackness names a fugitive escape from the confines of being, isn't the nothingness of apophatic divinity waiting for it in the darkness? Hasn't theology anticipated the no-thing-ness of Blackness? Doesn't Moten's use of the word "mysticism," as well as a host of other theological language, call upon spiritual and theological traditions of unsaying and unknowing to give Blackness its sense? Wouldn't we then need to say that *theology*, at least historically, but maybe even logically, precedes Blackness, and not the other way around? And wouldn't the implication be that Blackness ought to look for its fulfillment or its legitimation, or at least its precedent, in some version of negative theology?

Of course, not all negative theologies are the same. The question

---

88. Harney and Moten, "Base Faith."

89. Moten, "Blackness and Nothingness (Mysticism in the Flesh)," 752.

90. Moten, *Stolen Life*, 244.

91. Moten, *Stolen Life*, 245.

is how one puts the tradition of negative theology to work, or indeed, whether one regards it as a tradition at all. Catholic and Anglo-Catholic post-metaphysical theologies and philosophies, those of Jean-Luc Marion and John Milbank, for instance, tend to position apophasis as adjunct to ecclesial tradition and its institutions. For both Marion and Milbank, apophatic unsaying and unknowing enacts a deferral to the absolute transcendence and authority of the divine Word, whose authorized representatives reside in the church as overseers of the eucharist, that sacrament where the divine Word becomes flesh for the world as the sociality of the church. In *God Without Being*, Marion writes the following: "if finally only the [eucharistic] celebrant receives authority to go beyond the words up to the Word, because he alone finds himself invested by the *persona Christi*, then one must conclude that only the bishop merits, in the full sense, the title of theologian."[92] Only the male bishop, finally, can unsay and unknow properly, because only he can authorize the eucharist, that site where the faithful are brought beyond mere human words up to the divine Word. The political implication is that the church is sovereign over the earth because only in the church is there a proper deferral to divine authority: "All is given to the Church (space: the nations; time: the days) so that the Church may return it (keep the commandments) to the Word, because he already received all (exousia [authority]) from the Father."[93] Apophasis, going "beyond the words up to the Word," functions here to legitimize the gatekeeping authority of the bishop, who alone has access to divine mystery. Anthony Paul Smith calls it "weaponized apophaticism."[94]

It should be obvious that this sort of post-metaphysical ecclesio-centric theology is not exactly hospitable to Blackness, let alone able to think with or from it. If "blackness is the refusal to defer to. . . sovereignty,"[95] then any theology, no matter how negative, that amounts to a sovereign claim to know who or what gives proper(tied) access to divine mystery must, in the name of Blackness, be refused. Considering the possibility of Black queer theology, Amaryah Shaye Armstrong warns against the assumption "that it is a settled matter that the theological is adequate to name what is witnessed to in the queerness of black social worlds."[96] Any theology attuned to Blackness must refuse "the presumption that it could exhaust the joys of black

92. Jean-Luc Marion, *God without Being: Hors-Texte*. Trans. Thomas A. Carlson (Chicago: University of Chicago Press, 1991), 153.

93. Marion, *God Without Being*, 158.

94. Anthony Paul Smith, "Against Tradition to Liberate Tradition: weaponized apophaticism and gnostic refusal," *Angelika: Journal of the Theoretical Humanities* 19:2 (Sept 2014).

95. Moten, "Blackness and Nothingness (Mysticism in the Flesh)," 751.

96. Amaryah Shaye Armstrong, "Thinking Practice: Method, Pedagogy, Power and the Question of a Black Queer Theology," *Modern Believing* 60:1 (2019): 7.

life or satisfy the justice demanded by black death."[97] At its best, theology could only be "a witness and a failure."[98] Perhaps I might extend the thought here and say that "the theological" is also not adequate to *unname* the joys of Black life and the justice demanded by Black death. Theology, at times ready to admit its linguistic failure to capture God in words and concepts, is much less ready to admit that it cannot name, tame, save, and purify creaturely life. One name for this presumption is settler colonialism. Mark Jordan notes that Christian theology "long ago professed apophasis, but mostly relished imperial adventures"[99]—to which I want to add that it relished imperial adventures in part *by way of* apophasis, by claiming access to the proper paths of unknowing on which souls are saved and purified for God. Too quickly assimilating the unspeakability of Blackness, what Moten calls its "unspeakable, unrecitable vacation of decision and its metaphysics,"[100] which "description and narration cannot comprehend,"[101] to the unspeakability of God is to perform again the colonizing gesture. It is to fail to register how Blackness exceeds and disrupts both the naming and unnaming strategies of theological discourse.

But perhaps this is simply a problem internal to those more conservative post-metaphysical theologies that could be gathered under the name "Radical Orthodoxy." Perhaps an approach more hospitable to Blackness could be found in leftist deconstructions of Christianity. For instance, Moten's affirmation of Blackness as the no-thing-ness of flesh's unregulated sociality finds echoes in Jean-Luc Nancy's "deconstruction of Christianity." Nancy's deconstructive traversal of the Christian tradition finds "a resource—hidden beneath Christianity, beneath monotheism, and beneath the West, which . . . would open a future for the world that would no longer be either Christian or anti-Christian, either monotheist or atheist or even polytheist, but that would advance precisely beyond all these categories (after having made all of them possible.)"[102] The resource that Nancy identifies and then builds his whole philosophy around is *the very sense of*

---

97. Armstrong, "Thinking Practice," 7.

98. Armstrong, "Thinking Practice," 7. For a sustained meditation on what it might mean for thought and language to become adequate to black queer lives, see Saidiya Hartman, *Wayward Lives, Beautiful Experiments: Intimate Histories of Social Upheaval* (New York: Norton & Company, 2019). Becoming adequate would mean, "To love what is not loved. To be lost the world" (227).

99. Mark D. Jordan, "Writing-Terrors: A Dialectical Lyric," *Modern Theology* 30:3 (July 2014): 89.

100. Moten, *Stolen Life*, 264.

101. Moten, *Stolen Life*, 246.

102. Jean-Luc Nancy, *Dis-Enclosure: The Deconstruction of Christianity*, trans. Bettina Bergo, Gabriel Malenfant and Michael B. Smith (New York: Fordham University Press, 2008), 34.

being-with,"[103] which finds its most explicit theological articulation in the Christian affirmation of "God-with-us." To think God as incarnate withness is, for Nancy, a way of affirming existence as irreducibly social or shared. The essence of existence is that we are with each other because God is with us; and God is with us because the essence of God is being-with, or what theologians call the trinity. Mary-Jane Rubenstein elaborates the deconstructive trajectory of this thinking:

> Yet what kind of an essence is "with"? How is one to make any sort of substance out of a preposition? This, for Nancy, is precisely the point. Insofar as existence is essentially shared, it is *essentially inessential*: no thing is simply itself because being is not simply itself. Being is *shared (partage)*, which is to say both common and fragmented, shared and shared out, preventing beings from being themselves in the very gesture of making them. . . . The perhaps troubling implication of withness . . . is that it does not provide the ontological sturdiness some might want from it. If it is genuinely the case that sharing grounds Christian being, then sharing also ungrounds it from the outset, rendering each of its boundaries exposed to a *constitutive* outside. Sharing shares out that which it holds in common. Hence the deconstruction of Christianity, hence the dis-enclosure of all of the West's old conceptual bulwarks. The task of sharing, then, is neither to install new bulwarks nor to resurrect old ones, but rather, to participate in their undoing. To risk a tautology, to share would mean living into sharing, exposing oneself to exposure.[104]

The resonances here with Moten's "consent not to be one" are many, not least the affirmation that existence is essentially nothing, essentially inessential, because it is essentially shared. The materiality of this sharing is central for both, Nancy calling it "body" while Moten calling it "flesh." Both "body" and "flesh" come prior to their regulation by metaphysical or political regimes and are therefore the possibility and site of their deconstruction. For Nancy, as for Moten, existence as entanglement or sharing necessitates thinking elsewhere than from the position of the individualized "I" who would face the world, itself, and its others from the position of sovereign isolation. There is only ever a "mutual intrication or enveloping, such that 'I' am not 'in' the world, but rather *I am the world* and the world is me, just as it is you and us, the wolf and the lamb, nitrogen, iron,

---

103. Jean-Luc Nancy, "Church, State, Resistance," in *Political Theologies: Public Religions in a Post-Secular World*, ed. Hent de Vries and Lawrence E. Sullivan (New York: Fordham University Press, 2006), 112.

104. Mary-Jane Rubenstein, "Capital Shares," *Political Theology* 11:1 (January 2010): 115-6.

optical fibers, black holes, lichen, fantastical imagery, thought, and the thrust of 'things' themselves."[105] Each thing in existence, from human beings to quantum particles to oceans, "creates a gap from itself, not a distance that could defer its final advent, but rather a prox- imity whose open chink puts it into contact with the totality of beings and thus with the infinite of the opening that shares them all and reunites them all."[106] The infinite opening of existence that shares all with all and unites all with all is what is meant by "God."

While there is undeniable resonance here with Moten's own deconstruction of individual subjectivity, there yet remains a signif- icant, perhaps even qualitative, difference between Nancy's "body" and Moten's "flesh." Simply put, Moten thinks "flesh" from/as the underside of history, as its undercommon refusal and disturbance, whereas Nancy thinks "body" as the deconstructive fulfillment-with- out-fulfillment of European history, philosophy, theology, poli- tics, and aesthetics. Acknowledging the deconstructive potential of Judaism and Islam, Nancy ultimately privileges Christianity (and with it, Europe), as the site from which a sense of the world as irre- ducibly shared emerges. Nancy wants to open thought to a world beyond Christianity, but because *the* path to this beyond is the path of Christianity's self-deconstruction and dissemination as "being-with," it does not actually de-center European Christianity as the privileged site of the history of being. Nancy's philosophy reads not as a refusal of but as the deconstructive culmination of "the subject's long devel- opmental nightmare." It cannot therefore give witness to the night- marish quality of the subject's developmental history—it cannot think Blackness—because it positions itself too squarely within this history, even as it wishes to deconstruct it. By contrast, Blackness as flesh, or as nonperformance, occurs on a "lower frequency"[107] than the theo- logical-philosophical history that Nancy traces. To think Blackness is to give thought over to what both Nahum Chandler and Jared Sexton call "the figure of the unsovereign"[108] whose flesh holds the promise not so much of the deconstruction of the subject but rather its abo- lition: "To have been touched by the flesh, then, is the path to the abolition of Man: this is part of the lesson of our world."[109] When Betty returned to Tennessee, she was following the path of her flesh. Rather than submit to the law of freedom, the law of Man, or even to

---

105. Jean-Luc Nancy, *Adoration: The Deconstruction of Christianity II*, trans. John McKeane (New York: Fordham University Press, 2013), 69.

106. Nancy, *Adoration*, 70.

107. Moten, *Stolen Life*, 246.

108. Nahum Chandler, *X–The Problem of the Negro as a Problem for Thought* (New York: Fordham University Press, 2014), 163; Jared Sexton, "The Vel of Slavery: Tracking the Figure of the Unsovereign," *Critical Sociology* 42 (December 2014).

109. Alexander G. Weheliye, *Habeas Viscus: Racializing Assemblages, Biopolitics, and Black Feminist Theories of the Human* (Durham: Duke University Press, 2014), 138.

its deconstruction, Betty abolishes the law through her underground nonperformance. "It's not that she didn't return to a brutal lifeworld; it's that in so doing she turned to something else so that we might keep turning into something else."[110] Such "exorbitance," as Chandler would call it, or the fugitivity of Blackness, as Moten would call it, remains in Nancy, as in the whole western theological-philosophical tradition, unthought.

What I am trying to get at here is that neither ecclesial apophaticism nor philosophical deconstructions of Christianity are able to stay with or think from Blackness, because both, in their own ways, remain invested in forms of sovereign thinking. This is the case, I submit, even in those post-metaphysical theologies and philosophies that declare themselves "weak," those of John Caputo and Gianni Vattimo, for instance. To affirm the weakness or deconstructability of metaphysical categories is not yet to give up the position of sovereign thought, even though one declares it a failure. To think from *no position at all*, without investment in protecting the proper form or purity of any discourse, whether theology or philosophy, is what Blackness calls for. In other words, it calls for the thought of nonnormative flesh, flesh as nonnormative.

Ashon Crawley notes how even in those theologies that arise from communities and experiences of marginalization and oppression, theology emerges "as a pure category, as a purely distinct mode of thought."[111] He writes: "We can perhaps ask how theologies *black*, theologies *womanist*, theologies *mujerista*, theologies *liberation*, do the work of reifying the seeming import of theology as categorical. How is it the production of theology ends up being a mode of respectability, constricting [the radical potentiality of the object of study] to the strictures of an abstracted, delimited zone and field of inquiry?"[112] Considering Kelly Brown Douglas's book, *Black Bodies and the Black Church: A Blues Slant*, as an example, Crawley notes how the materiality or fleshiness of blues, its sound and vibration, ends up being muted through its submission to theology as a modality of thought:

> Does not the blues in all its varied enfleshed manifestations Douglas describes—blues bodies, blues hopes, blues bonds, blues song, as examples—act as an antagonism not merely to the black church's resistance to blues, to secularity, but to the very conceptual domain, zone, field of categorical distinction called theology? . . . Douglas submits the wildness and irruptive force of the blues to a *Christological* theological rendering,

110. Moten, *Stolen Life*, 246.

111. Ashon T. Crawley, *Blackpentecostal Breath: The Aesthetics of Possibility* (New York: Fordham University Press, 2016), 15.

112. Crawley, *Blackpentecostal Breath*, 14.

a doubled submission that abstracts and mutes—as so many trumpets in Harlem nightclubs—without the aesthetic adornment, excesses, or flourishes. The theologian's very identity is produced through the capacity to 'think theologically' as a pure category, as a purely distinct mode of thought. . . . The blues antagonize such distinctions grounded in the identity of the one making such a claim for thought. The aesthetic practices of blues moves us beyond simply interrogating who gets to make such a declaration about certain modalities of thought being theological in order to argue that the declaration itself—that some thought is theological over and against other kinds of thought—is a problem. It does not matter if the adjectival appendage is black, womanist, liberation, or queer. The capacity to make the distinction seems grounded in the necessity for exclusionary practice. What the blues demonstrate is not the working of theological thought but a critique of the capacity to make something theological, which is to say the capacity to make the pure distinction, the purely different.[113]

What Crawley is doing here is showing how Blackness, which is to say the enfleshed sociality of blues, the materiality of its sound, refuses the individuation by which the theologian could claim access to the distinct modality of thought called theology. Blues is consent not to be one; blues refuses the kind of proper distinction or isolation required to make the theologian beholden to theology as a sovereign discourse. The Blackness of blues is that it insists on its own nonnormative, impure flesh, and this insistence, this "drive that is never meant to be contained, never meant to reach some there," "undoes the project of theology."[114] This not to say that theology cannot or should not be done with or from the thought of Blackness. It is to say, though, that theology will have to consent to its own undoing as the work of thinking with Blackness, "in the name of theology, writ[ing] against the project of theology"[115] by writing with and from the flesh. What I have tried to say is that such undoing can be subsumed neither under apophatic or negative theology nor under philosophical deconstructions of theology. The undoing that Blackness might work or unwork or nonperform within theology remains an "otherwise possibility" that awaits.

113. Crawley, *Blackpentecostal Breath*, 13, 15.

114. Crawley, *Blackpentecostal Breath*, 20, 17.

115. Crawley, *Blackpentecostal Breath*, 17.

So what would it mean for theology to acknowledge the precedence and priority of Blackness as prior to the *logos* of any possible *theos*? If Blackness, as Jared Sexton puts it, "consists in the affirmation of the unsovereign slave," and if "the slave's inhabitation of the earth precedes and exceeds any prior relation to land,"[116] then what theology is given to think as its undoing is the unownership of the earth, another word for which is abolition. "The flesh of the earth demands it: the landless inhabitation of selfless existence."[117] Such selflessness is not that of the Christian mystics whose paths to nothingness typically remain structured teleologically by various points of orientation: the soul, eternity, church, the bible, liturgy. It is a selflessness that emerges as "the refusal of that which has been refused."[118] Rather than warring over who has access to the territory of proper subjectivity, Blackness consents to a shared unsovereign life that has no subject, no ideal self, as its regulatory and aspirational goal. "It's not mine but it's all I have. I who have nothing, I who am no one, I who am not one. I can't say it and I can't get over it. I can't fathom it and I can't grasp it. It opens everything and, in the exhaustion of what it is to acquire, a choir is set to work."[119]

What would it be to do theology without a subject? Without a human subject and without a divine subject. What would it be to do theology as an unsovereign choir of flesh who sing the sorrow, terror, and beauty of the unowned earth—"(en)chanted, (en)chanting matter, canted blackness (where flesh and earth converge beyond the planetary, in and as non-particulate differentiation)"?[120] Perhaps it might mean, as Marcella Althaus-Reid puts it with reference to the possibility of a queer theology, becoming "a stone on the road to force theologians to stop, fall down, while pausing in their pain and thinking during the pause."[121] If Pseudo-Dionysius is right that we need names for God that are not the technically proper ones, not even the proper negations, but ones that throw us off the path through their wild and material impropriety, then perhaps the best name for God

---

116. Jared Sexton, "The *Vel* of Slavery," 11.

117. Sexton, "The *Vel* of Slavery," 11. My citation of Sexton at this point is not meant to elide the debate within Black Studies between so-called "Afro-pessimism" and so-called "black optimism." It is an attempt to take from Sexton a point about the relation of Blackness to the earth that Moten's own thought affirms. I do not attempt here an ultimate adjudication of this debate. For more on this debate, see David Kline, "The Pragmatics of Resistance: Framing Anti-Blackness and the Limits of Political Ontology." *Critical Philosophy of Race* 5, no. 1 (2017): 51-69.

118. Moten, *Stolen Life*, xii.

119. Moten, *Stolen Life*, ix.

120. Harney and Moten, "Base Faith."

121. Marcella Althaus-Reid, *The Queer God* (New York: Routledge, 2003), 35.

is Blackness, which "bears or is the potential to end the world"[122]—in other words, our chance to touch the earth.

REFERENCES

Althaus-Reid, Marcella. *The Queer God*. New York: Routledge, 2003.

Armstrong, Amaryah Shaye. "Thinking Practice: Method, Pedagogy, Power and the Question of a Black Queer Theology." *Modern Believing* 60:1 (2019): 5-14.

Carter, J. Kameron. *Race: A Theological Account*. Oxford: Oxford University Press, 2008.

Chandler, Nahum. *X–The Problem of the Negro as a Problem for Thought*. New York: Fordham University Press, 2014.

Crawley, Ashon T. *Blackpentecostal Breath: The Aesthetics of Possibility*. New York: Fordham University Press, 2016.

Harney, Stefano and Fred Moten. "Base Faith" e-flux 86 (November 2017). https://www.e-flux.com/journal/86/162888/base-faith/

Hartman, Saidiya. *Wayward Lives, Beautiful Experiments: Intimate Histories of Social Upheaval*. New York: Norton & Company, 2019.

Jordan, Mark D. "Writing-Terrors: A Dialectical Lyric," *Modern Theology* 30:3 (July 2014): 89-104.

Kline, David. "The Pragmatics of Resistance: Framing Anti-Blackness and the Limits of Political Ontology." *Critical Philosophy of Race* 5, no. 1 (2017): 51-69.

Marriott, David. *Whither Fanon? Studies in the Blackness of Being*. Stanford: Stanford University Press, 2018.

Marion, Jean-Luc. *God without Being: Hors-Texte*, trans. Thomas A. Carlson. Chicago: University of Chicago Press, 1991.

Moten, Fred. "Blackness and Nothingness (Mysticism in the Flesh)." *The South Atlantic Quarterly* 112:4 (Fall 2013): 737–780.

Moten, Fred. *Stolen Life (consent not to be a single being)*. Durham: Duke University Press, 2018.

Nancy, Jean-Luc. *Adoration: The Deconstruction of Christianity II*, trans. John McKeane. New York: Fordham University Press, 2013.

Nancy, Jean-Luc. "Church, State, Resistance," in *Political Theologies: Public Religions in a Post-Secular World*, ed. Hent de Vries and Lawrence E. Sullivan. New York: Fordham University Press, 2006: 102-112.

Nancy, Jean-Luc. *Dis-Enclosure: The Deconstruction of Christianity*, trans. Bettina Bergo, Gabriel Malenfant and Michael B. Smith. New York: Fordham University Press, 2008.

---

122. Moten, "Blackness and Nothingness (Mysticism in the Flesh)," 739.

Prevot, Andrew. *Thinking Prayer: Theology and Spirituality Amid the Crises of Modernity*. Notre Dame: University of Notre Dame Press, 2015.

Robinson, Cedric. *Black Marxism: The Making of the Black Radical Tradition*. London: University of North Carolina Press, 1983.

Rose, Marika. *A Theology of Failure: Žižek Against Christian Innocence*. New York: Fordham University Press, 2019.

Rubenstein, Mary-Jane. "Capital Shares." *Political Theology* 11:1 (January 2010): 115-6.

Sexton, Jared. "The Vel of Slavery: Tracking the Figure of the Unsovereign." *Critical Sociology* 42 (December 2014): 583-597.

Sharpe, Christina, *In the Wake: On Blackness and Being*. Durham: Duke University Press, 2016.

Smith, Anthony Paul. "Against Tradition to Liberate Tradition: weaponized apophaticism and gnostic refusal." *Angelika: Journal of the Theoretical Humanities* 19:2 (Sept 2014): 149-159.

Warren, Calvin. "Black Mysticism: Fred Moten's Phenomenology of (Black) Spirit," *Zeitschrift für Anglistik und Amerikanistik* 65:2 (June 2017): 219-229.

Warren, Calvin, *Ontological Terror: Blackness, Nihilism, and Emancipation*. Durham: Duke University Press, 2018.

Weheliye, Alexander G. *Habeas Viscus: Racializing Assemblages, Biopolitics, and Black Feminist Theories of the Human*. Durham: Duke University Press, 2014.

Wilderson, Frank B. *Red, White, and Black: Cinema and the Structure of U.S. Antagonisms*. Durham: Duke University Press, 2010.

Williams, Delores. *Sisters in the Wilderness: The Challenge of Womanist God-Talk*. New York: Orbis Book, 2013.

Wynter, Sylvia. "Unsettling the Coloniality of Being/Power/Truth/ Freedom: Towards the Human, After Man, Its Overrepresentation— An Argument." *CR: The New Centennial Review* 3, no. 3 (2003): 257-337.

INDEX

ABOUT THE EDITORS

ROBERTO SIRVENT is an educator interested in race, law, and social movements who has taught at Hope International University, Pomona College, Scripps College, Claremont School of Theology, and Yale's Summer Bioethics Institute. He is Coordinator of Outreach and Mentoring for the *Political Theology Network* and currently serves as Associate Editor of the *Political Theology* journal. With Linn Tonstad, he edits the Political Theology Undisciplined book series for Duke University Press. He is coauthor (with Danny Haiphong) of the book, *American Exceptionalism and American Innocence: A People's History of Fake News—From the Revolutionary War to the War on Terror* (Skyhorse).

ASHON CRAWLEY is Associate Professor of Religious Studies and African American and African Studies at the University of Virginia. He is author of *Blackpentecostal Breath: The Aesthetics of Possibility* (Fordham University Press), an investigation of aesthetics and performance as modes of collective, social imagination and *The Lonely Letters*, an exploration of the interrelation of Blackness, mysticism, quantum mechanics and love, to be published with Duke University Press in 2020. He is currently working on a third book, tentatively titled "Made Instrument," about the role of the Hammond Organ in the institutional and historic Black Church, in Black sacred practice and in Black social life more broadly. All his work is about otherwise possibility.

ABOUT THE CONTRIBUTORS

HANNAH BOWMAN is a graduate student in the M.A. in Religious Studies program at Mount Saint Mary's University, Los Angeles, and the founder and director of Christians for the Abolition of Prisons (christiansforabolition.org).

MICHAEL COX is an advocate for prison abolition and LGBTQ prisoners in Massachusetts. He is the administrator for the Massachusetts Bail Fund, where he and his colleagues secure the release of hundreds each month. As Executive Director of Black & Pink MA, he cultivates state and federal legislation that reduces incarceration and improves conditions of confinement.

PETER KLINE is the Academic Dean and Lecturer in Systematic Theology at St Francis College, University of Divinity. He is the author of *Passion for Nothing: Kierkegaard's Apophatic Theology* (Fortress Press, 2017).

ANDREW KRINKS is an educator, writer, scholar, and movement builder working at the intersections of racial justice, religion, mass criminalization, and abolition in Nashville, Tennessee. He teaches college and seminary courses on theology, ministry, social justice, carcerality, and abolition, and conducts participatory action research on the impacts of prisons and policing. His book *White Property, Black Trespass: The Religion of Mass Criminalization* will be published by New York University Press in 2024. He educates and organizes with the Nashville People's Budget Coalition for a world of abundance and safety beyond cops, courts, and cages. www.andrewkrinks.com.

RAE LEINER is a Black identified multi-racial Queer organizer, activist, and parent residing in the Hudson Valley. Rae's professional trajectory is primarily focused on social justice and movements for transformative change. Rae is currently the cofounder and Co-Director of the Newburgh LGBTQ+ center, former director of the Empire State Poverty Reduction Initiative in the city of Newburgh and a former Community Voices Heard organizer in Orange County. Rae brings fifteen-plus years of professional experience in the not-for-profit field and social justice work. An experienced facilitator and organizer, a strategic thinker, embodied practitioner, relationship builder, Rae's creative thinking and radical dreaming help to inform their analysis and work towards an equitable society.

JASON LYDON is a Unitarian Universalist minister in Boston, Massachussets. Reverend Lydon focuses much of his time and ministry on penal abolition while specifically meeting the current needs of gay, lesbian, bisexual, transgender, and gender-nonconforming prioners.

FATIMA SHABAZZ is an African American warrior transwoman activist and social Justice Advocate and founder and President of Fatima Speaks LLC, a Black Trans-owned and operated LGBTQ+ consulting concern specializing in cultural sensitive training in how to onboard members of the trans community into a safe, inclusive and productive work space.

JASMINE SYEDULLAH is a black feminist theorist of abolitionist movement scholarship as well as coauthor of *Radical Dharma: Talking Race, Love, and Liberation* (North Atlantic Books, 2016). She joined the faculty of Vassar College in 2019 and holds Africana Studies' first Assistant Professor line there. In addition to teaching, she advises the development of Prison Studies curriculum and programming. Her current book project centers the truant emancipation and timecraft of Harriet Jacobs's 1861 abolitionist narrative as a protofeminist foundation for critical carceral race and gender studies.

JARED WARE is a cohost and producer of the podcast *Millennials Are Killing Capitalism,* which covers revolutionary history, social movements, and political theory. He was a member of the media relations team for the 2018 National Prison Strike. He is also a freelance journalist covering prisoner movements and abolitionist struggles.

AK WRIGHT is a Jamaican first-generation healer-scholar who is a Black Feminist Thought postdoctoral fellow at Northeastern University in Africana Studies and Women, Gender, and Sexuality Studies. Their book project, *Embodied Abolition: Healing Justice, Black Feminism and Ending Carcerality,* investigates how Black individuals communally and intimately live, resist, and care amid carceral forces. Situated in Black feminist thought, queer and trans studies, and carceral studies, their research explores communal healing justice approaches to carceral abolition.

ABOUT COMMON NOTIONS

Common Notions is a publishing house and programming platform that fosters new formulations of living autonomy. We aim to circulate timely reflections, clear critiques, and inspiring strategies that amplify movements for social justice.

Our publications trace a constellation of critical and visionary meditations on the organization of freedom. By any media necessary, we seek to nourish the imagination and generalize common notions about the creation of other worlds beyond state and capital. Inspired by various traditions of autonomism and liberation—in the US and internationally, historical and emerging from contemporary movements—our publications provide resources for a collective reading of struggles past, present, and to come.

Common Notions regularly collaborates with editorial houses, political collectives, militant authors, and visionary designers around the world. Our political and aesthetic interventions are dreamt and realized in collaboration with Antumbra Designs.

commonnotions.org
info@commonnotions.org

BECOME A COMMON NOTIONS
MONTHLY SUSTAINER

These are decisive times, ripe with challenges and possibility, heartache and beautiful inspiration. More than ever, we are in need of timely reflections, clear critiques, and inspiring strategies that can help movements for social justice grow and transform society.

Help us amplify those necessary words, deeds, and dreams that our liberation movements and our worlds so need.

Movements are sustained by people like you, whose fugitive words, deeds, and dreams bend against the world of domination and exploitation.

For collective imagination, dedicated practices of love and study, and organized acts of freedom.

By any media necessary.
With your love and support.

Monthly sustainers start at $12 and $25.

Join us at commonnotions.org/sustain.

MORE FROM COMMON NOTIONS
& ABOLITION COLLECTIVE

Abolishing Carceral Society
Abolition Collective

978-1-942173-08-3
$20.00
256 pages

Beyond border walls and prison cells—carceral society is everywhere. In a time of mass incarceration, immigrant detention and deportation, rising forms of racialized, gendered, and sexualized violence, and deep ecological and economic crises, abolitionists everywhere seek to understand and radically dismantle the interlocking institutions of oppression and transform the world in which we find ourselves. These oppressions have many different names and histories and so, to make the impossible possible, abolition articulates a range of languages and experiences between (and within) different systems of oppression in society today.

Abolishing Carceral Society presents the bold voices and inspiring visions of today's revolutionary abolitionist movements struggling against capitalism, patriarchy, colonialism, ecological crisis, prisons, and borders.

In the first publication of the series, the Abolition Collective renews and boldly extends the tradition of "abolition-democracy" espoused by figures like W.E.B. Du Bois, Angela Davis, and Joel Olson. Through study and publishing, the Abolition Collective supports radical scholarly and activist research, recognizing that the most transformative scholarship is happening both in the movements themselves and in the communities with whom they organize.

Abolishing Carceral Society features a range of creative styles and approaches from activists, artists, and scholars to create spaces for collective experimentation with the urgent questions of our time.

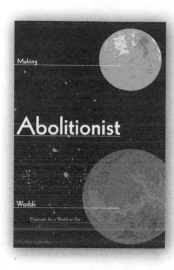

Making Abolitionist Worlds:
Proposals for a World on Fire
Abolition Collective

978-1-942173-17-5
$20.00
272 pages

What does an abolitionist world look like? Insights from today's international abolitionist movement reveal a world to win.

Making Abolitionist Worlds gathers key insights and interventions from today's international abolitionist movement to pose the question: what does an abolitionist world look like? The Abolition Collective investigates the core challenges to social justice and the liberatory potential of social movements today from a range of personal, political, and analytical points of view, underscoring the urgency of an abolitionist politics that places prisons at the center of its critique and actions.

In addition to centering and amplifying the continual struggles of incarcerated people who are actively working to transform prisons from the inside, *Making Abolitionist Worlds* animates the idea of abolitionist democracy and demands a radical re-imagining of the meaning and practice of democracy. Abolition Collective brings us to an Israeli prison for a Palestinian feminist reflection on incarceration within settler colonialism; to protest movements in Hong Kong and elsewhere, who use "abolition democracy" to advocate for the abolition of the police; to the growing culture in the United States of "aggrieved whiteness," which trucks in fear, anger, victimhood, and a need for vengeance to maintain white supremacy; to the punitive landscapes that extend from the incarceration of political prisoners to the mass deportations and detentions along the U.S. southern border.

Making Abolitionist Worlds shows us that the paths forged today for a world in formation are rooted in antiracism, decolonization, anticapitalism, abolitionist feminism, and queer liberation.

MORE FROM COMMON NOTIONS

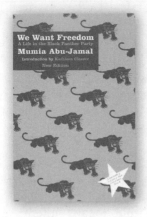

We Want Freedom: A Life in the Black Panther Party (New Edition)
Mumia Abu-Jamal

978-1-942173-04-5
$20.00
336 pages

In his youth Mumia Abu-Jamal helped found the Philadelphia branch of the Black Panther Party, wrote for the national newspaper, and began his life-long work of exposing the violence of the state as it manifests in entrenched poverty, endemic racism, and unending police brutality. In *We Want Freedom*, Mumia combines his memories of day-to-day life in the Party with analysis of the history of Black liberation struggles. The result is a vivid and compelling picture of the Black Panther Party and its legacy.

. . .

New Bones Abolition: Captive Maternal Agency and the Afterlife of Erica Garner
Joy James

978-1-942173-74-8
$20.00
240 pages

Joy James spent a year in which she addressed the legacy of Erica Garner, the daughter of Eric Garner. From this she offers us a new framework for inspired abolitionist organizing and risk-taking today, one that situates the everyday and ordinary acts of revolutionary love and caretaking at the radical root of resistance to anti-Blackness. *New Bones Abolition* addresses "those of us broken enough to grow new bones" about the new traditions we inherit and renew in the struggle for freedom. James introduces us to a powerful figure in these struggles, the "captive maternal," who emerge from communities devastated by or disappeared within the legacy of colonialism and chattel slavery, and who sustain resistance and rebellion toward the horizon of collective liberation.